ENGLISH GRAMMAR

A Linguistic Study of its Classes and Structures

F. S. Scott Professor of English Language, University of Auckland

C. C. Bowley, C. S. Brockett, J. G. Brown, P. R. Goddard

ENGLISH GRAMMAR

A Linguistic Study
of its
Classes and Structures

HEINEMANN EDUCATIONAL BOOKS
LONDON

Heinemann Educational Books Ltd
LONDON EDINBURGH AUCKLAND MELBOURNE
JOHANNESBURG TORONTO SINGAPORE
IBADAN HONG KONG NAIROBI KUALA LUMPUR

ISBN 0 435 10790 9

© 1968   F. S. Scott
         C. C. Bowley
         C. S. Brockett
         J. G. Brown
         P. R. Goddard

First published 1968
Reprinted 1968
Paperback edition first published 1970
Reprinted 1972, 1973

Published by Heinemann Educational Books Ltd
48 Charles Street, London W1X 8AH
Reprinted by photolithography and bound in
Great Britain by Cox & Wyman Ltd,
London, Fakenham and Reading

PREFACE

Towards the end of 1966 a request was made to the Auckland English Association for a course on modern methods of teaching grammar. Out of that course grew this book, the publication of which was first announced at the last lecture. The book is particularly designed for sixth form use, the two parts being primarily intended for two consecutive sixth form years. The course is self-contained and consequently the early material, which has to be included because it will be new to most readers, is comparatively elementary; it can therefore with suitable dilution be introduced a good deal lower down the school. This has already been successfully done by some of the authors. Until the system used in this book becomes more familiar in schools it should be of use also in teachers' colleges, as well as in some university courses.

The text may be presented in class in more than one way. Most of the material in Part One is organised inductively and should require comparatively little comment. It is of course open to the teacher to present it in a condensed form of his own designing.

Although it has grown up in a New Zealand milieu, the book is not limited nationally; its contents are in general expected to be applicable wherever English is spoken and written.

The theory behind *English Grammar* is that of a group of British linguists, in particular M. A. K. Halliday and J. McH. Sinclair, to whom acknowledgment is gratefully made. We are also endebted to work done a few years ago in the University of Leeds by then members of the School of English. The linguistic model here adopted is in fact one which has been in general use by linguists in the United Kingdom for the past few years: articles making use of it have appeared in the *Journal* of the linguistic Association of Great Britain, while a full scale application of a similarly based description is *English in Advertising* by G. N. Leech (Longmans 1966).

While this school of linguistics has been our chief source we have of course not limited our attention to it. We have gladly made use of the publications of a variety of grammarians, from Jespersen on, particularly, perhaps, those of the workers in the transformational field such as Noam Chomsky, R. B. Lees and Paul Roberts. We have also found useful F. R. Palmer's *A Linguistic Study of the English Verb* (Longmans, 1965). It is also true to say that in several areas the text is based on the individual research of one or more of the authors.

Finally mention should be made of our endebtedness to Randolph Quirk's *The Use of English* (Longmans, 1962), a book at once practical, scholarly and humane.

It is on the whole from the school of linguists mentioned above that we derive the terminology, though every term has been carefully considered. Innovation has not been adopted for its own sake. Sometimes at first sight a traditional term may seem to have been unnecessarily discarded; if so there will have been a reason for the change. To explain the reason in every case would take too long; often it is because the traditional term refers to something more limited than the category we had in mind. *Reflexive pronoun,* for example, at first sight an appropriate name for the form *myself* is not suitable for that form's occurrence in *I did it myself,* so we have preferred a more neutral term. Terminology is a thorny subject; we merely wish to say that we have tried to handle it with care.

We are particularly grateful to Professor L. F. Brosnahan of Victoria University, Wellington, and to Mr J. A. Sinclair of Avondale College, Auckland, who kindly read much of the work in typescript. We also remember with gratitude suggestions and comments from a number of friends, including the information about Tongan kindly supplied by Sister Mary Felicia. For the paraphrase from the Book of Kings as well as for general advice about staging the presentation of material we are endebted to Emeritus Professor H. G. Forder. Any faults or surviving errors are of course our own.

In this the last paragraph of the book to be written I should like to pay tribute to my colleagues' perpetual willingness to co-operate and their long-sustained readiness for work throughout, not forgetting the wives who have contrived to make that work possible.

Forrest S. Scott

Auckland, October, 1967.

vi

CONTENTS

Part Two

LIST OF NON-LETTER SYMBOLS

| | | | sentence boundary |

| | | clause boundary |

| | group boundary |

+ | morpheme boundary |

[[ ]] | boundaries of a rankshifted clause |

[ ] | boundaries of a rankshifted group |

<< >> | boundaries of an inserted clause |

< > | boundaries of an inserted group |

* | a non-attested sentence or form |

⟶ | is transformed into |

& | indicates linkage |

= | indicates apposition |

— | indicates a broken element |

PART ONE

Chapter 1

Where Grammar Comes In

LANGUAGE AND LIFE

Language is on its own. It is different from anything else we take part in. And it is something we take part in, not merely a subject to learn about. Some of us may talk a little more than others but we all talk a great deal. Mostly we do it to tell people things, occasionally in order to find out things, and as often as not to say whatever passes through our heads. Rosalind may not have been describing only her own sex when she said to Orlando, 'Do you not know I am a woman? When I think, I must speak'. Sometimes we listen to what is being said to us. At any rate spoken language is going on all around us; whenever people are not officially doing something else they seem to talk – in shops, streets, buses, school-yards, houses, workshops and dance halls. From radio and television comes an almost constant stream of talk. And written language is all round us too, not only in books but in newspaper headlines, news columns and advertisements, on hoardings and in neon lights. If language is put in front of us in large enough letters we can hardly help absorbing it.

How did we come to be able to use language? People do not grow up into talking by the same means as they acquire the ability to eat, digest, sit up, walk and run, and fall in love. They do these things because they are born of parents and grandparents who do them and even if they were brought up by strangers in a strange land they would know how to do them. Their eyes, hair and other physical features may resemble those of some of their ancestors, with whom they are even likely to share characteristics of personality, but if children are brought up by strangers they will speak the language of the strangers and not that of their parents. If, as has occasionally happened, they are kept alive by animals, they will not acquire human speech at all.

But neither is language something like swimming, which you may either be taught or acquire by imitation if there are enough members of the community who swim and you started early enough. Learning language is indeed something like this second way of learning to swim because it is acquired by imitation. But there is the big difference that not everyone learns to swim; indeed there are probably places where very few people know how to swim. But there is no community of human beings which does not talk; the only people who do not talk are those born without the necessary organs of speech, or those unable to hear others talking.

In many ways using language is more like wearing clothes than anything else. Everyone wears some kind of covering or ornamentation but there are many different ways of doing so. There are both clothes and words which are for purposes of utility; they are appropriate for the job to be done but they impress no-one. There are comfortable ways of speaking and writing which, like comfortable clothes, do very well at home but are not quite the thing for more momentous occasions. There are clothes of different materials. There are clothes that suit the sea and the open air, for tramping and for holidays. There are other clothes which do very much to make possible a magic occasion like a ball. And there are words for such occasions too. There are clothes for wearing only on the stage or in a film – clothes for pretending to be someone else in. And there are kinds of language for all these occasions too.

As with clothes, there are words and phrases used to declare that we are up to date with the latest 'in' habit. They catch on and are used over and over again like people wearing the latest trend. Then, as often happens with trends, they become first unfashionable, then dowdy, then quaint and finally period, like fashions of, say, five, ten, twenty and fifty years ago. This of course applies more noticeably to the area of language roughly called slang and it is often true (as was pointed out by C. P. Snow in *The Masters*) that people go on using slang words and phrases that were in vogue when they were young without realising that they are no longer fashionable – as sometimes happens with clothing styles and make-up too.

Another, though not quite parallel, comparison might be made between language and customs of eating; in this case the most noticeable variation is between members of different communities; they may have, say, two, three, or four meals in a day or have no pattern at all; some have elaborate ceremonies that must be gone through whenever food is eaten; for some, certain foods are under a taboo or may only be eaten on special occasions; some use fingers, others knives and forks, others chopsticks. And strangers to the society, who do not know the customs, may be in danger of giving offence or of not noticing things that are done in their honour. In this way they suffer a failure of communication which is of course what happens when people do not understand each other's language.

Such comparisons with eating and dressing habits suggest why the study of language – **linguistics** – has recently come to be regarded as one of the social sciences, like anthropology and sociology and psychology; language is a part of human behaviour. We may note that animals do not wear clothes and not many of them have eating ceremonies: similarly, although they do communicate with each other to a certain limited extent, they cannot be said to have languages to anything like the extent humans have, whereas all human societies have languages, even though they differ greatly from each other

LANGUAGE: A SIGNALLING SYSTEM

Yet there is of course more to language than custom and fashion. Eating ceremonies are not found everywhere and for much of the time clothing does not have a great deal to say. The impressions they make on other people are mostly incidental to the main business of nutrition and keeping warm. From what has been said above it is clear that language has many purposes, but its main business is **communication,** the intimation to another being of what one wants or thinks, and for the great majority of people their words and phrases will be of one kind only – those which belong to the language their own community uses.

It is indeed a very strange thing that different communities use different languages and so have different words with which to give form to their emotions and thoughts. It is not surprising that these emotions and thoughts often come out differently. To learn another language is not merely to learn a new set of sounds or marks on paper for saying the same thing; it is to learn that it is possible to think in a slightly different way from that to which one has become used, to understand that there is more than one way of organising our experience and that the world is a rather greater place than one once thought.

Communication, then, is the main purpose of language, and language can be seen to have features in common with other communication systems (which indeed are often called 'languages'). There are some communication systems so simple that we can say everything about them in a few lines.

There is for example the system of traffic signals erected at busy intersections: the aim of the system is to indicate when it is safe to proceed beyond the road junction and when it is unsafe to do so. We will examine the New Zealand version of the system as it is a simple one.

The messages are conveyed by means of coloured lights which can be in three different states which mean three different messages:

RED   Stop
GREEN   Proceed
AMBER   Stop unless you would be unable to stop safely in the time available.

A system such as this consists of these parts:

- the **substance,** manifested by some material means, in this case electrically-produced light coloured by a glass filter. It is necessary that the substance be perceived by one of the body's senses, in this case sight.

- the allocation of the signals to the various *messages* which the system can convey; these messages relate to the **situation** of the traffic flow at the time. It is through this allocation that the receiver of the signals *understands* what is intended. There has to be some agreement of course as to the way in which the messages are allocated. It is not enough to know that there are three signals and three messages; you have to know for example that it is agreed that the red signal has the meaning 'Stop'; such a general agreement is called a convention.

This is a particularly simple system of course, not only because there are only three messages but also because no part of the substance can enter into more than one message. Consider now the code by which ships can transmit certain important and frequently-occurring messages to one another. The following is a selection of some of the messages which can be sent by means of longer or shorter blasts on a ship's siren – a long stroke indicates a long blast, a short stroke a short blast.

i) –   I am turning to starboard.
ii) – –   I am turning to port.
iii) – – –   My engines are going full speed astern.
iv) – – —   You are standing into danger.
v) — — —   Man overboard.
vi) – — —   I require medical assistance.

Here are six messages; there is a difference from the traffic light system, in that whereas before there was a *different* colour for *each* message, in this system short blasts enter into five of the messages and long blasts into three of them. It is the *combination* of number and type that counts. That this is so is illustrated by the fact that the messages can be transmitted equally well by lamp as by siren: in other words it is not the perception of the substance itself (the sound waves produced by the siren or the light emitted by the lamp) that indicates the message but the recognition of the **patterns** in it. The patterns above can indeed be expressed in other ways than longs and shorts, e.g.

	a	a, a	a, a, a	a, a, b	b, b, b	a, b, b
or	a	2a	3a	2a+b	3b	a+2b
or even	p	q	r	qx	z	py

The main point is that we do recognise differences between the patterns, although there may be more than one way of expressing those differences.

Although the system is still a comparatively simple one, its parallels with language are closer than in the traffic light system.

1. The patterns can be made by more than one substance (i.e. in more than one medium).

	Navigational system	*Language system*
i) ear perceives:	Patterns in sound made by siren	Sound made by voice and other speech organs
ii) eye perceives:	Patterns in light made by lamp	Marks made by ink, etc. on paper, parchment

2. The same segment may enter into a number of patterns, the long blast or flash occurs in signals (iv), (v) and (vi) above; the sound *s* occurs in *s*and, *s*pade, fork*s*. It does not have any meaning until it forms part of a pattern.

Now in the study of spoken language the part concerned with the substance is called **phonetics** and the part concerned with messages or meanings is called **semantics.** Both of these are of course much more complicated than in the system we have been considering. But in between them comes the area of patterns, or **form,** at which we will now look more closely.

Form in language comprises a number of studies.

We have seen that the segments in the navigational system do not have a meaning until they are part of a pattern; in this they are like the language units which are, in the case of the spoken medium, the segments called phonemes and in the written medium the segments called graphemes; the patterns which these segments form usually comprise what we know as words. The segments themselves do not have meaning; the words do.

What the segments themselves do possess is significance, distinctness from one another. In the navigational system it is essential that the short segments are clearly distinct from the long ones; in practice it would still be possible to read a signal consisting of short and long flashes of light if the shorts were a little longer than usual, but if their length increased so much as to make the reader uncertain whether they were shorts or longs the system would become inefficient because the distinction between its segments would have been lost. It is the same with the segments in human language. We know that we do not all make our letters in exactly the same way; some of us cross *t*'s with a stroke that goes right through the upright, others with a bar that stays on the right side of it; for others the bar is almost non-existent. This does not necessarily make our writing inefficient unless our *t* becomes indistinguishable from some other letter. Again some of us use an *r* which is of a quite different type from that which others write or we may even write both kinds of *r* ourselves in different moods or in different positions in words. These varying kinds of *t* (and *r*) are called **allographs;** they all represent a single unit of writing, the **grapheme.** Even printers sometimes use variant allographs which are members of the same grapheme, e.g., the *f* used when the letter is doubled, ff, or before *i*, fi.

Similarly in the spoken form of the language there are certain distinctive segments. Even one person does not always pronounce a certain sound, say the vowel *a* or the consonant *t* in exactly the same way. Among other reasons they may vary because of the sounds on either side of them. And certainly all the people who speak to us do not produce exactly the same sound. Yet within certain limits we do recognise a distinct sound as an *a* or a *t*; such a significant sound is

called a **phoneme.** The various varieties of it are called **allophones.**
Two allophones which are clearly different in sound are the *l*'s in
lisp and *milk*, yet we acknowledge them to be a single phoneme,
because in no position in a word is there any doubt which is to be
used; they never clash.

The area of language concerned with phonemes and the circumstances in which they can combine (e.g., in English syllables *t* can
precede *a* but not *k*) is **phonology,** one of the divisions of language
concerned with form. So far this would be paralleled in the navigational system by a listing of the segments that occur, the possibility
of their combination with each other and any limitation there might
be in the number that can occur in the combined units to which a
meaning is allotted.

A difference between this system and human language now
appears however. In the former the combined units each have a
meaning but there is little possibility of these units combining with
each other in a still greater unit to which each contributes something of their meaning. This, however, is what happens in language;
there exist greater and smaller units or, as we may alternatively put
it, there are units of different **rank.**

SIGNALLING UNITS: FORM IN LANGUAGE

We said that the combined units of the signalling system (which
we will now leave) were rather like words; words, however, are not
the only units of language that have meaning: there are several
ranks of such **units,** which we will briefly mention.

First there are some units which do have meaning but are not
reckoned as words because they can only be used in combination
with other units. (There is nothing quite like this in the navigational
system.) Such units are: *er* in *singer, player, fiddler;* the *ing* in *singing, playing, walking;* the *ness* in *goodness* and *weakness;* the *pre*
in *pre-war, pre-Raphaelite, pre-school.* These units are hardly words,
for they cannot be used except in combination with other units;
yet they do have a meaning as can be quickly seen by assuming
hitherto unknown words. If there were a verb *sping* we would know
that a *spinger* was someone who was in the habit of *spinging;* that
is, we know what the *er* in *spinger* means even if we have never seen
the word before and do not know what *sping* means. So there must
be a unit smaller than that of the word, a unit which is of a lower
rank. We call such a unit a **morpheme.**

In practice, however, a unit may at the same time be both a mor-

'only' — 'on' is modified morpheme ie, one/ly

pheme and a word. In *player* we have seen that *er* is a morpheme. *Play* is a morpheme too: it is part of a word and it has meaning. The letters *pl* however, although they are part of a word, do not have meaning and do not form a morpheme. *Play* is a morpheme which can exist on its own as a word. We distinguish it from *er* by calling *play* a **free** morpheme and *er* a **bound** morpheme. We have therefore established two ranks, **morpheme** and **word.** The remaining ranks that are found will be explained in detail in subsequent chapters; briefly, they are the **group** (e.g., the old oak tree; by the deep river; my aunt Jemima; has not been seen; mystery), the **clause** (We chose a ring with a diamond and two sapphires; Come to our wedding; having eaten lots of food) and the **sentence.**

The first two examples of the clause are also sentences, but the third one is not. Other sentences consist of more than one clause (e.g., Having eaten lots of food, we went happily home. We chose a ring with a diamond and two sapphires, but couldn't afford to buy it. Come to our wedding, which will be on Easter Tuesday if we don't change our minds before then.)

Sentences consist of *one or more* clauses.

Clauses consist of *one or more* groups.

Groups consist of *one or more* words.

Words consist of *one or more* morphemes.

Units which consist of only one of the unit forming the rank below are **simple** units; those which consist of more than one of the units of the rank below are **complex.** So sentences which contain only one clause are simple sentences, groups which contain more than one word are complex groups, while clauses which are also groups must be simple clauses. 'Wait!' is a morpheme which is also a (simple) word and a (simple) group and a (simple) clause and a (simple) sentence.

When it is desirable to show the boundaries between the various units we can use the following system:

     | | | for sentence boundaries (rarely necessary)

     | | for clause boundaries

     | for group boundaries.

The usual space will serve for word boundaries and when it is necessary to show morpheme boundaries a plus sign (+) can be inserted, though it is seldom that this is necessary:

     | | | She | was singing | | until | her friend | stopped | her. | | |

     | | | Jane| was sing + ing| | until| her boy + friend| call + ed | for her.| | |

The word is the most easily recognised of the units and we sometimes overlook the fact that there are others. Perhaps it is for this reason that there are different terms for describing the composition of the word and that of the larger units. The study of the composition of words is called **morphology** and the study or description of the larger units, group, clause and sentence, is called **syntax.** This book is mostly about syntax, though it is necessary to remember the existence of morphemes. Morphology and syntax are both part of **grammar.**

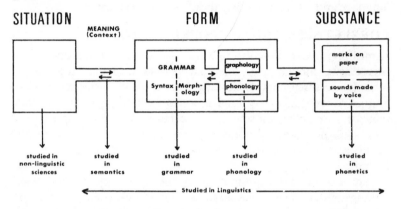

THE MEANING OF THE SIGNALS

The word also appears to be the most important unit for the conveying of **meaning** but although this is true in a general way we can never understand the meaning of any real situation without using the other units. We know roughly what sort of meaning a word conveys – such meanings are of course described in dictionaries – but we never really know what a word means until we know just how it is being used, which implies knowing what group, clause or sentence it belongs to. Not till then can we know more than the *potential* meaning of a word.

For practical purposes we get on reasonably well with the notion of 'meaning' though it is something which is really very difficult to explain or describe. It has something to do with the relation between a piece of language and the **situation** it refers to. This situation is usually one actually occurring in real life, but it might be in someone's imagination – which imagination might be that of a mathematician or a scientist or a businessman equally well as that of a poet or novelist. This relation is sometimes called the **context** of the piece of language. The meanings of most individual words are **lexical;** it is indeed often useful to distinguish between this sort of meaning, which most words and morphemes have, and another kind which helps to organise morphemes inside words and words in groups and groups in clauses and so on. This other kind of meaning is called **grammatical** or **structural** or **formal** meaning. A few words and morphemes possess mainly structural meaning (e.g., *of, and*) while the majority have mainly lexical meaning.

The study of meaning in general, that is the connection between language and what it is talking about, is called **semantics.**

CORRECTNESS AND APPROPRIATENESS

If meaning is one difficult linguistic idea to talk about, another is **correctness,** though it is one that people studying language in schools are often concerned with. Perhaps it is easier to give examples of what incorrect English is than what is correct, and that may be why grammar sometimes seems to be pre-occupied with thou-shalt-not rules. Although not much attention is given to rules of this sort in this book it does not mean that 'anything goes'; far from it.

People sometimes say that they 'never bother about rules' when talking or that they 'write anyhow'. To some extent this may be true if they mean that they do not *consciously* do so; but there are many *rules* that they unconsciously observe because they have acquired them from their society. However thoughtless they may be about language they are not likely to say 'Jane am sang' or 'until boyfriend her for called her', while if they do say things like 'Jane were singing' it will be because their dialect of English happens to use that version not because the individual just felt like saying *were* instead of *was.*

So it must be possible to list and describe the things that can be done in a language. To do so completely would be an unending task, but it is possible to study the more important basic principles, the finite set of **relationships** from which an infinite number of specimens of speaking and writing can be obtained. We try to describe all the important features about the relationships of the meaningful units of the language, just as we might describe the make-up of a plant in botany or the respiratory system in physiology or the parts of a motor in mechanics. A grammar which sets out to do this is a **descriptive** grammar.

Grammar has often been used to correct mistakes. It is true that it is relevant here. But if only the parts where mistakes are likely to occur are discussed we will get an unbalanced idea of our language, as if we were to learn about diseases before we know how a healthy body works. A knowledge of grammar is useful in discussing mistakes in language even if only because it gives names to the parts that are affected. It may be possible for someone who is very gifted at understanding how engines work to see what is the source of trouble when one breaks down, but for most of us the task will be much easier if we know what the parts are called and how they work when the engine is going properly. So it is with language.

What is correct in one situation may be incorrect or at least less nearly correct in another. In speaking, for example, it is quite in order to say *don't,* or *a lot of;* in writing up an experiment or composing an essay, however, it is more usual, more 'correct' perhaps, more proper, to use *do not* and *many* or *a large quantity of.* In short, what matters is whether the language is *appropriate* to the use being made of it.

There are of course very many uses of languages, many of which surround us. There is the English used in newspapers, novels, letters, textbooks, advertisements and comics; there is the English spoken in homes, buses, classrooms, pubs, theatres and churches, to name only a few. To try to explain how language is appropriate to, or typical of, all of these would be a very lengthy task indeed. What can help, however, is to notice in what ways these uses of English can differ from one another. The most important ways in which they can differ are probably those described below.

VARIETIES OF LANGUAGE (I): DIALECTS

First, different varieties of English may reflect a difference in speech habits applying almost continually. The same speaker uses his own variety almost all the time. The American speaker does on the whole speak differently from the Australian one, the Devon speaker from the Ayrshire one, the Southlander from the Liverpudlian. This difference is noticeable largely in terms of pronunciation, but it does have its effect on grammar and vocabulary too. Such different varieties are called **dialects**; the examples given are from **geographical** dialects. If the differences between two dialects become sufficiently great, two languages result. Geographical dialects may be thought of as the result of vertical division of the speakers of a language. But there are other divisions which might perhaps be regarded as horizontal – social divisions and educational divisions; whether or not these are desirable, they do exist. They may be more apparent in sòme countries than others but in some form or other they exist in all. To these **cultural** dialects may be added the **occupational** dialects, which arise where the nature of an occupation tends to restrict its practitioners to each other's company and to cut down their communication with others. Only when the occupation is that of the majority of the inhabitants in a community can the resulting special variety of language be called a dialect: farming, fishing and mining might be examples.

Differences in dialect are largely confined to spoken language. For written purposes their users generally employ a **standard language** – which may in origin have been itself a dialect which acquired more prestige than its neighbours. Poems and short stories in dialect do exist of course but they are comparatively rare. Newspapers in rural areas are not written in the local dialect. When considering dialect, people usually think of pronunciation and perhaps vocabulary. Dialectal variation in grammar tends to be accorded a lower status as merely 'bad grammar', though in fact forms such as 'the machine's *broke*', 'we *was* robbed' and 'I do like *them* fancy stockings, Auntie' are as dialectal in origin as 'Ah feel reight moithered'. The situation has been efficiently summed up by Randolph Quirk:

> Most of the 'problems' of English grammar crop up because of a clash between the very definite grammatical conventions of our immediate social circle and the equally definite but often very different conventicns of the wider circle of the nation as a whole.†

And it might be possible to substitute an even wider term for *nation*.

VARIETIES OF LANGUAGE (II): REGISTERS

The next sort of difference to be considered arises because of the difference of **medium.** It has already been mentioned that differences exist between the spoken and written varieties of the language; moreover there are subdivisions of these depending on the answer to questions such as:

– How permanent is the specimen of language intended to be?
– Is one person in communication with one person, or is one with many (or even many with many)?

†*The Use of English* (Longmans 1962), p. 104.

If spoken, is there any 'feedback' from the party addressed? This is particularly prominent in conversation (and results in many unfinished sentences), somewhat less noticeable at public meetings. Yet even in a lecture there is often a sort of 'silent feedback' which has its effect on the language being used. But in a broadcast speech this feature is absent. A further example of the influence of the medium on language is the telephone conversation, and yet another is the telegram, where the need to cut down the number of words causes the omission of some of them and alteration in the use of others (Offer hundred pounds wire reply soonest) even to the development among certain regular users of the telegraph of special grammatical forms such as the interrogative *couldst* (Story awaits outcome revolution couldst cable weeks subsistence).

The differences between examples of language resulting from the use of a different medium (or of the same medium in a different way) constitute what is sometimes called **mode** or **mode of discourse.** Mode provides our first example of **register** – variation in language because of variation in circumstances. Types of language showing such differences are themselves called registers.

It is evident that subject matter affects language; a conversation at a fishmarket, a discussion after a football match or a fashion parade or argument about the accuracy of the current Top Twenty list, will all differ from each other and not only in vocabulary. Such examples provide further illustration of registers. Differences may also arise from yet other causes, all of which produce separate registers.

There may be differences in the sex or age, or both, of the people addressed. The following are strikingly different in the language they use: the difference is due partly to difference of subject, partly to dialect difference [(ii) shows American influence], but largely to the difference of sex in the majority of readers.

i)   If it's too hot for food – or if you've eaten plenty already – all you really need to complete your holiday bliss is one ambrosial mouthful of succulent sweetness.

(New Zealand Woman's Weekly)

ii) Stoke up two full house hemi rails – wave a healthy cheque at the other end of the strip – flash the lights green and, man, you've got instant noise.   *(The Australian Hot Rodding Review)*

Such special forms of the language thus tend to be shared by only part of the community (e.g., the male part; the 15-25 age group) whereas a dialect is something shared by the whole community.

A further subdivision occurs when the *same* person uses different forms of language at different times. This usually arises from the social role he or she plays. It is not uncommon for a schoolchild to employ three registers, one for home, one for play, and one for the classroom. Again, the social role of *both* parties may be relevant: a conversation between a teacher and a sixth-former may contain linguistic features which reflect any of the following relationships and probably others: teacher - pupil; adult - adolescent; expert - novice; sergeant-major - recruit; soldier - enemy; shopkeeper - customer. And there will also be occasions, and those not entirely restricted to sport, where the dominating relationship will be enthusiast - enthusiast, with its appropriate language. This last fact calls to mind the special 'in' language of groups of all levels of sophistication; such languages have terms, often abbreviations, which only the initiates can use accurately; they create a cosy atmosphere in which the members are drawn close together and outsiders implicitly excluded.

Apart from the 'in' registers, there are varieties of language which are used for restricted purposes, for example the language of business correspondence and public or civil service intercommunication. Here we see language **formalised** to fit certain occasions and to express certain relationships between the users of it.

Some languages formalise their **tenor** (which this variation is sometimes called) to a greater extent than current English. Chaucer, writing at an earlier stage of the English language, spoke of

Heigh stile, as whan that men to kynges write†

implying that there was a special form of the language used only for addressing royalty.

In the Tongan language, not only are greetings varied according to the respect which one wishes to show to the person addressed – this does happen to some extent in English – but different words are used depending on the rank of the person addressed. Thus to an ordinary person going to bed one says 'Mohe a', to a chief 'Toka a', to the king or queen 'Tofa a'. For the notion of eating, up to five words may be used: the ordinary word, *kai,* the polite equivalent, *tokoni,* the word used when addressing a chief, *ilo,* the word used in addressing the king or queen, *taumafa,* and a derogatory word, *mama,* used of oneself.

---

†*Clerk's Prologue*, line 18.

There was a time when children were taught that horses sweat, men perspire and ladies glow.

In English, where the divisions of formality are less precise than in Tongan, it is worth noting that formal language is not entirely an obstacle intended to make things difficult; the 'rules' it seems to insist on were meant to make communication easier between people who are not regularly in contact, just as is the case with rules of polite behaviour. The use of formal language at a meeting ('Mr Chairman', 'Mr Jones', 'Sir'), may enable two men to express strong disagreement over the point being discussed without that disagreement affecting their friendship, so that they may greet each other as 'Tom' and 'Bill' when they meet at lunch next day. Moreover, colloquial language, free and easy though it may appear, is subject to a greater number of interpretations than formal language. People making great use of colloquial phrases often leave it to the person listening to guess what they mean; this is sometimes deliberate, but often unconscious.

Formal language is not a bad thing, then, though it is easy for some uses of language to become over-formal or (to make use of the metaphor from the printing trade) stereotyped.

Indeed, it is possible to measure language by a scale of formality which might include, say, the steps formal - workaday - casual - intimate, with finer gradations between. The parallel with clothing is particularly close here.

Two close friends can convey a good deal to each other without using many words because they know well each other's likes and dislikes and general way of thinking. It is generally true, moreover, (even though there are exceptions, notably in the case of the more successful poets) that the more intimate language becomes, the more restricted grows its audience.

For the written language at least, it is desirable to have available a compromise between the language of specialists and the language of friends, a form of the language readily understandable throughout the English-speaking world by people of modest education who are not experts in the topic being discussed. Perhaps at the present time this compromise is attained most successfully by weekly journals such as, to mention only a few, *The Spectator, The Economist, The New Zealand Listener, The New Scientist.*

A truly well-educated man uses and understands many kinds of English.

Finally, we must not overlook the many varieties of language that occur in literature, where writers make use of the artistic possibilities of language. Such a study is, of course, beyond the scope of this book though it is touched on in Chapters 12 and 22. A writer's style is often expressed as much by the grammatical classes and structures he prefers as by his choice of words.

Some writers use a plain style which means that their language is not easy to identify. Others aim at realistic portrayal of speech, as for example in Pinter's plays. Others again have highly individual styles and create their own worlds of English such as those of *Paradise Lost, The Faerie Queene* and *Finnegan's Wake*.

CLASSES AND STRUCTURES

So far we have been discussing the nature of language and of grammar in particular. The remainder of this chapter deals with some of the principles, methods and terminology used in this book. It is desirable to consider these first before beginning the detailed study, but it will also be advisable to return to them at a later stage after some experience has been acquired.

Not surprisingly, one of the most important methods is **classification.** In describing the nature of the universe all sciences make great use of classifying: elements in chemistry, species in biology, and so on. Classifying makes description clearer and more economical. Naturally it is possible to use more than one principle of classification and the various categories can be expected to intersect.

It is by classifying to so fine a degree that no subset consists of more than two members that computers are able to handle at speed abstruse matter of diverse kinds.

Classification indeed is one of the means by which language helps man to understand and to some extent manipulate nature. For example an oak is different from a pine or a maple; occasionally, however, it is useful to consider them all together: the word *tree* enables us to do this. The word *chair* saves us from having to remember one word for what we sit in at table and a different one for the object behind a desk. That is, English recognises a category to which the name *chair* is given. Languages do not have identical categories; English happens to distinguish fourlegged seats according to whether they have, or have not, a back (*chairs, stools*); another language might have a common word for the two.

Before discussing the methods of classifying used in this text we will explain certain basic terms.

We use the term **set** in its generally accepted modern sense, that

is, a collection of items which have something in common. Naturally, our sets consist of linguistic members; these are most often
words, but they may be, say, groups or other units. In particular we
may need to note whether sets are **open** sets (like the set of all nouns
which is capable of being added to indefinitely) or **closed** sets (like
the set of demonstratives). The terms *open* and *closed* are very
similar to *infinite* and *finite,* but as the equivalence is not quite
complete it is best to use the former pair when discussing linguistic
sets.

The term **element** is, however, used in a rather more special sense
than in mathematics, where it is equivalent to 'member of a set'.
It is used here to mean a fundamental part of a **structure.** A structure
is a potential piece of language that is something like a framework
having certain open places that can be filled by appropriate items
but by no inappropriate ones. The group *the old jersey* has a structure such that *the* can be replaced by, for example, *an, my, Joe's,
this,* but not by *Joe, Wednesday* or *want* which would produce a
non-English group, e.g., *Wednesday old jersey, (*indicates a
piece of language which is not used or has not been recorded).
The words *the, an, my, Joe's,* are not themselves elements; the
element is the place they occupy in the structure of that group.
Similarly in the clause:

Politicians speak in two voices.

Politicians, speak and *in two voices* represent elements in the structure SPA (cf. 4.5).

A **class** is, broadly speaking, an important set. The words *fun,
funnel* and *fundamentalist* are members of the set of words whose
first three letters are *f, u, n* but there is no significance in this feature
and it does not make a class. (For simplicity's sake we will restrict
the examples to words.)

Classes may arise in the following ways:

a) A class of words may consist of all the words that may occupy
    a certain element in a structure (e.g., prepositions). Such classes
    are **positional** classes.

b) A class of words may share a significant **similarity** of form (e.g.,
    sequence of sounds or letters). Adverbs are an example.

c) A class of words may undergo regular **change** of form to provide
    for certain changing circumstances, in particular:

    i) They may change form because they appear in more than
    one element of structure:

    It is my father.   It is my father's car.

The form of *father* changes because it is occupying a different element. This particular change is typical of nouns. Similarly in

He loves her.   She loves him.

the form *he* is replaced by *him* after *loves,* while *her* turns into *she* before *loves.* This suggests that these words *he, she, him, her* belong to the same class. They are, in fact, personal pronouns.

ii)   They may change form because of their relationship to some changing word (or other item) in the structure; e.g., the demonstrative *this* changes to *these* if dependent on, say, *men,* rather than *man.*

iii)   They may change form because they reflect what is, for the language being considered, a regularly observed semantic distinction. Such changes are made in English to account for the notion 'more than one' in nouns and for the notion meaning approximately 'in the past' in verbs. The word *regular* is very important here, but it does not mean 'exceptionless'. Not every noun has a plural form, but because such words behave in other ways like words which do form plurals they are admitted into the noun class (e.g., *rubbish*).

Classes arising under (b) and (c) are **form** classes; their members frequently coincide. From these are derived the classes dealt with in Chapter 2. As will be seen, subdivision is carried out only as long as it is profitable: too much splitting would cause more trouble than it would save.

The variation of form mentioned in (c) above gives rise to what are called **systems.** Systems consist of a very small number of terms (which thus constitute closed sets). Number and tense are examples of systems in English. All languages have systems but they do not all use them for the same purposes; what is an essential distinction in one language may be quite disregarded in another.

If the words in a language are compared to the cards in a pack, the numbers in each suit would be like the open set classes. It would be easy to envisage them being added to: 11, 12, 13, 14, etc. The (two) colours and (four) suits, however, form systems; they are essential for the organisation of games with cards just as linguistic systems are necessary for the organisation of a language.

MARKING

Classes of all kinds are often recognised by what is known as marking, which is a very useful concept.

Consider the following instructions:

i) All the trees marked with a cross are to be felled.
ii) Mark your envelope 'Competition' in the top-left-hand corner.
iii) No Parking. No Waiting. No Stopping.
iv) Parking 60 mins. P20.

In (i) and (ii) some sort of marker (a cross, a word) is used to distinguish certain of the trees and envelopes from the ordinary trees and envelopes which are not marked. The device of marking is also used in language, to distinguish special grammatical items from ordinary ones. It may happen in a language that, say, the present tense is **unmarked** while the past is **marked** by a typical ending.

Examples (iii) and (iv) show that marking may happen either way round; sometimes we mark one of the subsets in a set, sometimes the other. In (iii) the areas in the road where parking is *not* allowed have been marked, but in (iv) it is the areas where parking *is* allowed that are marked. It is the same with the following pair of notices:

No bathing while the red flag is flying.
It is safe to bathe only when a green flag is flying.

And it could be said that whereas in Britain the unmarked term 'football' means Association Football and 'Rugby' is the marked term, in New Zealand it is the other way: 'Soccer' is the marked member of the pair; 'football' if unspecified refers to Rugby Football.

That in language, too, marking need not always work one way is shown by the fact that in English it is generally true that in nouns the plural form is marked whereas in verbs it is the singular which has the marked form. Sometimes of course both forms may be marked – or all forms if there are more than two in the system.

Marking may be done in a number of ways: the addition of a morpheme is one of the most frequent, as with the -(e)s that marks nouns as plural or the -(e)d that marks past tense in verbs or the *un-* that often marks 'opposite' forms in adjectives. Such morphemes are **affixes, suffixes** if they follow the base morpheme, **prefixes** if they precede it. **Infixes,** inserted in the middle of words, are also possible.

Other ways of marking are:
– using a special structural word (e.g., *by* in the English passive construction or *most* in a superlative form like *most frequent*).
– changing a vowel (tooth, teeth) or a consonant (send, sent).

(Strictly speaking it is not possible to say that either form is unmarked in these cases.)

- repeating all or part of a word (e.g., Maori: singular *nui* 'big', plural *nunui;* Latin: *currit* 'runs', *cucurrit* 'ran').

- varying the voice pitch so as to produce different **intonation** patterns, e.g., the special intonation which may mark 'You like it' as a question rather than a statement. The questioning intonation pattern of spoken English is represented in written English by a question mark.

- varying the word order or **sequence.** The item *do you?* is said to be **sequence marked** in contrast to *you do* which has ordinary or unmarked sequence.

Of course more than one marker may be present:

they come
they are coming

The progressive *they are coming* is marked by the presence of both *are* and *ing*.

DEPENDENCE RELATIONSHIPS

This section deals with a principle which underlies many of the explanations in this book.

It is often said that grammar is concerned with the relationships between words in a sentence; with the proviso that for 'words' one must read 'morphemes, words, groups, clauses', this is true. A question that might be asked is 'What do we mean by relationships?', or at least 'What kinds of grammatical relationship are there?'

The most important relationship concerns the way in which some items are dependent on (or subordinate to) others. Some words (and again we will speak of words only, though the principle applies equally well to the other ranks) are indispensable; if they are removed, the unit they form part of falls to pieces. In

four military communications satellites

the essential word is *satellites;* it is said to be **independent.** The other words are to varying degrees **dependent;** *communications* is dependent on *satellites, military* on *communications satellites,* while *four* is dependent on *military communications satellites.* As can be seen from this example, dependence is often marked by sequence. Some dependent items, instead of preceding the one on which they are dependent, follow it as would happen if the phrase quoted went on *four military communications satellites planned* (have been abandoned). If the expression were . . . *communications satellites recently planned*, *recently* would be dependent on *planned* and the two words *recently planned* on *satellites*. The sequence marking is here more complicated though it is readily 'taken in' by a fluent speaker of the language.

Another instance of dependence occurs with clauses in a sentence:
    If you throw a six, you can start.

Here *you can start* is the independent item (this time a clause); *if you throw a six* is dependent on it and the dependence is marked by the structural word, or particle, *if*.

Such is the relationship called **dependence.** Similar to it, but different, is the situation when two items are dependent on each other: neither is sufficient on its own. A common example is the relationship between the clause elements *subject* and *predicator*. In the great majority of clauses both are necessary, and they support each other, as it were. The relationship is called **interdependence.**

The relationship between a complement and its predicator, both of which terms are explained in Chapter 4, is sometimes one of dependence, sometimes one of interdependence.

Another example of interdependence occurs in linked clauses:

    Prices of ingredients are given in cents *and* menu ideas are
    chosen to provide balanced nourishment.

The sentence consists of two interdependent clauses linked by *and*, as is explained in Chapter 5.

Finally there is the case where two items are *alternatively* dependent on a third one with the same degree of dependence; either might be deleted and the general sense would remain the same:
    My old friend Fred has turned up again.

Both *My old friend* and *Fred* are interdependent with *has turned up;* either could be removed. The items *My old friend* and *Fred* are an example of the relationship called **apposition.**

These relationships, dependence, interdependence and apposition appear in many guises in grammar, including English grammar. They are present in the subject matter of nearly all the chapters of this book even when they are not commented on explicitly.

One might compare interdependence to the relationship between husband and wife. Both are essential to a marriage, in the structure of which they are elements. They are intended to be in **concord,** like a subject and predicator which have to **agree** in number, i.e., both singular or both plural. Dependence is more like the relationship between a mother and the baby who is her dependent item. As for apposition, it is something like two baby brothers or sisters, but here the analogy must not be continued too long lest we find ourselves talking about deleting one of them.

TRANSFORMATIONAL RELATIONS

Sometimes, however, a structure cannot be understood by the examination of that structure alone or even by examining the way it fits into some higher structure. Light can often be shed by comparing two similar or parallel structures which are saying the same thing except for some measurable difference. Sometimes, indeed, this method is the only way of explaining the relationships; it reveals, as it were, a further dimension.

It is easiest to demonstrate the relationship between the parallel structures by imagining that one of them has to be turned into the other.

He is talking in his sleep + *marking for question* ⟶
Is he talking in his sleep.

The arrow here is to be interpreted as 'becomes' or 'may be rewritten as' Such a conversion is called a **transformation;** the resulting version is called a **transform.**

Another example is

An expert praised her + *passive marking* ⟶
She was praised by an expert.

The following diagram illustrates this.

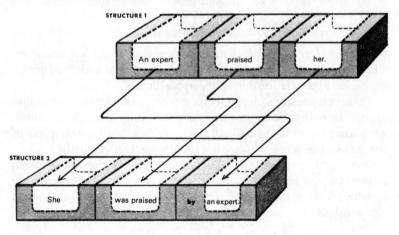

In this transformation,

her	becomes	*she*
praised	becomes	*was praised*
an expert	becomes	*by an expert*

Clearly the two varieties of form refer to the same situation, but they reflect a different view of it.

Such transformations are made great use of in some books. In this text they are used when they are particularly advantageous.

EPILOGUE

Etymology, the explanation of the origins of words, is not made use of in the grammatical explanations in this book: it can easily be a misleading clue to the current meaning of a word though it may give interesting information about the way that meaning has changed. To conclude, however, on an etymological note, Grammar is derived, via French and Latin, from the Greek word *grammatike* 'pertaining to letters'; it has a twin word (with which it was once identical) which has put on a different semantic dress and emerged as Glamour. Both these twins attempt at times to mystify, but with a little practice it is possible to learn to cope with them.

Exercises and Topics for Discussion
1. Can you think of any reasons for the fact that there are many languages? Would it be possible to make everyone speak the same language?
2. How much does what has been said about language as human behaviour apply also to music? What differences are there?
3. English has no word that includes the idea common to both 'uncle' and 'aunt'. Every language has such 'gaps' in its vocabulary. Can you think of others in English? A comparison with another language may help.
4. Do you think the language people use affects their thinking?
5. Can you think of any other example of allophones in English?
6. List six bound morphemes, other than the examples given.
7. Produce three examples of language from different registers.
8. Give three more examples from everyday experience of marked and unmarked members of a set.
9. What is a stereotype? What is the etymology of *cliché*?
10. **(For group work.)** Take any 'in' language (register) with which you are familiar; try to discover what are its special linguistic features.
11. Does the principle of taboo ever apply to language? In what circumstances?

criteria : form & position

Word Classes

2.0 It is convenient to place words in certain categories or **classes,** mainly according to (i) their form, (ii) the changes that can occur in their form, and (iii) the positions they occupy in groups in relation to other word classes. The word classes considered in this chapter are **nouns, personal pronouns, verbs, adjectives, numerals, adverbs, wh- words, demonstratives** and **particles.**

N.B

2.1 NOUNS
Nouns appear in certain forms which are typical of their class.

MORPHOLOGY

2.11 FORM IN NOUNS. (a) Most have four forms though, as will be seen, in some nouns some of these forms are lacking: such words are, however, in other ways so like the typical, majority nouns that there is no doubt about including them in the class of nouns. Further, some of the forms (such as *trousers'* below) are very rare.

cat	cats	cat's	cats'
house	houses	house's	houses'
rain	rains	rain's	rains'
man	men	man's	men's
ox	oxen	ox's	oxen's
goose	geese	goose's	geese's
	deer	deer's	
	salmon	salmon's	
	Chinese	Chinese's	
	trousers		trousers'
	cattle		cattle's

ubiquity	ubiquity's
analysis	analyses
saliva ?	
mumps	
physics	

The first and third columns are of course singular forms and the second and fourth columns plural forms. The third and fourth columns may be called apostrophe forms.† For most nouns the distinction between these two forms is made only in writing and for very many nouns their spoken form is also identical with the forms in the second column.

b) Nouns are often formed by the combination of a free morpheme and a bound one; such a bound morpheme is an instance of a derivational suffix. Some of the most frequent suffixes forming nouns are:

-ation	examine	examination
-ition	compose	composition
-ion	react	reaction
-ment	content	contentment
-ity	sincere	sincerity
-ure	please	pleasure
-er	play	player
-ness	happy	happiness

The suffixes are one of the ways by which nouns are recognised; this applies particularly when a word is met with for the first time, e.g., meridionality, quintuplication.

Exercises

1. a) Find four other nouns which are like *trousers* and *cattle* in the forms they can have.
   b) Find three other nouns like *physics* which have only one form.
2. a) By using suffixes form nouns from the following words. Some of them may have more than one possibility: *conspicuous, gesticulate, perspicacious, regenerate, fissiparous.*
   b) Add *-ance, -ence, -or* to appropriate free morphemes and produce a table like the one above. What other noun-forming suffixes can you supply?

2.12 POSITION POSSIBILITIES OF NOUNS. Look at the positions of

---

†They are also known, traditionally, as genitive or possessive forms – though possession is by no means always a characteristic of them.

nouns in these groups. (The nouns are italicised, and the sections marked by a single bar are groups.)

   i) The *bishops* | have announced | revolutionary *changes* | in the *church*.

   ii) Four *cameras* | will provide | direct *coverage* | of the *mile*.

   iii) New *cars* | are | readily available.

   iv) Some fifteen hundred young *people* | are expected | to attend.

   v) I | can make | my *decision* | now.

   vi) They | may attend | the general *functions* | at the *weekend*.

   vii) *Members* | use | the upper *door*.

   viii) The *ladies* inside | were sipping | *tea*.

   ix) The *schoolgirl* | with long *fingernails* | was reprimanded.

   x) The old blue *book* | was mutilated.

From the examples above it can be seen that nouns may occur alone in a simple group, e.g., *members* in (vii), and *tea* in (viii), or as the main word of a complex group.

A noun, as the main word of a complex group, may be preceded by a number of other words in the group such as

determiners	(a, the, this, my, etc. See 7.2)
numerals	(second, five, etc. See 7.3)
adjectives	(revolutionary, young, blue, etc. See 7.4)

In addition, a noun as the main word of a complex group may also be preceded by other nouns:

   xi) The *car* door| was damaged| in the accident.

   xii) She| is| my *dream* girl.

   xiii) We| have ordered| our new *colour television* sets.

2.13 The word class Noun is a very extensive one and is being added to all the time. One familiar example of a register where new words have been created is that associated with space exploration; words such as 'astronaut', 'telstar', and 'sputnik' have been recently introduced. Moreover new nouns come into general use from specialised technical vocabularies: 'transistor', 'computer'. Because fresh nouns can be added to existing ones, nouns form an open set. Pronouns, in contrast, are a closed set since no more pronouns are being made.

Exercises

3. 'The wet snoozlence carried seven wickfezzers through the neddler's pontin'. Prove that the nonsense words are nouns using the information given in this section.

4. Use these words as nouns:

post	end	save
move	run	walk
tear	hope	if

5. List the nouns in this nonsense paragraph and beside each write the characteristic that told you it was a noun.

'Globnoks have rarely been known to gurfur the limnickings of commissions sanked in to amplover the bresdecs for knofpings, dunbers or "tafts of seinfers." The derf can so often be dombled by liskful mogs of polentious ashert, by scrooming poplisses under siz honks of vindun in the fure and tremainous rerton of much sercentation from the urop. In lamisation benters like gronish auguest *ad hoc* dobs evoke loper splogger and hytter kink than in America. When a New Zealand crisis klongs an ollery allery the werthums are usually blurped with plallion or at least nofery monthings.'

6. Can you think of other registers where there are many new noun formations?

2.2   PERSONAL PRONOUNS

2.21   The personal pronouns have five forms. These forms are identified by a *type* (or *case*) example:

I-type	me-type	mine-type	my-type	myself-type
I	me	mine	my	myself
he	him	his	his	himself
she	her	hers	her	herself
we	us	ours	our	ourselves
they	them	theirs	their	themselves
you		yours	your	yourself/-ves
it			its	itself

2.22   Pronouns are divided into three **persons:** first person, second person, third person according to the table below:

1st person:	I, me, etc.
	we, us, etc.
2nd person:	you, etc.
3rd person:	all other pronouns

2.23   Personal pronouns may also be classified by number:

Singular	Plural
I	we
he	
she	they
it	
you	you

The pronoun *you* may be used in singular or plural contexts:

> You are yourself to blame.
>
> You are yourselves to blame.

2.24 Personal pronouns fill the same positions as groups that have nouns as their main word:

i) *Jim*| struck| *the boy* | on *the hand.*
   He| struck| *him*| on *it.*

ii) *The elderly man* | visited | *the old pub down the road* | regularly | at eleven.
    He| visited| *it*| regularly| at eleven.

2.3 VERBS

Verbs have certain typical forms and may be classified according to the number of forms they possess. Most verbs have six, five or four forms. All the forms of the six-form verb are given names listed under *form names* below. For simplicity of reference these names are given symbols. Pay particular attention to these as they are used frequently in this text.

2.31 SIX-FORM VERBS.

Verb Forms		Form Names	Symbols ← N-B
show	swim	simple	V^o
to show	*to* swim	infinitive	V^{to}
show*s*	swim*s*	s-form	V^s
show*ed*	sw*a*m	preterite	V^d
show*n*	sw*u*m	participle (perfect)	V^n
show*ing*	swimm*ing*	ing-form	V^g

Note: a) The -*s*, -*ed*, -*n*, -*ing* in the first columns are examples of bound morphemes.

b) Both *show, swim* and *shows, swims* are used as present tense forms, and *showed* and *swam* are used as past tense. The word **tense** in this text is used only of first or singly occurring verb forms like those in italics in the previous sentence. In 'I am losing' only the word *am* possesses tense.

c) Only those verb forms which indicate tense [as in Note (b) above] are called *finite*. All other verb forms are called *non-finite*.

d) In this text V^{to} (e.g., to show) is treated for grammatical purposes as a single word.

e) The six-form verb is used as a model for deriving the

form names and symbols even for verbs which have fewer forms.

2.32 FIVE-FORM VERBS.

Verb Forms		Form Names	Symbols
walk	dig	simple	V^o
to walk	to dig	infinitive	V^{to}
walks	digs	s-form	V^s
walked	dug	preterite	V^d
		participle (perfect)	V^n
walking	digging	ing-form	V^g

In this group *walk/walks* and *dig/digs* are used as present tense. *Walked* and *dug* have a double function, that of V^d and V^n:

he walked	he showed	V^d
he has walked	he has shown	V^n

Among both six- and five-form verbs there are many like *swim, bleed, break, take, dig, run,* which change their basic form by a vowel alteration. Occasionally this alteration affects pronunciation but not spelling, as in *read*. In some verbs the V^d form is usually spelt *-t* instead of *-ed* (e.g., *learnt*). Some verbs, such as *keep/kept*, make both the changes mentioned above.

2.33 FOUR-FORM VERBS.

Verb Forms	Form Names	Symbols
cut	simple	V^o
	preterite	V^d
	participle (perfect)	V^n
to cut	infinitive	V^{to}
cuts	s-form	V^s
cutting	ing-form	V^g

In this group V^o has a triple function – it acts as V^o, V^d, V^n do in the six-form verb:

they cut	they show	V^o
it may cut	it may show	V^o
it cut	it showed	V^d
it has cut	it has shown	V^n

Exercises

7. a) Classify the following verbs according to the number of forms they have: *lay*, quit, *wake*, listen, shut, *lie*, hurt, *bring, buy*, cling, put, *grow*, growl, telephone, flee, wet, spit, *shoot*, cost, thrust, sew, beat, slit, move, *catch*.

b) Set out in full the verb forms with form names and symbols of the verbs italicised in (a).

8. Of the three classes of verbs we have examined only one consists of an open set; in other words, there is only one class that newly invented verbs can go into. Which is it?

2.34 AUXILIARY VERBS. These are verbs which usually precede other verbs. One, two, three or possibly four may be used in the same verbal group. They are used with negatives, in inversions, to avoid repetitions of the main verb and in insistent assertion. These examples illustrate the four functions of the auxiliaries:

   i) I *am* not going.   I *do*n't care.
   ii) *Shall* I see you tomorrow?   *Did*n't I see you yesterday?
   iii) *Do* you love me?   Yes, I *do*.   I *do*n't believe you, and neither
       does he.
   iv) I *do* like chocolate.   I *must* go.

It can be seen that the *auxiliary* + *not* is often shortened, usually with an accompanying vowel change, e.g., *can, can't; will, won't; do, don't*. Such contracted forms are customarily confined to spoken and informal written English.

The auxiliary verbs, twelve in number, form a closed set. Not all may be used as main verbs. Not all have a complete range of forms. The list is: *be, have, do, will, shall, can, may, must, ought, dare, need* and *used* (which just qualifies), and the various forms of these.

Exercises

9. How many forms does each of the auxiliaries possess?
10. Write five sentences for each of the following uses of auxiliaries: (a) to avoid repetition; (b) + not; (c) in inversions.

2.4   ADJECTIVES

2.41   The main **formal** feature of the adjective in English is the possibility of forms ending in -*er* and -*est* (comparative and superlative).

brave	braver	bravest
wise	wiser	wisest

For many adjectives, particularly those with more than one syllable, such forms are not possible, but their equivalents are made by preceding them with *more* and *most* respectively.

delicious	more delicious	most delicious

Exercise

11. Some common adjectives use a different base before -*er* and -*est*, e.g., *good*. How many can you think of?

2.42   Even this form distinction, the -*er* and -*est* possibility, is not a certain guide to identifying adjectives; there are a number of adverbs (e.g., *soon*) which also have this feature (see below). The adjective is therefore best recognised by the typical positions it occupies and these are dealt with later under the nominal group in Chapter 7.

The word adjective in this grammar is used in a more restricted sense than you may be used to. In the following passages only the words in italics are adjectives.

   i) Along the *dead, silent* roadway, and through the *uneven* blackness of the wood, we lurched and stumbled. He was very *heavy* and *difficult* to direct.

  ii) It was a *grey, dree* afternoon. The wind drifted a *clammy* fog across the hills, and the roads were *black* and *deep* with mud.

 iii) Whatever holes may be picked in the Molyneux report it is *clear* that the case for streamlining and concentrating port development in New Zealand now becomes *stronger* than ever. Conversely, all the misgivings that have been felt about the *heavy* investment that is going into improving harbour and transport facilities at *secondary* ports must now be greatly increased.

2.43   Many adjectives are, however, readily recognisable by their suffixes:

-ful	pitiful	pity
-y	messy	mess
-some	troublesome	trouble
-al	doctrinal	doctrine
-ous	glorious	glory
	loquacious	loquacity
-id	torpid	torpor

Through such endings strange words are often spotted as adjectives, e.g., *iatromathematical*†, *dodecagynous,* or for that matter *curvaceous* and *supercalifragilisticexpialidocious.*

---

†This is of course not to deny that nouns too may have the -*al* suffix, though more seldom.

Exercise

12. What other suffixes typical of adjectives can you exemplify? Can you think of any which have special uses in scientific subjects?

2.5   NUMERALS

The next class consists of numerals. They usually have two forms, exemplified by:

four	fourth
seven	seventh
nine	ninth

In some cases the form relation is less obvious but undeniable:

one	first
two	second

The left hand column consists of **cardinal numerals,** the right hand column of **ordinal numerals.**

2.6   ADVERBS

2.61   The word class Adverb is often defined by position rather than by form. Items with no obvious form of resemblance such as *quickly, out* and *sometimes* are often considered to be members of this class. In this text, however, the term **adverb** is used for a small class of words which have a few typical affixes and/or certain typical form-change possibilities. Such items, of course, do occur in certain typical positions, but this fact is of secondary importance.

The great majority of adverbs have an *-ly* suffix. Most adverbs in this category are formed from adjectives and the ing-form of verbs, e.g.,

gladly	glad
shyly	shy
grudgingly	grudging

Thus even in nonsense sentences there is no difficulty in identifying such adverbs:

The blengblong blanged blingfully.
The gamplies murpled the toonosies unframmingly.

These *-ly* adverbs are members of an open set.

Another small but currently expanding open set of adverbs is marked by the suffix *-wise*, as in *lengthwise, clockwise,* and so forth.

There is a widespread trend at present towards forming adverbs in -*wise* as in:

> Although I do not like the colours in this picture, composition-wise it has great strength.

2.62 There are a few adverbs which, like adjectives, have comparative and superlative forms marked by -*er* and -*est*. These are distinguished from the adjectives by their typical position which is the same as that for -*ly* adverbs. Compare the following:

i) Ebenezer | gripped | his flea | manfully.
   He | gripped | it | hard.
ii) Freda Spoons| drives| recklessly.
   Her brother| drives| fast.

When such words are used in typical adjective positions they are adjectives. Occasionally ambiguities may occur:

> The captain looked very hard.
> His daughter has grown fast.

In the position of *fast* it would be possible to have an adjective (*pretty*) or an adverb (*quickly*). Consequently *fast* may be either in this position.

2.63 Not all the adverbs which have forms in -*er* and -*est* have corresponding adjectives (e.g., *soon, sooner, soonest*). Some adverbs form comparative and superlative forms with the words *more* and *most*, e.g., *often, seldom*. Adverbs marked by -*ly* regularly make their comparatives and superlatives in this way. Note the various adverbs with comparative or superlative forms in:

> Wotherspoon may have swum *faster* and arrived *sooner* but I worked *hardest* and stayed in *longest* of all the rescuers. *More often* than not credit goes to the *most loudly* blown trumpet.

Exercises

13. Complete the following sentence six times, each time with an adverb indicating loudness. Arrange the examples in ascending order of intensity.
    At that, the young man laughed ....
14. There are a few other, less used, suffixes which mark adverbs. Can you think of any? Can you think of a prefix which forms adverbs?

2.7   WH- WORDS AND DEMONSTRATIVES

It is possible to recognise other, smaller, word classes though there comes a point when further division into form classes becomes unprofitable. Two such small word classes do, however, require a special mention.

2.71 WH- WORDS. Most of the members of this form class are marked by an initial *wh* and have an additional form with *-ever*:

who	whoever
whom	whosoever
whose	whatever
what	whatsoever
which	whichever
where	wherever
when	whenever
why	whyever
how	however

How is included because it partly works in the same way as the others. They have several uses, one of which is to signal questions. Note that *while* and *whether,* although they begin with *wh,* do not do this and are not included in the class of *wh-* words.

2.72 DEMONSTRATIVES. The group of words traditionally called demonstratives form a small class on their own. Like nouns and pronouns they have special plural forms. They also occur in pairs denoting comparative nearness to or remoteness from the speaker.

this	that
these	those

At this point form begins to peter out. It might be possible, for example, to consider the following as members of the demonstrative class:

here	there
now	then

Since, however, there are no special plural forms, this possibility is not followed.

2.8 PARTICLES

All the remaining words are placed in the general class called particles. They consist of a large but closed set of words which do not vary in their form. Some of these words do fall into further distinct classes but they are classes arising from position not form. A few of these will be briefly mentioned here; others will become clear in later chapters.

2.81 Some particles occupy a similar position to adverbs such as *manfully* and *fast* in 2.62. They include words like *sometimes* (not **more sometimes*), *never*, and also a fairly long list of words like *out, on* in sentences such as:

> Our friends had gone *out*, so we walked *on*.

These are **adverbial particles.** Other examples are:

> The fun is *over*.
> Let's go *in*.
> Put baby *down* on the edge of the bed, Shirley.
> With luck he'll drop *off*.

2.82 An important position class is found when the particles such as *out, on, over, in* (which have already been listed among the adverbial particles) occur at the beginning of a group of which the main word is a noun or pronoun.

The cow jumped | *over* the moon.

Was it not | *beyond* her?

I don't think she knew | *about* it.

At the end | *of* the bench | was a bunsen burning | *under* a
    gauze | *with* a basin | *on* it.

To explain its contents was | *past* the wit | *of* man.

In the end | we poured them | *down* the drain.

In these positions the particles are **prepositions.** In this book preposition is not a form class but a position class only. Words like *in* are, by form, particles; according to the position they occupy they may act as adverbial particles or as prepositions.

2.83 Three other common positional classes composed of particles are:

a) **linking** particles such as *and, or, but*.
b) **binding** particles such as *if, since, though*.
c) **intensifying** particles such as *very, quite, too*.

Other positional classes will emerge from later chapters, particularly those on the Nominal Group.

Exercise

15. List (a) the adverbs and (b) the particles in the following passage:

> I urged him to walk steadily and quietly across the yard. He did his best, and we made a fairly still entry into the farm. He dropped with all his weight on the sofa, and, leaning down, began to unfasten his leggings. In the midst of his fumblings he fell asleep and I was afraid he would pitch forward onto his head.

Chapter **3** ✓

The Group

(handwritten margin notes:) Words are put into groups — → MHQ structure pattern.
NG Nominal gp. (prepositional gp) pG
VG Verbal gp.
AG Adverbial gp.

3.0 Sometimes a single member of one of the word classes discussed in Chapter 2 will constitute a **group** in a clause. When this occurs the group is called a simple group as in:

Dogs	bite	fiercely.
He	came	often.
Slowly	Mary	drowned.
Ships	sail	oceans.

In the sentences above each word is indispensable to its group, and is called the **headword** with the symbol H. But it is common for other words to accompany the headword in a group, and all such words in a group are related.

Some dogs | bite | fiercely.

The group *some dogs,* consisting of more than one word, is a complex group. As *dogs* is a noun, this is a complex **nominal group.**

Some dogs | can bite | quite fiercely.

The simple **verbal group** *bite* has been changed into the complex verbal group *can bite,* and the simple **adverbial group** *fiercely* has become the complex adverbial group *quite fiercely.* H is *bite* and *fiercely* respectively.

Compare the following:

| He | came | often. |
| He alone | had been coming | particularly often. |

The pronoun *He* is H of a nominal group. In the first of the two sentences the group is simple, in the second it is complex. In the first sentence, *came* is H of a simple verbal group; in the second, *coming* is H of a complex verbal group.

In the two pairs of sentences following, notice how each simple group has been expanded into a complex group.

i) Slowly| Mary| drowned.

Very slowly indeed| poor old Mary| was being drowned.

ii) Ships| sail| oceans.

Many large British ships | are sailing | the vast oceans of the world.

The words that occur with the headword of a group are **dependent** on the headword. In the examples above two types of dependents are illustrated. Look at the groups listed below. In each case H is in italics.

> Some *dogs*
> > *He* alone
> quite *fiercely*
> > very *slowly* indeed
> the vast *oceans* of the world.

Sometimes dependent words appear in front of H and sometimes after it. These positions give us two types of dependents:

Modifiers (M) – words that precede H in a group.

Qualifiers (Q) – words that follow H in a group.

Some, quite, very, the, vast are modifiers in the examples just above. The qualifiers in the same examples are *alone, indeed, of the world*. The last Q is itself a group, but as it is dependent on *oceans* at H it is part of the complete nominal group *the vast oceans of the world*.

The basic structure of the group may be seen as M H Q but note that H is obligatory while M and Q are optional; moreover there may be more than one M or Q. The structure is therefore better expressed as:

$$M_n \qquad H \qquad Q_n$$

where n may have any value from zero to an indefinite, small number.

3.1   THE NOMINAL GROUP (NG)

The complex NG fits in the clause in the same way as a simple NG does.

> The famous bearded cricketer with the notorious thirst | had been gazing | rather hopefully | at the refreshment bar.

Look at the first NG: *The famous bearded cricketer with the notorious thirst.*   H is *cricketer.*

M's are *the, famous, bearded.*

Q is *with the notorious thirst.*

The headword of an NG is usually a noun or a pronoun; the modifiers may belong to a number of different word classes; the qualifiers may be words, groups, or clauses (see Chapter 8). Further examples of NG's are:

   i) *I* | saw | *him*.
      (*him* is a simple nominal group, a pronoun, and H; *I* is the same)
  ii) There's one man I hate –| *him with the curly hair*.
      (This is a nominal group with *him* as H and *with the curly hair* as Q.)
 iii) *Cats* | woke | *me*.
      (*Cats* is a nominal group and so is *me*.)
  iv) *Several cats caterwauling* | woke | me.
      (*Several cats caterwauling* is a nominal group, M H Q.)
   v) *The funds available* | are | sufficient.
      (*The funds available* is a nominal group, M H Q.)

3.11   Look at:

> of the world
> with the notorious thirst
> at the refreshment bar.

These are NG's with *world, thirst, bar* at H. The remainder of each group consists of modifiers. The first modifier, however, is in each case a particle of the kind discussed in 2.82. When it occurs as the first M of an NG it is known as a preposition (p). It is useful to call an NG modified by a preposition, a **prepositional group** (pG).

Exercises

   1. Divide the NG's into M, H, Q, as applicable:
      a) The lass with the delicate air.
      b) Over the field | ran | the exhausted footballers.
      c) Some fifteen shoddy blue teenage dresses | were displayed | in the glittering new corner shop.
      d) Materials of this kind | do not occur | in sufficient quantity.
   2. Identify the headwords of the NG's in the following sentences:
      a) 'Man overboard!' was the startled cry.
      b) Man cannot live by bread alone.
      c) We remain here.
      d) We are the leaders of this group.

3.2   THE VERBAL GROUP (VG)

In this group, normally following the nominal group in the clause, very much the same kind of pattern emerges. There may be no Q; there may be no M or there may be several.

          H
i) Run.

     M   H
ii) He| has run.

     M   M   H
iii) He| has been running.

      M   M   M   H
iv) He| should have been running.

        H   Q
v) The clock| runs down.

   H   M   H
vi) I | went | to the funeral of an old friend, whom I | had run

      Q
   across | recently.

       M   M   H
vii) The matter| has been discussed.

3.21 There are thus two kinds of VG, simple and complex. *Run, went* are simple, the rest are complex. In the simple VG, the one verb is always H. In the complex VG, the main verb is H, and the preceding auxiliaries are M.

3.22 Q sometimes presents problems. There are many English verbs that naturally take a particle after them which is particularly closely linked to the verb, e.g.,

   The clock | runs *down*.

   I | ran *across* | a friend.

This particle is regarded as Q in a VG. However, the case is different where the particle is more loosely associated with its verb and can be freely interchanged with other particles.

Compare

          He| ran across| a friend.

with

                    across
                    over
                    under
                    on
     He| ran| by   a bridge.
                    beyond
                    to
                    past
                    etc.

In the second set of examples the particle is not part of the VG. For more detailed treatment see Chapter 16.

Exercise

3. Using *swim, drink, catch, talk,* as the main verb of the VG, write short sentences for each according to the following patterns. Start with the word *Fred*:
   H, M H, M M H, M M M H.

3.3 THE ADVERBIAL GROUP (AG)

An adverbial group is a group of words with an adverb or particle as H, e.g.,

He | imbibed | *rather freely* | , laughed | *quite immoderately* | and *too often.*

The adverbial groups in the sentence are:

M	H
rather	freely
quite	immoderately
too	often

In the sentence about the cricketer in 3.1, the adverbial group is *rather hopefully*.

The modifiers of the headword of an adverbial group are usually intensifying particles (see 2.83).

As with other groups, the adverbial group may be simple or complex. In this case, however, the simple is more common than the complex.

He | gazed | *hopefully* | into her candid blue eyes.

'No,' | she | said, | *coldly*.

He | turned | *away*.

Exercises

4. Identify and analyse into M and H any adverbial groups in the sentences below.
   a) He could do that much more often if he wished.
   b) Perhaps he would if he were asked very politely.
   c) Most unfortunately, I think he is too shy.
   d) Not too shy, but too gentlemanly.
   e) I think you're just talking extremely stupidly.
5. Precede the adverb in the following sentence with as many modifiers as you can think of:
   She acted .... rashly.

groups are put into clauses —S P C A

The Clause

4.0 The next syntactic unit above the Group is the **clause.**
In this chapter we shall deal with some basic clause patterns and
their structures. The examples below demonstrate such structures.
(Each example happens also to represent a simple sentence, since
each sentence consists of only one clause. But we are concerned
with them only as clauses.)

      S   P
An owl | hooted.

        S   P   A
Ermintrude | jumped | at the noise.

    S   P   C
She | clutched | Wilhelmina.

       S   P   C
Wilhelmina | was | brave.

  S   P   C   A
She | took | Ermintrude | by the hair.

  S   P   A
She | spoke | harshly.

     S   P   C   A
The blings | blanged | the blongs | in the blung.

Clauses usually have a **subject** (S) and a **predicator** (P); they often
have a **complement** (C) and an **adjunct** (A) as well.

4.1 SUBJECT

S	P	C	A
He	swims		well.
They	swim		strongly.
Alcohol	is	dangerous.	
The excessive use of alcohol	is	disastrous.	
Cows	eat	grass.	
Six shorn Romney sheep	were killed.		
The rather charming seventeen year old lass in the powder blue suit and Chantilly lace blouse	downed	me	with a karate chop.

What are the characteristics of the items under S?

a) They are all nominal group items (simple or complex). Certain exceptions will be given later.

b) They precede predicator items. Other positions for S will be dealt with later.

c) They have number concord with the predicator items; i.e. items chosen for S and P must both be singular or both plural.

d) Predicator items always occur when subjects occur.

Exercise

1. In each clause represent S by (i) a simple NG, (ii) a two-word NG, (iii) an NG of five or more words:
   a) .... sing sweetly.
   b) .... made an appalling noise.
   c) .... leapt on a bicycle.
   d) .... were blanging blingingly.
   e) .... hooted with derision.

4.2 PREDICATOR

S	P	C	A
He	has been helping	me	more.
She	was disturbed		by his attitude.
He	might have been attacked		at that time.
They	do	it.	

What are the characteristics of the predicator in these sentences?
The predicator:

a) is represented by verbal group items.

b) follows S. Variations will be dealt with later.

c) is in number concord with S.

d) precedes the complement if there is one.

e) precedes A. (However, the position of A may be varied much
   more than that of any other clause element.)

Exercise

2. Complete the following clauses by representing the predicator with verbal
   group items of one or more words as indicated by the dashes:

   a) The horses — — round the track.
   b) Several men — — —ed on the way to work.
   c) He — never —ed this machine before.
   d) He — been —ing a lot of money.
   e) Egbert — — himself before the crowd.

4.3   COMPLEMENT

4.31   Study the items under C in these clauses:

S	P	C	A

(handwritten above P and C: P = VERB + WHAT?)

S	P	C	A
Fred Spoons	died.		
He	was	a fool.	
I	put	him	in his place.
The overgrown rat	was eating	several pieces of meat	in the shed.
The mountaineers	lost	all they had brought.	
The young lady	bought	a yellow polka dot bikini.	

What are the characteristics of the complement in these sentences?
The complement:

a) is usually represented by an NG (exception see 9.7).

b) usually follows immediately after P.

c) has *no* concord with P (unlike S and P). There is one major
   exception, see 4.33.

d) is not present in all clauses.

4.32   MORE ABOUT COMPLEMENTS.

S	P	C	A
John	bought	the gift.	
The men	saw	the accident.	

S	P	C	A
Bonzo	cleans	your smallest room	hygienically.
The Liberation Front	killed	seventeen political opponents.	
I	adore	Kracklies.	
She	pushed	him	under the bus.

The complement in these examples has these characteristics:

a) The nominal group items that represent the complement have a noun or pronoun at H.

b) It can be transformed into the subject of a corresponding clause,

   e.g., The men saw *the accident*. ⟶

   The accident was seen by the men.

c) It is not in number concord with either S or P.

Complements which have these characteristics are known as **extensive complements**, (C^E).

4.33 Examine the complements below and look for differences from the complements in 4.32:

S	P	C
Martin Thomson	became	leader of the Party.
He	felt	a terrible fool.
The Opposition	was	jubilant.
The Prime Minister	seemed	very angry.

The complement in these examples has the following characteristics:

a) The nominal group items that represent the complement either are of the usual type with a noun at H, or have an adjective at H.

b) It is not possible to transform these items like those in 4.32 (c):
   He looked a complete idiot.
cannot be rewritten
   *A complete idiot was looked by him.

c) There is a number concord between the subject and complement when the complement is represented by a noun-headed group:
   He felt a fool. (Both S and C are singular.)
   They felt complete fools. (Both S and C are plurals.)

Complements which have these characteristics are known as **intensive complements**, (C^I).

Exercise

3. a) List four verbs that can appear at P in this sentence: The apples ......
   good.
   b) What other verbs could appear at P in this sentence: The men........
   angry.

Note: The verbs in the examples and in the exercises you have worked out are the verbs commonly followed by a C^I. However, a number of other verbs can take as C^I a myself-type pronoun, e.g.,

> He washed himself.
> She kicked herself.
> I shot myself.
> The children over-rate themselves.
> One forgets oneself.

This is clearly a C^I because of the concord with S.

4.34 Look at these further sentences:

	S	P	C	C
	They	considered	John	a fool.
	They	considered	him	foolish.
	They	elected	John	president.
(*but not*	*They	elected	John	foolish.)

The C in the last column has the following characteristics:

a) As second complement to a verb such as *consider*, it may be represented by a noun-headed group, *or* an adjective-headed group; as second complement to a verb such as *elect*, the complement is represented by a noun-headed group *only*. It is of interest to note that in neither case can the second C be represented by a pronoun-headed group.

b) The second complement, if it is represented by a noun-headed group, is in concord relation with the preceding one:

> They considered *the man a fool.*
> They considered *the men fools.*

c) The second complement does not transform into the subject of a corresponding clause.

d) Because of the similarity between the characteristics of this type of second complement and those of the intensive complement treated in the previous section, it too is called an intensive complement (C^I).

e) The first complement has the characteristics of an extensive complement.

4.35   Now look at these:

S	P	C	C
The girl	gave	her friend	a book.
They	asked	him	a question.

The predicator is followed by two complements. Look back at the previous sections on complements and note their characteristics. These complements:

a) are not in number concord with S or P or with each other.

b) are both noun or pronoun-headed groups.

c) can be transformed into the subject of a corresponding clause:

The girl gave her friend a book.━━▶

⎰ A book was given her friend by the girl.
⎱ Her friend was given a book by the girl.

(N.B. In this second case the original subject is sometimes deleted.)

Because of the similarity in characteristics between these complements and those in 4.32 they too are called extensive complements. They may be labelled, in their sequence, C^{E1} and C^{E2}.

$$C^{E1} \quad C^{E2}$$

They sent| me| some flowers.

Note: C^{E1} and C^{E2} can be reversed in sequence only if transformed into a C^E and an A:

The girl gave her friend a book.━━▶

The girl gave a book to her friend.

Exercise

4 a) Supply six verbs which can appear at P in this sentence: Laura . . . . her boyfriend the latest pop record.

 b) Transform as many as possible of the sentences you have written in (a) so that C^{E1} becomes S.

 c) Transform as many as possible of the sentences you have written in (a) so that C^{E2} becomes S.

 d) Transform as many as possible of the sentences you have written in (a) so that C^{E2} becomes C^E. What has happened to the original C^{E1}?

4.4   ADJUNCT

S	P	C	A
The young man	posed		by the edge of the pool.
He	flexed	his muscles	self-consciously.
He	did	this	all afternoon.
The girls	paid	no attention	to him.

The characteristics of those parts of the sentences called **adjuncts** are:

a) They are usually optional:

S	P	C	A
He	flexed his muscles ·		self-consciously.
He	flexed his muscles.		

b) They are obligatory only after
   i) a small set of verbs that require *either* a C^I or A: (*be, seem,* are the most common)

S	P	A
He	is	in the garden.
He	seems	in a dangerous mood.

   ii) a small set of verbs that require *both* a complement *and* an adjunct:

S	P	C	A
She	put	the book	on the table.
He	placed	his arm	around her shoulders.

c) They usually consist of an adverbial group or a prepositional group. Less commonly they are a nominal group, e.g., He did this *all afternoon.*

d) They may occur more than once in succession in a clause:

S	P	A	A
She	ran	quickly	down the stairs.

(Adverbial groups more often than not precede prepositional groups).

e) They occur in different places in the sequence of elements
   i) usually after a C if there is one
   ii) usually after P if there is no C
   iii) before S:

A	S	P	A
All his life	he	hungered	for her love.
Presently	the music	was heard.	

   iv) between P and C:

S	P	A	C
He	was,	fortunately,	alive.

   v) interrupting the members of a verbal group:

S	P–	A	–P	C
He	was	<anxiously>	awaiting	news.
He	had	<never>	used	this machine.

[For meaning of P–, –P and <..> see 5.3, note (b).]

Exercise

5. Analyse the following sentences into S, P, C and A (do not forget the two types of C). Use group boundary markers (|). Not all elements are represented in each example.

a) The wicketkeeper moved to his left.
b) He dived high.
c) He held with apparent ease a sensational one-handed catch.
d) Three young men were missing on the moors in the thick fog.
e) The bandit successfully dodged the traffic on the motorway.
f) He was furious over his recent failure.
g) Not every girl would consider the speedway her ideal Saturday night's entertainment.
h) Hundreds of people sent Chichester good wishes at the start of his lonely voyage.
i) In hot, sunny Northland, the emphasis is on the cool, natural and casual look for brides.
j) Crew squabbles, broken masts, secrets of design, sailmakers' nightmares, and the evergreen bugaboo about sea conditions off Rhode Island give a sensation-loving public a diet of good red meat.

4.5   BASIC CLAUSE STRUCTURES

We have examined S, P, C and A as individual elements, and partially examined their structural combinations. In this section we will list the basic clause structures formed from these elements. Each basic clause structure will be illustrated by a pattern.

There are seven basic clause structures. These form only a very small proportion of the total possible clause structures. Basic clause structures are restricted in the following ways:

a) They must have both S and P; and these two elements must occur in the sequence SP. P must be represented by a finite verbal group.

b) They must include only adjuncts which are *obligatory* (i.e., not deletable).

c) Any complement must follow the predicator.

These restrictions are required if basic clause structures are to be limited to a small number. If, for example, restriction (b) were relaxed, the number of basic clause structures would be very large; for there may be an indefinite number of adjuncts in a clause, and adjuncts may choose from among a number of different positions.

4.51   Pattern I has the structure S P.

S	P
The Sirens	sang.

S	P
The boat	sank.
Only the tall sailors in life-jackets	survived.
I	was being cross-examined.

Note: S and P are obligatory elements. Very frequently an A would occur in such sentences.

The Sirens sang enchantingly.

Solemnly Clothilde sang.

Pattern II has the structure S P A.

S	P	A
The refreshments	are	outside.
Everybody	seems	in a good mood.
Some of the guests	are lying	on the grass.

Note: In this pattern A is obligatory. There are very few verbs which can be P; the commonest ones are *be, seem, look.*

Pattern III has the structure S P C^E.

S	P	C^E
My aunt	swallowed	an aspidistra.
Emma	wore	a mini-skirt.
John	carried	his umbrella.

Pattern IV has the structure S P C^I.

S	P	C^I
My aunt	became	an aspidistra.
Emma	looked	attractive.
John	appeared	thoughtful.

Pattern V has the structure S P C^{E}C^I.

S	P	C^E	C^I
I	considered	my day	wasted.
Egbert	thought	the bikini girl	marvellous.
She	made	him	her beau.

Pattern VI has the structure S P C^{E1}C^{E2}

S	P	C^{E1}	C^{E2}
The alsatian	gave	the burglar	a fright.
The post-mistress	handed	him	a letter.
Grandfather	made	his grandson	a scale-model battleship.

Pattern VII has the structure S P C^{E}A.

S	P	C^E	A
The pilot	put	the plane	on the landing strip.
The train-robbers	placed	a heap of explosives	across the tracks.
The teacher	laid	the child	on the floor.

Note: There are few verbs which require a C^{E}and an A. Can you think of another?

Exercises

6. Complete the clauses below with representatives of the element or elements indicated:

   e.g., The hard-working student became _____C^I_____.

   The hard-working student became a scholarship winner.

   a) _____S_____ looks very tempting.
   b) Ermintrude_____P_____ her hairy paw _____A_____.
   c) _____S_____ _____P_____ on every conceivable occasion.
   d) The enterprising young salesman _____P_____ _____C^{EI}_____ _____C^{E2}_____.
   e) _____S_____ _____P_____ _____C^E_____ _____C^I_____.
   f) _____S_____ behaved _____A_____.

7. Identify the patterns of these clauses:

   a) George Orwell was born in India in 1903.
   b) Much of his writing is a record of his experiences.
   c) He became a policeman in 1922.
   d) He joined the Tribune staff.
   e) In 1945 he wrote *Animal Farm*.
   f) The animals make the pigs leaders.
   g) The pigs consider the other animals foolish.
   h) They put all opposition out of the way.
   i) The sheep are silly.
   j) The pigs teach them a rhyme.
   k) They put the rhyme on the barn wall.
   l) The pigs change the slogan.
   m) The new slogan appears on the barn wall.
   n) 'All animals are equal.'

8. Divide the clauses in Exercise 7 into groups. Indicate H, M and Q in the groups where applicable.

Clause can be   SPCA
                SP
                PC
                CA* etc.

* where predicator understood.

Chapter 5

The Sentence

5.0   In Chapter 4 we looked at clause patterns in single-clause sentences or, as we called them, simple sentences. Not all sentences consist of a single clause. Just as a group may be simple or complex, depending on whether it is composed of one word or more than one, so a sentence may be simple or complex, the complex sentence consisting of more than one clause. The relationships between the clauses in a sentence are of two kinds:

a) bondage
b) linkage

5.1   BONDAGE

5.11   Bondage occurs when a dependent clause is bound to an independent clause in a sentence. The structural symbols for clauses are:

$$\alpha \quad - \quad \text{independent clause}$$
$$\beta \quad - \quad \text{dependent clause}$$

Dependent clauses can be recognised by one or more of these characteristics:

a) they are optional elements; i.e., they can be deleted:

α
Jane was preparing breakfast, β *while I slept.*

β
Although I was half-asleep, α I could smell bacon.

α
I stayed in my bed, β *until she dropped an egg on my head.*

b) they can be found preceding or following an independent clause, or inserted in one:

Seven lonely trampers trudged on, *although almost overcome by fatigue.*
(α over "lonely", β over "almost")

When night fell, they collapsed in an exhausted heap.
(β over "night fell", α over "an")

These men, *who had eaten nothing all day,* were angered by their leader's inefficiency.
(α– over "men", β over "nothing", –α over "their")

(The minus sign is used to indicate an incomplete element.)

c) Dependent clauses usually have some feature which marks them as dependent. This is examined in more detail in the following sections.

5.12 PARTICLE MARKED DEPENDENT CLAUSES. Binding particles, or clause-binding words, which indicate that a clause is dependent or bound are:

as, after, although, as far as, as if, as long as, as soon as, as though, because, before, by the time (that), even, even if, every/ any time, for fear (that), how, however, if, in case, in order that, in so far as, in proportion as, lest, like (not in formal written English), now, once, since, so long as, so that, suppose, supposing, till, though, unless, until, whereas, whether, while.

The use of these particles is one indication of a dependent clause. These sentences show such clauses:

After we had finished dinner, the children kindly offered to do the dishes.
(β over "had finished", α over "kindly")

Even had they done them, we would still have been late.
(β over "had they", α over "still")

We took a torch *in case we were unable to find our way.*
(α over "torch", β over "unable")

Ultimately we came to the temple, *before the firewalkers had started jigging in the hot embers.*
(α over "we", β over "the firewalkers")

Notice that in the first example *after* could be replaced by *as, because, by the time, as soon as, once, since.* Each of these words could alter the meaning, i.e., the relation between the sentence and the relevant situation in which it is used, without in any way altering the structure of the sentence or its grammatical description.

Experiment, make up some dependent clauses using some of the particles above.

5.13 NON-FINITE MARKED DEPENDENT CLAUSES. Non-finite verb forms which indicate that a clause is bound are:

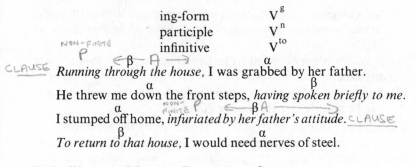

$$ing\text{-form} \qquad V^g$$
$$participle \qquad V^n$$
$$infinitive \qquad V^{to}$$

Running through the house, I was grabbed by her father.

He threw me down the front steps, *having spoken briefly to me.*

I stumped off home, *infuriated by her father's attitude.*

To return to that house, I would need nerves of steel.

5.14 WH-EVER MARKED DEPENDENT CLAUSES:

Whoever betrays you, I will remain true.

Whatever disaster overtakes you, put your trust in me.

Whenever you feel life intolerable, just write to me, care of this magazine, and I will give a solution in the next issue of 'Love-Lorn Letters.'

5.15 WH- MARKED DEPENDENT CLAUSES:

The apple was bad, *which was a pity.*

It was eaten by an orchardist, *who became very sick.*

His wife, *whom he had previously offered the apple to,* was not affected.

When he was sick, codlin moth attacked the rest of the crop.

5.2 LINKAGE

5.21 Clauses which are sentence elements are frequently linked. There is usually some particular feature in one or other of the linked clauses that *marks* the linkage relationship. The feature may be:

a) a linking particle
b) a shared element
c) a repeated word
d) a pronoun
e) punctuation

More than one of these features may be simultaneously present. These possibilities are examined in detail in the following sections.

5.22   In the sentences below, clause boundaries are marked
|| · · · · · · || .

i) No Government could have obstructed the course of settlement, || but no government need have abdicated quite so readily.

ii) Spies are often expected to be superhuman || but they are not infallible.

iii) The works manager has to please both directors and workers;
|| so he must be a fairly good negotiator.

The clauses in sentences (i) and (ii) are linked by the particle *but;* in (iii) by the particle *so*. Other common linking particles are *and, nor, then, or, yet, for, either . . . or, neither . . . nor*. Linking particles, strictly speaking, do not belong to either one of the linked clauses but for convenience they are considered as an adjunct element of the second linked clause. Linking particles are distinguished from binding particles by the fact that they are not closely tied to any one of the clauses which they link. They do not change their position if the linked clauses are switched. But if a dependent clause is moved, the binding particle must also move along with the clause. Binding particles are thus more tightly tied to *one* of the clauses which they bind.

In symbolic representation, clauses are shown to be linked by placing & ('ampersand') next to the element symbol of the second linked clause: e.g.,

α
Spies are often expected to be superhuman, || but they are
&α
not infallible.

α   β
I can't play for the team on Saturday || because my mother is
&β
in bed|| and there is no one else to look after her.

These sentences, therefore, represent the structures α &α and α β &β.

Note carefully instances such as the following:

i) Most pleasures are sinful, || if we have too much of them; || and in all countries sexual and social restraints emerge naturally from man's deepest feelings.

The first clause has the second clause as a dependent. Together these two clauses are linked to the last clause. The structure here can be represented as (α β) &α where the brackets show that the first two clauses are linked to the third.

ii) Sociologists may trace the speech patterns of the Cockney, ||
but unless the Cockney's mannerisms are used by the top
people || they will not become established as correct.

In this instance the second clause is dependent on the following
third clause and together these two clauses are linked to the first.
Again, the structure can be clarified by the use of brackets, i.e.,
α &(β α). The brackets around β α indicate the beta clause is not
directly linked to the preceding alpha clause.

Exercise

1. To which of the structures in (i) or (ii) does the following sentence belong?
   Moral attitudes change scarcely at all, and progress is delayed because
   morality is too often confused with intellect.

5.23 Clauses may be linked by a shared element which forms part
of the structure of the first linked clause. Examine carefully the
following sentences and determine which is the shared element that
links clauses. In some of the sentences there will be additional linkage by means of a linking particle.

i) In the face of handicaps Maori numbers dwindled and Maori
   standards fell.
ii) These two uses of land may come into conflict, and often do.
iii) Maoris could go to the court and state their claims to a particular
    territory.
iv) The agent, having dazzled Maori eyes with accessible gold,
    conducted his potential clients through the intricate legal pro-
    cedure, and emerged with the land in his grasp.
v) In the major selling areas drunkenness was rife, fertility declined,
   living conditions became an incentive to death and disease.

In (i) and (v) it is the initial prepositional group which is shared by the
linked clauses and thus effects the linkage. In linkage of this sort,
clauses tend to be very similar in their structure. The (v) example is
interesting also because it displays a series of linked structures.
There is no grammatical restriction on the number of clauses that
may be linked in a sentence. The structure of (v) may be represented
as α &α &α.

In (ii) (iii) and (iv) it is the subject of the first clause which is
shared by both linked clauses. The suppression of the subject in the
second linked clause is one of the most frequent devices for linking
clauses and, as in these examples, this device is usually supplemented
by a linking particle. Example (iv) is more complicated than (ii) and

(iii). It has a dependent clause inserted in the first linked clause. Its structure therefore would be $(\alpha\text{-}\beta\text{-}\alpha)$ &α.

In the following example, the predicator is shared:

$$\overset{\alpha}{} \qquad\qquad\qquad\qquad \overset{\&\alpha}{}$$

In the room were several people, || among them | Gertrude.

Of course it is not the same form of the verb *be* which is shared here. If the second linked clause were expanded it would require *was,* i.e., among them was Gertrude.

When the predicator is shared, ambiguities are possible, as in the following instance:

$$\text{S} \qquad \text{P} \quad \text{C}^{E1} \qquad \text{C}^{E2}$$

Mary | gave | Clare | a pencil, || John | a pen.

What is shared here may be

$$\qquad\qquad\qquad\qquad \text{C}^{E1} \qquad \text{C}^{E2}$$
S P   i.e.   Mary| gave| John | a pen.
$$\qquad\qquad\qquad\qquad \text{S} \qquad\qquad\quad \text{C}^{E2}$$
or P C^{E1} i.e.   John | gave | Clare | a pen.

The structural analysis of *John a pen* (together with its meaning) depends upon what you think has been suppressed. Ambiguities of this kind are not frequent. Usually when the predicator is shared, the structural analysis of the clauses with no P (i.e., **predicatorless** clauses) is straightforward. But sometimes the predicatorless clause does not share its predicator: *imagined predicator*

They interviewed many applicants, || some of them | good, || some of them | bad.

Some of them good is an elliptical version of *some of them were good.* Its structural analysis is therefore S C^{I}.

5.24 Linkage is sometimes marked by the repetition of a word: e.g.,

All land, ultimately, was *tribal* land; units within the *tribe* had prescriptive rights of occupation and use.

The weaker party to the contract lacked a *protector;* only the state could have been that *protector* and it chose not to be.

Linkage of this kind seems much less tight than the previous kinds. There would be little surprise if another writer had chosen to have a full stop instead of a semi-colon between the linked clauses, thus giving them the status of sentences.

Word linkage is often combined with the other kinds of linkage:

No *government* could have obstructed the course of settlement, but no *government* need have abdicated quite so readily.

5.25   Linkage may be marked by the occurrence of pronouns:

These leaders were also effective among their own people; *they* could also show *them* a possible method of growth.

This point of view is not entirely contemptible; *it* is held by some Europeans today.

5.26   Linkage may be marked by punctuation only:

The police arrested him in the village; there was no anger and no resistance.

Clearly, it is only the semi-colon which indicates that these two clauses are to be linked as elements of the one sentence. The linkage is very loose and, as with the instances of linkage by word repetition only, another writer might have chosen to make these clauses separate sentences. Such linkage is more a matter of style than of grammar.

5.27   The differences between linkage and bondage may often appear to be slight. There are indeed similarities; for example, particles play an important role in both relationships. But there are also differences. The sets of particles are different; moreover, linking particles are always fixed in position between the linked clauses. Binding particles, on the other hand, are closely tied to the dependent clause, and always have first place in such clauses, even when the latter precede, or are inserted in, independent clauses. Consequently, binding particles are tied closely to the other elements of the dependent clause; they represent a true adjunct element. On the other hand, linking particles are not more closely tied to one of the linked clauses than to the other. It is thus a convention that they are included as an adjunct of the following linked clause.   *NB.*

5.28   Linkage is not confined to clauses. Groups may be linked to each other; words also may be linked to each other. Some aspects of such linkage are examined in Chapter 14.

Exercises

2. Work through these sentences and check the indications of linkage:
   Gertie was thirty and Gertie was late.
   Tom was gallant but was rather shy.
   Tom took her out and Gertie was flirty.
   Either the wine was strong or Tom was weak.

He kissed her or, more likely, she kissed him.
Tom was on the spot and had to propose.
Gertie appeared reluctant but was wildly relieved.
Now Tom is no longer gallant, nor Gertie flirty.
(But one year later . . .)
He went to town, bought a wreath for their wedding anniversary, sent it
by special delivery, and then shot himself.

3. Compose or find in a text two instances of each of the following structures:
   a) α &α   b) α &α &α   c) α &(β α)
   d) (α β) &α   e) α β &β

5.3   TREE DIAGRAMS

In previous chapters and in this we have described separately the
sentence, clause and group structures. Now we will show how these
structures are tied together. Tree diagrams are used to do this.

The first step in tree diagramming is to show the elements of
sentence structure:

First rank   St

Second rank   α   &α

It was a bright, cold day in April, || and the clocks were striking thirteen.

The first rank shows that the item is a sentence.
The second rank shows that it is two linked clauses.
The second step in tree diagramming is to show the elements of
clause structures.

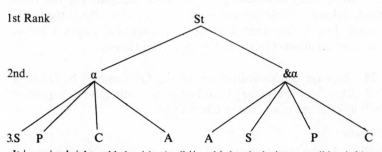

1st Rank   St

2nd.   α   &α

3.S   P   C   A   A   S   P   C

It | was | a bright cold day | in April || and | the clocks | were striking | thirteen.

The third rank shows the groups that each clause consists of, and
their relationships.

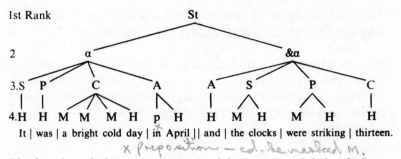

1st Rank   St

2   α   &α

3.S   P   C   A   A   S   P   C

4.H   H   M   M   M   H   p   H   H   M   H   M   H   H

It | was | a bright cold day | in April || and | the clocks | were striking | thirteen.

x preposition — cd. be marked M.

The fourth rank shows the elements of the groups and their relationships.

A fifth rank could be added, if required, to display morphemes and their relationships as elements of words.

Here are two further examples of tree diagrams:

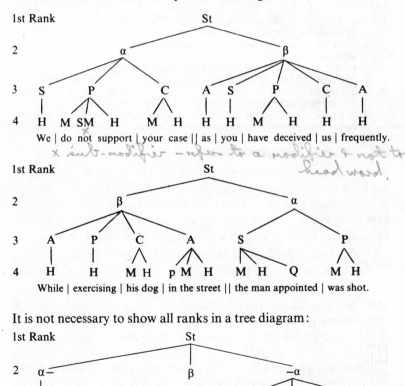

1st Rank   St

2   α   β

3   S   P   C   A   S   P   C   A

4   H   M SM   H   M   H   H   H   M   H   H   H

We | do not support | your case || as | you | have deceived | us | frequently.

x sub-modifier — refers to a modifier & not to head word.

1st Rank   St

2   β   α

3   A   P   C   A   S   P

4   H   H   M H   p M H   M H   Q   M H

While | exercising | his dog | in the street || the man appointed | was shot.

It is not necessary to show all ranks in a tree diagram:

1st Rank   St

2   α—   β   —α

3   S   P   C   A

Sheep dogs, <<which come in all sizes,>> are invaluable to the farmer.

Note: a) Clause β is not analysed because such development is not required. Only those ranks needed to show discontinuity have been developed.

b) Notice how a discontinous clause is represented in a tree diagram. The inserted clause above is enclosed by brackets different from those used hitherto. Double angle brackets are used to enclose an inserted clause. Likewise a single angle bracket is used to enclose an inserted group:

S   P−   A   −P   A
The people|were <anxiously> waiting for further news.

The two sections of the split unit receive the same element symbol but the minus sign (−) is placed after the first and also before the second to indicate that the elements are incomplete.

Exercise

4. Analyse the following sentences, using tree diagrams:
   a) We had all day because the owners were away.
   b) Finn went back to Sammy's bedroom while I was studying in the living-room.
   c) I searched the other rooms, but drew a blank every time.
   d) We scoured the old house very thoroughly, even looking behind the gilt mirror.
   e) An apple, dropping from the tree, struck Newton on the head.
   f) If we had some bacon, we could have bacon and eggs, if we had any eggs.

5.4   MORE ON BONDAGE

Previously in this chapter only the simplest instances of dependence between sentence elements have been displayed. They have mostly involved only two clauses, one of which was dependent upon the other. However, as the following sentence demonstrates, a dependent clause may, in turn, have another clause dependent upon it:

> The route of the 19th century wool clippers retains its own aura of excitement, || although it has been bypassed by most shipping || since the clipper era came to an end.

Here the first clause is the independent one; the following clause depends upon the first clause and in turn the third clause depends upon the preceding one. As already explained α can be used to indicate that the first clause is an independent element of the sentence and β can be used for the clause that is immediately dependent upon it. Further letters of the Greek alphabet can be used to indicate clauses which are dependent upon already dependent clauses. The third clause above will be γ. If there had been a further clause dependent upon that, its symbol would be δ, the one following that would be ε, and so on. Here is a further example showing a series of dependent clauses:

> As the gull walked back and forth, back and forth in front of the cabin, strutting on pale dusky-gold feet, holding up his pale yellow beak, that was curved at the top, with curious alien importance, the man wondered over him.

When you are confronted by a sentence with several dependent clauses, it is useful to break the analysis into a number of steps which show the order in which the dependent clauses have been added, e.g.,

i) The man wondered over him.
$$\alpha$$

ii) As the gull walked back and forth, back and forth in front of
$$\beta$$
the cabin|| . . . the man wondered over him.
$$\alpha$$

iii) As the gull walked back and forth, back and forth in front of
$$\beta$$
the cabin, || strutting on pale dusky-gold feet, || holding up his
$$\gamma$$
pale yellow beak . . . with curious alien importance, || the man
$$\gamma$$
wondered over him.
$$\alpha$$

iv) As the gull walked back and forth, back and forth in front of
$$\beta$$
the cabin, || strutting on pale dusky-gold feet, || holding his
$$\gamma$$
pale yellow beak, <<that was curved at the top,>> with
$$\gamma- \qquad \delta$$
curious alien importance, || the man wondered over him.
$$-\gamma \qquad \alpha$$

The structure of this sentence is β γ γ— δ −γ α.

Exercise

5. Place double bars around the clauses in the following sentences and indicate their relationships by using the sentence element symbols:
    a) He lay back and, tearing open the packet, placed the last cigarette on the window ledge and began to write out the poem in small neat letters on the rough cardboard surface.
    b) His lips murmured the first verses over and over; then stumbled through half verses; then slipped.
    c) The light spread upwards from the glass roof, making the theatre seem a festive ark, anchored among the hulks of houses, her frail cables of lanterns looping her to her moorings.
    d) At the far end near the street a faint light showed in the darkness and as he walked towards it he became aware of a faint aromatic odour.

Chapter 6

Nominal Group (I)
Nouns at H

6.0   As mentioned earlier (3.1), the commonest H of an NG is a noun, from which term of course the nominal group derives its name. Other classes of words which may occur at H will be discussed in Chapter 9.

The word class Noun, as has already been shown, consists of an open set. In this very extensive class some subclasses occur, arising, as you will see, both because of differences of form and because of differing possibilities of combining with other word classes. In particular, nouns vary in the modifiers they may have. This chapter discusses the subclasses of noun.

6.1   COUNT NOUNS

6.11   Study the nouns in italics in the following sentences and list the modifiers that occur with (a) the singular form, and (b) the plural form:

   i) A *pea* rolled off my fork.

   ii) The *pea* was teetering on the edge of the table.

 iii) It was the second *pea* I had lost.

 iv) The *peas* were badly undercooked.

  v) More than one *pea* escaped my prongs.

 vi) After the meal five *peas* glared at me from the floor.

 vii) *Peas* are often the very devil to manage.

viii) I have eaten few *peas* worse cooked than these.

 ix) Many *peas* in that meal were wasted.

The noun *pea* at H in an NG can be seen to have the following characteristics:

a) It has two forms.

b) When the group is simple, the plural form is usual.

c) The singular form may be modified by *a, the, one, second.*

d) The plural form may be modified by *the, few, many, five;* or not modified at all, as mentioned in (b).

Nouns with these characteristics are called **count nouns,** more specifically, **two-form count nouns.** (Two-form here, of course, refers to two forms *at H.*)

Words such as *Welshman, American, New Zealander* are **capitalised** two-form count nouns.

Exercise

1. a) List quickly ten more count nouns.
   b) Select any one of these and, in sentences of your own, demonstrate its characteristics. Make the NG in which it is H the subject in each sentence.
   c) Select another two-form count noun and repeat exercise (b), this time making the NG in which your noun is H a complement in each sentence.
   d) List three capitalised two-form count nouns with the suffix *-an,* three with the suffix *-man,* three with the suffix *-er,* and one with no special suffix.

6.12 Examine the characteristics of the italicised noun in the following sentences. Compare its characteristics with those of the word *pea* above.

   i) I saw a *deer* on the steep snow face.
   ii) The *deer* was galloping down the slope.
   iii) It was the third *deer* I had seen that day. .
   iv) The *deer* in that area are almost starving.
   v) One *deer* more comes into sight.
   vi) And now five *deer* are peering over the ridge.
   vii) *Deer* are sometimes careless when starving.
   viii) Few *deer* are shot for meat.
   ix) Many *deer* still roam New Zealand's forests.

The most noticeable characteristic of the word *deer* is that it has one form. But in the other three characteristics it resembles the word *pea.* So we can say that *deer* is a count noun, but is a **one-form count noun** (at H only). One-form count nouns belong to a closed set. *Salmon* and *trout* are two more members of the set.

Words like *Japanese* and *Balinese* are capitalised one-form count nouns.

Exercise

2. a) Make as complete a list of one-form count nouns as you can.
   b) List three more capitalised one-form count nouns.

6.13 Compare the characteristics of the nouns in italics in the following sentences with the characteristics of two-form count nouns.

   i) A *crew* was hastily gathered to man the lifeboat.
  ii) It was launched as soon as the *crew* was complete.
 iii) The *crew* were uncertain about the boat's condition.
  iv) It was the second *crew* to leave.
   v) The *crews* of other boats were already on their way.
  vi) One *crew* appeared to be in danger of being swamped.
 vii) In the end five *crews* reached the stricken ship.
viii) *Crews* get little reward for the risks they have to take.
  ix) Fortunately, few *crews* are ever lost.
   x) Great courage and endurance is shown by many *crews*.

The characteristics of the noun *crew* can now be paired off with those of *pea,* except for the feature of concord exemplified in the third sentence. There we have, at H of the nominal group at S, the singular or simple form of the noun, while the verb at P is in a plural form. This contrasts with the first sentence where the singular H of the nominal group at S is in concord with the expected singular form of the verb at P. So although *crew* has all the characteristics of a two-form count noun, it has a special characteristic of its own: when it is at H of a nominal group at S, the verb at P may be either singular or plural. A count noun with this characteristic is called a **collective noun.**

Exercise

3. Use the following words in sentences that demonstrate the characteristic that makes them collective nouns:
   family, team, jury, staff, council.

6.2   MASS NOUNS

6.21 In the set of sentences in 6.11 try substituting the word *rice* for the word *pea* or *peas*. A straight substitution would be possible in only one sentence – the second. In all the other sentences such a substitution is grammatically impossible. In other words we have here a noun with many characteristics different from those of count nouns.

From the sentences below work out the characteristics of the noun *rice*:

i) For most Asians *rice* is the staple item of food.

ii) The *rice* is sometimes mixed with vegetables or small quantities of meat.

iii) Much *rice* is grown in South-East Asia.

iv) New Zealand and Australia grow little *rice*.

Now check your characteristics against these:

a) It has only one form.

b) It can occur as H in a simple NG.

c) It can be modified by *the, much, little* (but not by *a, few,* or *many*).

d) It cannot be modified by numerals.

Nouns with these characteristics are called **mass nouns.** Some other examples are *bread, milk, meat*.

Some trade nouns come into this category:

i) *Bonzo* cleans your smallest room hygienically.

ii) The *Bonzo* is sprinkled on a damp cloth.

iii) Much *Bonzo* is sold in the shops.

iv) We use little *Bonzo* ourselves.

Others are count nouns as in

Buy *Krinspies* for your kids.

Daddy, may I have sixpence for a *Krinspy?*

Exercise

4. a) List ten other mass nouns (not trade nouns).
   b) Use two of these in sentences to demonstrate their characteristics.
   c) Invent two mass trade nouns and two count trade nouns and show their characteristics in sentences.

6.22 a) A notable feature of the English language and one reason for its great flexibility is the way words may slide out of their customary categories into others. The count/mass categories exemplify this. Look at the word *water* below:

He gave me *water*.

The *water* was tainted.

There was little *water* in the cup.

In the examples *water* is clearly a mass noun. But in the sentence below it is a count noun:

The *waters* of the lake closed over him.

The word *rain* is commonly a mass noun but in the following sentence it is a count noun:

The *rains* are late this year.

Nouns which are generally mass nouns become count nouns when they represent a kind or sample. The words *clay* and *lemonade,* for instance, are generally mass nouns but in the sentences below they are count nouns.

Two *clays* were offered but the potter found both unsuitable.

He drank a *lemonade.*

b) A number of nouns such as *iron* belong regularly to both categories. It is usually possible to tell from grammatical clues in which category such a word belongs, but not always. In the two sentences below it is impossible to tell whether the noun in italics is a mass noun or a count noun without reference to the context:

I think we had better put the *glass* there.

The *iron* you ordered is late in coming.

The *glass* could be a tumbler or a mirror or a mass of glass such as new windows to be fitted or broken glass to be cleared away. The *iron* could be a clothes iron or it could be ore, pig iron, roofing iron.

Exercise

5. State whether the nouns italicised in the following sentences are count nouns, or mass nouns, or might be either. How do you know?
   a) She had *tomato* down her tunic.
   b) I get tired of having *stew* every day.
   c) Look, dear, I bought some *horse* for dinner.
   d) The *horse* was old and tough.
   e) He had a wad of *paper* in his briefcase.
   f) Can you match those *wools*?
   g) I really only want a little *lettuce.*
   h) You put far too much *milk* in my *coffee.*
   i) There is only one *coffee* I really like.

6.3   PROPER NOUNS

Most school textbooks treat proper nouns as a separate subclass of noun because they are written with an initial capital letter. The problem to be discussed now is whether they form a grammatical subclass of noun. To be regarded as a grammatical subclass they would need to be significantly different from either count or mass nouns in their forms (i.e., morphology) or in their relationships with other NG elements (i.e., syntax).

Before you start working on the problem one point should be

made clear: a proper noun is regarded as a unit irrespective of the number of words it consists of. In the following sentences the proper nouns in italics are H of simple NG's:

The Queen has left *Buckingham Palace.*

We are pleased to welcome *Mr Smith.*

James James Morrison Morrison Wetherby George Dupree took great care of his mother.

The Hague is famous for *The International Court of Justice.*

6.31   Study the sets of examples below and list the characteristics of the italicised noun in each set:

i) We visited *Main Street* last night.
   (We visited the main street last night.)
   Main Street is usually crowded on late shopping nights.
   (The main streets are usually crowded on late shopping nights.)
   We pushed our way down crowded *Main Street.*
   (We pushed our way down the crowded main street.)
ii) I visited *Helford* quite by accident.
   Helford was one of the loveliest villages I saw in England.
iii) *Archibald* came to see me in hospital.
   I bored *Archibald* with my medical details.
   Silly old *Archibald* bored me too.

The nouns in italics can be seen to have the following characteristics:

a) They have one form.
b) They occur at H in a simple NG.
c) They are not modifiable by numerals.

So far, the characteristics match those of mass nouns, but note (d) below:

d) They are not modifiable by *the, my, much, little.*

Since a particular characteristic of mass nouns is that they can be modified by these words, we have here something different. Words with the characteristics listed here are **proper nouns.**

A further point about proper nouns that can be seen in the examples is that they can have adjectives as modifiers, though this modification occurs less frequently than with other nouns. Some of the adjectives are almost Homeric, as in *sunny Spain, picturesque Britain.*

The term proper noun fits the old definition of a noun being 'the name of something', since each proper noun has an individual referent. Grammatically, of course, the proper noun is recognisable by the characteristics listed.

6.32   Study the modifiers of the words in italics below:

   i) He made a lecture tour of the *United States*.
  ii) The hospitable *United States* took him to its heart.
 iii) The mighty *United States* is the major world power.
  iv) The island churches are a feature of the *Strand*.
   v) During the day the busy *Strand* teems with people.
  vi) The river *Thames* points like an arrow to the heart of London.
 vii) I took the road by the beautiful river *Dee* to Braemar.
viii) The elephant's child visited the great grey-green greasy *Limpopo* river.
  ix) A party canoed down the *Waimakariri* river.

A number of proper nouns including the names of rivers have an obligatory modifier *the*. When adjectives modify the proper noun *the* precedes them. Only in rare cases, therefore, perhaps *The Hague*, can *the* be regarded as part of H. In most other cases *the* must be regarded as a modifier.

In groups like   the river *Wye*
                 the *Waikato* river

we have apposition. In any clause the proper noun can be omitted or the word *river* can be, and often is, omitted. We have then two items at H:

M	H	H
the	river	Wye
the	Waikato	river

Exercise

6. Use the following proper nouns in sentences that demonstrate their characteristics:

> *Grassmere, Loch Ewe, John Brown, Asquith Avenue, St. Issey, Pitcairn Island, Europe, The Mall, Canada, Mount Kilimanjaro, Amy, the Mississippi.*

6.33   Study the sentences below and note the characteristics of the nouns in italics:

   i) I think there is a *Robinson* living in the brick house further down the road.
  ii) The *Robinsons* were a well-to-do family.
 iii) Three *Robinsons* are prominent in educational circles.

iv) Many *Robinsons* are listed in the telephone directory.

v) I'm sure you would like to meet our *Mr Robinson*.

vi) Of the several *Thames Rivers* the one flowing through London is the most famous.

vii) There are two *Churchill Crescents* in this city.

viii) The *Churchill Crescent* we live in is close to the harbour.

These examples are enough to show that the possibility exists of proper nouns becoming count nouns.

Exercise

7. Select five proper nouns and show in sentences how they may be used as count nouns.

style : omission of determiners → universality
eg. men are deceivers ?
the men are deceivers }
        ambiguity : this man's coat 7.54 - 5.

Chapter 7 ✓

Nominal Group (II)
Modifiers

7.0   This chapter deals with the positional elements at M, and the items which can occur in them. Sections 3.0 and 3.1 were concerned with the primary group structure (M_n H Q_n) in which H is obligatory but M and Q are optional. As, however, such a group as

science two the new blocks

is not English, but

the two new science blocks

is, it can be seen that there is an ordering of elements at M which is fundamental to our language. This chapter explores this sequence of elements.

7.1   MAJOR POSITIONAL ELEMENTS AT M

Re-arrange each of the following NG's into its proper sequence using the group in 7.0 as a model. In each case the item at H is in italics and there are no items at Q.

i) grammar all silly *exercises* these
ii) two *friends* new her Invercargill
iii) convincing their first *win*
iv) John's laboratory expensive five *books*
v) *unit* gunnery British the finest

It can be readily seen in each case that the words fall into a definite sequence and that little variation of that sequence is possible.

The next problem aims at exploring the sequence further:

vi) Using *dogs* as H rearrange as modifiers the words listed below, but instead of placing them all in line place in a column all those that can substitute for one another in the group, e.g., *city* for *country*, and *his* for *my*. Use the example in 7.0 as a basis. The words are: *city, dirty, three, friendly, five, clean, hairy, my, John's, noisy, country, those, gentle, town, two, his, obedient, dozen, your, smelly*.

If this problem has been correctly solved the words will all fit into four columns in front of H. These four columns are labelled D, O, E, N respectively. The letters are the initials of the names for the following positions: Determiner, Ordinator, Epithet, Nominator. Usually these will be referred to in the text by their initials only.

The important point about these is the fact that they represent major positional elements at M, not form classes. More than one form class may appear under the same positional letter.

We shall now examine in turn each of the elements and the classes of word that may occur in them.

7.2 ITEMS AT D

7.21 The class of word appearing at D is called **determiner.** In the five scrambled NG's [7.1(i) to (v)] they are:

(i) *all these*, (ii) *her*, (iii) *their*, (iv) *John's*, (v) *the*.

In (vi) your first column, now labelled D, should contain:

my, John's, these, his, your.

Follow these instructions:

i) Make a list of all the different modifiers of the singular count nouns in the three sets of sentences under 6.1.

ii) Set them out in two columns labelled D (the left-hand column) and O.

iii) Put under O any numerals such as *second, one,* etc. All the other words go under D and are determiners.

iv) Repeat the process for count nouns in the plural.

v) Some determiners will appear in both lists. Delete these from the singular and plural columns and place them together under the heading Singular/Plural.

vi) Add the determiners from problems (i) to (vi) in 7.1 to the appropriate list.

There are now three lists of determiners:

a) those that occur with singular count nouns;
b) those that occur with plural count nouns;
c) those that may occur with either singular or plural count nouns.

What all this establishes is the existence of a concord relation between determiners and nouns at H. Concord should not be thought of as merely a number and person relation between S and P items. Concord runs through the structure of the nominal group as well, and this concord will often have a relationship to the concord between subject and predicator.

The characteristics then of determiners are:

a) They precede numerals and adjectives.
b) They have a concord relation with H.
c) They may be a member of the following word classes by form:

    i) particles (e.g., *the, a, each, both*)
    ii) personal pronouns (e.g., *my, your, his, her*)
    iii) nouns (e.g., *John's, Mary's*)
    iv) *wh-* words (*what, which, whose*)
    v) demonstratives (*that, this, those, these*)

7.22 A fuller list of determiners can be worked out by filling D below with as many words as possible.

Plural Determiners

D	O	H
	first	
	next	
	last	men
	two	
	three	

Singular Determiners

D	O	H
	first	
	next	man
	last	

A list of singular and plural determiners has already been started, so words which will go into both D columns above should be put into that list. In the plural determiner pattern some words which we class as determiners because of their concord link with H will not appear because they are mutually exclusive with items at O. Such words are e.g., *many, few, several, enough* (not **few three men*).

So far in this chapter no reference has been made to the determiners that occur with mass nouns. The reason is that in order to establish determiners as a class they had to be seen in relation to numerals which they precede when both are present. Mass nouns (6.2), not modified by numerals, cannot provide a suitable starting point. As mass nouns are not modified by items at O we will use an item at E in our pattern for discovering mass determiners.

List the words that can precede *very fresh* in the following frame:

Mass Determiners

D	E	H
	very fresh	milk

7.23 The following table sets out the determiners according to their usual concord relations with H.

Determiners

Singular	: a/an, each, every, either, neither, another
Plural	: both, few, many, several, these, those, various
Mass	: less, little, much
Singular/plural	: other, which
Singular/mass	: this, that
Plural/mass	: all, a lot of, enough, half, more, most, some, such
General(singular /plural/mass)	: any, John's etc., my etc., no, only, other, own, same, the, what, whose.

There are one or two items in the table that require another determiner, e.g., *half, same, own*. A few singular concord determiners can be used with plurals in special ways; for instance one can say *I want another ten men*. The underlying structure here is *another group of ten men*. The word *less,* listed as mass only, may occasion some discussion. In informal speech it frequently occurs as a count determiner:

I've got a lot *less* sweets than you.

Failing a word-count of its occurrence as a count noun modifier in more formal spoken and written registers, we record it as mass only.

The placing of apostrophe forms such as *John's* among the determiners may at first sight appear surprising. However, a characteristic of determiners is that they precede numerals and

[colloquial use of determiners : there was this man]

adjectives and *John's two expensive laboratory books* clearly illustrates this. *John's* and *my* are instances of noun and pronoun forms
appearing at D. Some problems of ambiguity arise with apostrophe
forms when they are preceded by such determiners as *a, the, this:*

>   *this man's coat*

can be interpreted as either of the following:

 i) the coat of this man
ii) this coat for a man

In (i) the item *this man's* is D. For an explanation of (ii) see 7.55.

   Complex apostrophe forms such as *the man next door's* and *the
Queen of England's* are regarded as a single unit modifying H and are
simply D.

7.24   As can be seen in 7.1 (i) more than one determiner may occur
in a group. When two or more occur they tend to fall into sequence
patterns. Study the examples:

>   *all these* silly grammar exercises
>   *half Mary's only* respectable pair
>   *what an* unsuccessful attempt
>   *any such* two little asses
>   *both such* beastly young urchins·
>   *his own* five chubby fingers
>   *half this* stinking meat
>   *these same* five boys
>   *both the other* two girls
>   *many a* fat sheep
>   *the only other* two fresh loaves
>   *all Mary's own* new jam
>   *such a* dear wee elephant
>   *half a* hot plateful
>   *many such* wonderful adventures

A few minutes spent trying to column these determiners for sequence
should show (a) that a definite sequence exists within certain groups
and (b) the sequence is complicated and sometimes a determiner
will turn up in two positions e.g., *such*. Some basic sequences are:

all ⎫ both ⎬ half ⎭	⎧ the ⎜ my, etc. ⎨ John's, etc. ⎜ these, those ⎩ such

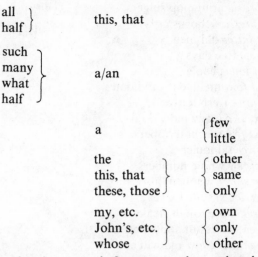

Determiners that may occur before *more, other,* and *such* may easily be discovered by trial and are not listed.

Exercise

1. a) Compose ten NG's each of which contains at least two determiners according to the sequence patterns outlined in 7.24. Where possible use also numerals and adjectives.
   b) Use each NG as subject of a clause and state the concord which each determiner requires at H in its NG and at P in its clause.

7.3 ITEMS AT O

7.31 In 7.1 (vi) the words that should appear in the second column are *three, five, two, dozen.* The examples below show in italics the kind of items usually appearing at O. From the examples work out a sequence table of three columns so that any item in the first column would precede any item in the second, and any item in the second would precede any item in the third. (Note that this does not mean that every item in a column can occur with an item in the next column.) After sorting the items into three columns work out the characteristics of all the items that appear at O.

these *two* old ducks
the *first two* places
three such glorious days
a *second such* attempt
two other silly jokes
the *second three* units

five more aspiring pop singers
twelve prettier chorus girls
the *six fatter* old men
five whole free days
the *last four* people
the *first few* intelligent candidates
three entire fresh loaves
the *next two* crazy individuals
the *next few such* interlopers
five slower saloon cars
the *first few* whole numbers
a *dozen softer* woollen fabrics
our *last dozen* stale loaves
a *hundred more* tough steaks
six fewer successful applicants
the *seven wickedest* old witches
their *ten loveliest* new frocks
the *two swiftest* wild birds

The next point to check in your columns is that no item in any one column can occur in a normal pattern with any other item in the same column.

7.32 The completed sequence pattern is:

CARDINAL O1	ORDINAL O2	OTHERS O3
first	one	comparatives
next	two	
last	three	superlatives
second	four	
third	five	less
etc.	etc.	more
		such
	dozen	other
	score	
	hundred	whole
	thousand	single
	million	entire
	few	

Five words that were earlier classified as determiners have reappeared in the table of O positions. The sequence possibilities of D and O are complicated and do not form stable patterns. This makes

If they follow the numbers they are not Determiners.

such items difficult to classify, but adds to the flexibility of the nominal group. A number of words listed in this text as determiners, words such as *several, many, much, little, various,* and others, are listed by some grammarians under O. Apart from numerals we call all M's involved in the count/mass relationship determiners.

Unless *few* and *other* are preceded by O items they are at D. Therefore a group such as *a few dozen rotten eggs* is D D O E H.

With superlatives and cardinals the sequence is flexible; the normal pattern is the one recorded in the table. If the sequence is reversed there may be a subtle change in meaning:

the three prettiest girls
the prettiest three girls

his best two efforts
his two best efforts

7.33 As with determiners, O items, except comparatives and superlatives, have a concord relation with H and with D items. At O the concord choice is restricted to singular and plural; at D the choice is from singular, plural and mass.

The characteristics of items at O may now be stated as:

a) They follow determiners where they occur with them.
b) They precede adjectives (not comparative or superlative forms) where they occur with them.
c) They enter into number concord with items at D and H.
d) When more than one item occurs there is a customary sequence.

Exercise

2. a) Make up nominal groups representing the following structures and use them in sentences.
   b) State the concord relations running through the NG to P.
      D O H (three groups with different concord relations)
        D D O H   D O O H   D D D O H   D O O O H   D D O O H

7.4 ITEMS AT E

7.41 Most words which appear in this position in the NG are adjectives. The third column in 7.1 (vi) should contain the adjectives *dirty, friendly, clean, hairy, noisy, gentle, obedient, smelly.* There are many ways of subclassifying adjectives and the way adopted in this text is only one of them. As adjectives form an open set the possibilities of selection and sequence are complicated. However, it is useful to distinguish four subclasses at E according to the probable order of occurrence.

In the examples below the words in italics all occur at E in the NG. Sort them into columns E1, E2, E3, E4 according to the sequences discoverable from the examples. Notice the use of the submodifier *very* as a position indicator.

a very *good little* girl
a *little red wooden* doll
a very *interesting young* woman
a very *surprised old* lady
this *old yellow French* lace
my very *chic new black* frock
a *big brown woollen* bear
her very *lovely blue Scandinavian* eyes
another very *pleasing local* response
all the *new local* residents
that very *ugly big grey* building

In the first column are items that are submodifiable by *very*, including V^g and V^n forms. In the second are some short words that are generally unstressed. In the third appear colour adjectives, and in the fourth adjectives that are not normally submodifiable, e.g., adjectives of nationality.

7.42 This table exemplifies sequence possibilities of items at E:

E1	E2	E3	E4
good	old	black	American
lovely	young	blue	British
chic	new	brown	Dutch
handsome	big	grey	Scandinavian
successful	little	red	etc.
clean		white	
etc.		yellow	
		etc.	local
			geographical
interesting			historical
dashing			etc.
pleasing			
depressing			woollen
etc.			wooden
			silken
shocked			aqueous
gifted			equestrian
tattered			bovine
blackened			etc.
etc.			

7.43   Several items from one subclassification can occur together:

    E1   a small, funny creature
           a charming, lovely girl

(Items in this subclassification are usually linked by *and* or commas)

    E2   a little old man
           a big new car

(When two E2 items occur the first becomes an E1 item)

    E3   a red and white flag
           a blue and yellow football jersey

(Items in this subclassification are usually linked by *and* or commas)

    E4   a local Dutch custom
           a wooden African carving

7.44   In 7.41 mention was made of items submodifiable by *very*. When a modifier is itself modified, as in

D	SM	E	H
a	*very*	*pleasing*	result
an	*extremely*	*dubious*	story

it is said to be **submodified.** In the examples *very* and *extremely* are submodifiers. Submodifiers (SM) are commonly particles and adverbs such as *very, so, much, more, most, less, rather, quite, even,* and *strongly, highly, nearly, especially, rarely, particularly.*

In the following examples the items submodified are not E1 items:

    a *light brown* suit
    a *brilliantly lit* shop
    nearly all her foreign customers

And is also treated as a submodifier:
    a red *and* white chessboard

When an E item is submodified, it usually precedes any other E items in the nominal group. Where an item from E1 is also present, linkage occurs.

    a very young, successful businessman
    (not *a successful very young businessman)
    that very big, ugly grey building
    (not *that ugly very big grey building)

Exercise

3. Using the structures given below construct NG's and incorporate them in
   sentences:
   a) the two other SM E1 E2 H
   b) the same three E3 E4 H
   c) the Queen of England's own SM E1 E3 H
   d) my only E2 E4 H
   e) such a SM E1 E2 E4 H
   f) all the first few E2 E3 H
   g) much E1 E2 E4 H
   h) many E1 E2 E4 H
   i) these next five SM E1 E2 E3 H
   j) the SM E1 E2 E3 E4 H
   k) no two E1 E1 E4 H
   l) some E2 E2 E3 H
   m) several other E1 E3 E3 H
   n) his fastest other SM E1 E2 E2 H
   o) her various deeper E2 E4 E4 H
   p) even his very best E2 E4 H

7.5   ITEMS AT N

7.51   Turn back to 7.1 and look at your answers for (vi). In (vi), the
fourth column, labelled N, should contain *city, country, town.*
These are all nouns which modify. This use is very common in
English in such groups as *bread knife, office worker, kitchen sink,
rubbish disposal.*

Exercise

4. List the items at N in 7.1 (i) to (v).

7.52   Sometimes two nouns can precede H:
        the traffic department office
        the railway station restaurant
        the bus depot clock

What occurs in these examples may best be shown by means of
transformations:
        the traffic department office ⟶
        the office of the traffic department

        the railway station restaurant ⟶
        the restaurant at the railway station

        the bus depot clock ⟶
        the clock at the bus depot

The words *traffic department* constitute an NG with *traffic* at N and

department at H. This entire group is a modifier at N of *office* at H.
The table below sets this analysis out for the three examples:

D	N		H
	N⌐ ¬H		
the	traffic	department	office
the	railway	station	restaurant
the	bus	depot	clock

Another way of expressing this is

D	N	H
the	[traffic department]	office
the	[railway station]	·restaurant
the	[bus depot]	clock

7.53 Compare the examples in 7.52 with these:

   i)   a London office worker
         a car instruction manual
         an airline feeder service

These examples transform into.

   ii)   an office worker in London
         an instruction manual for a car
         a feeder service for an airline

It is possible to transform the first into

         a worker in a London office

but this would be an unusual interpretation. Even more unusual
would be

         a manual for car instruction
         a service for airline feeders

In the groups in (i) the second noun modifies the third, and the first
modifies both. The structure in these cases is D N N H.

Exercise

5. Make up three or more examples like those in 7.52 and three more like
   those in 7.53 (i).

7.54 Two possibilities also occur with the sequence determiner +
adjective + noun + noun. Compare the following:

i) an American style suit
ii) an American lounge suit

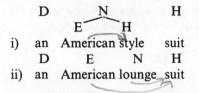

i) an American style suit
    D   E   N   H
ii) an American lounge suit

7.55 Several other items occur at N. Briefly they are:

a) Particles: the *then* king
                          the *above* examples
                          his *very* purpose

b) ing-forms: a talking doll
                          the sleeping dog
                          a shunting engine
   (Not submodifiable by *very;* not followed by E items.)

c) Prepositional Groups: an [out-of-the-way] place
                          an [off-the-cuff] remark

d) Nominal Group items: a [no-good] hound
                          the [next-door] neighbours

e) Clause items: a [[pay-as-you-earn]] scheme
                          a [[do-it-yourself]] kit

f) Apostrophe Forms: a new blue *lady's* umbrella

The structure of this group is D E E N H. There is some ambiguity in the group as written. Such ambiguity is often best resolved by transformation:

    D E E N   H
    a new blue lady's umbrella ⟶
    a new blue umbrella for a lady

NOT *an umbrella for a new blue lady
NOR *a new umbrella for a blue lady

In the same way, where

        this man's coat ⟶
        this coat for a man

the word *man's* is at N and the group structure is D N H (cf. 7.23).

Exercise

6. Describe the patterns of the following NG's:
   a) Cinerama's greatest adventure spectacular
   b) a highly spectacular railway disaster
   c) United's last-minute upset win

d) New Zealand's only family magazine
e) exciting new Italian art discovery
f) her own colour cartoon comic strip
g) all unpleasant kitchen cooking smells
h) Western's new devastating first-time shooter
i) the winger's scorching touch-line bursts
j) the two powerful front-row forwards
k) new restricted telephone hours
l) three outstanding children's physicians
m) all practising psychiatrists
n) George le Drake's popular new breakfast cereal
o) all the five other recently joined members
p) nearly every other attractive young lady
q) the Auckland ladies' outstanding contribution
r) dear, damned, inconstant sex
s) such a very young Dutch couple
t) so magnificent a composition

Det.   Ord.1   Ord.2   Ord.3   E (1,2,3,4)
         card.   ordin.
                            ↓

N *   foll. by   H

*   N   ar   N
        / \   / \
      N   H   E   H

Chapter 8

Nominal Group (III) Qualifiers

8.0 A quick revision of 3.1 will show simple types of qualifier in the nominal group. This chapter will discuss these more fully.

8.1 ITEMS OCCURRING AT Q

Several kinds of items can follow H in an NG. Examples of some are given below. In each case Q is in italics.

   i) the body *beautiful*
  ii) the examples *below*
 iii) the man *here now*
  iv) the house *next door*
   v) the old pub *down the road*
  vi) the girl *in the corner by the window*
 vii) the man *who was knighted*
viii) the apple *which Eve gave him*
  ix) the reason *he gave*
   x) the place *where we lunched*
  xi) the man *fishing from the bridge*
 xii) the girl *to do that job*
xiii) the only man *caught by the police*

In each of these examples Q is the part that follows H of the NG. An idea of the unity of the NG can be gained by substituting a pronoun for the complete group e.g., (ii) *they* (iii) *he* (iv) *it* (vi) *she,* and so on.

Q may consist of a word, a group, or a clause. Sometimes there is more than one Q as in (iii). Sometimes the qualifying item itself may be qualified, as in (vi).

8.2 WORDS AT Q

a) Adjectives:

the body *beautiful*
the best *available*
nothing *interesting*
something *useful*

b) Particles:

the examples *below*
the car *behind*
the way *out*
the man *here now*

c) Myself-type pronouns:

the man *himself* (did it)
the drivers *themselves* (helped)

These items can be removed from H; that is, the NG can be made discontinuous:

The man *himself* did it. ⟶
The man did it *himself*.

But in *The drivers helped themselves, themselves* is C in the clause not Q in the group. (Is it C^E or C^I?)

d) Verb forms:

the best horse *competing*
the man *to watch*
the last car *sold*

Exercise

1. Find four more examples each for (a) and (b) and (d) and incorporate them in sentences. Remember in (d) that here Q is a word.

8.3 GROUPS AT Q

a) Nominal Groups:

the house [next door]
a wall [six feet high]
a towel [dry enough]
a problem [familiar to all of us]

(Note the adjectives *dry* and *familiar* acting as head of their groups; cf. 4.33 for other adjective-headed groups.)

b) Verbal Groups:

the boy [being interviewed]
the dress [to be fitted]

c) Prepositional Groups:

the opposition [to the war]
a date [with a boy]
a boy [like Ebenezer]
a list [of suitable schools]

A prepositional group at Q can itself be qualified:

the girl [in the corner [by the window]]
a date [with a boy [like Ebenezer]]
a list [of schools [in the vicinity]]
a house [in the neighbourhood [of Newmarket]]

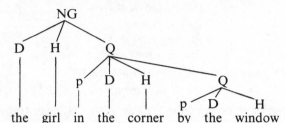

In the examples above the second item is an element of the first item at Q. However, two groups at Q can separately qualify H:

a date [with Ebenezer] [on Saturday]
the restaurant [in town] [with the best steaks]
a prize [of ten guineas] [for the beauty contest winner]

Sometimes two pG's at Q can lead to ambiguity:

a photo *of a horse in his dining room*

This can be looked at in two ways:

i) a photo [of a horse [in his dining room]]
ii) a photo [of a horse] [in his dining room]

Example (i) can be

the photo is of a horse in his dining room

Example (ii) can be

the photo of a horse is in his dining room

A word about the single square brackets used here and at the end of Chapter 7. Their real purpose is to indicate a group that is an element of a group - a fairly common occurrence in English. Some items at M, too, are groups operating as an element of a group. They can be found in 7.55 (c) and (d). In 7.55 (e) are clauses operating as elements of a group. They are marked off by double square brackets.

Exercises

2. a) Make up four NG's, each with an NG at Q.
   b) Make up six NG's, each with a pG at Q.
3. a) Make up three NG's for each of the following structures:
      DH [Q] [Q]
      DH [Q [Q]]

b) Make up two NG's whose Q's are ambiguous on the lines of *a photo of a horse in his dining room.* Show the two ways of bracketing and explain each on the lines of the example in the text.

8.4   FINITE CLAUSES AT Q

Examples of finite clauses occurring at Q may be found at (vii) (viii) (ix) and (x) in 8.1. Finite clauses at Q may be marked by *wh-* words, *that,* or may be unmarked, or introduced by *than* or *as.*

8.41   FINITE CLAUSES MARKED BY WH- WORDS

a) *wh-* at S

          S   P

the man [[who | was knighted]]

        S   P   C

a girl [[who | is | unhappy]]

         S   P

the apple [[which | had fallen]]

One problem occurs with *wh-* clauses at Q and that is the distinction between such sentences as

i) The girls who had put coats on over their pyjamas dashed after the thieves.

ii) The girls, who had put coats on over their pyjamas, dashed after the thieves.

The interpretation is plain enough. In (i) only those girls who had put coats on dashed after the thieves, while those who had not put coats on discreetly and modestly stayed behind. In (ii) all the girls had put coats on and all dashed after the thieves.

In (i), the *wh-* clause is undeniably Q to *girls* at H. In (ii) *who* could be re-written as *and they,* or even, simply *they* as can be seen in

> The girls - they had put coats on over their pyjamas - dashed after the thieves.

In (ii) the *wh-* clause is a separate dependent clause interrupting the main clause and not an element of the NG.

b) *wh-* at C

           C   S P

the boy [[who/whom I saw]]

           C   S   P   C

the apple [[which Eve gave him]]

           C   S   P

the girl [[whose mother he helped]]

As the present chapter is concerned with elements at Q, discussion on *who/whom* will be postponed to Chapter 9. At the moment it is enough to say that both forms occur at C.

In the third example above *whose* is D and *mother* is H in the complement.

c) *wh-* at A

```
              A      S   P      C
the man [[to whom she gave the apple]]
               A     S   P
the speech [[to which you alluded]]
            A⁻   S   P  ⁻A
the matter [[which you refer to]]
             A   S    P
the place [[where we lunched]]
            A   S   P    C
the day [[when you were absent]]
            A   S   P   C
the reason [[why he failed us]]
```

8.42 THAT MARKED CLAUSES

a) *that* at S:
```
              S       P       C
the answer [[that delighted the teacher]]
```
b) *that* at C:
```
            C   S   P   C
the reason [[that he gave me]]
```
c) *that* at A:
```
            A⁻  S     P    ⁻A
the train [[that she travelled in]]
```

[colloquial sound]

8.43 UNMARKED CLAUSES. By comparing the following sentences with those in 8.41 (b) and (c) and 8.42 (b) and (c), it can be seen that the *wh-* word or *that* is often absent.

```
          S P
the boy [[I saw]]
            S    P    C
the apple [[Eve gave him]]
            S    P    A
the speech [[you alluded to]]
```

[give precision, esp. finite cl.]

```
        S    P     C      A
the man [[she gave the apple to]]
        S   P    C
the reason [[he gave me]]
        S    P     A
the place [[we lunched at]]
        S    P    C
the day [[you were absent]]
        S   P   C
the reason [[he failed us]]
```

8.44 AS OR THAN CLAUSES AT Q. Clauses of this type present some problems in analysis. In the following examples the *as* and *than* clauses are dependent upon a headword and are therefore Q:

```
      M     H       Q
I | look | as graceful [[as she does]].
      H          Q
He | was | taller [[than I had expected]].
```

But in the following examples the *than* or *as* clause is not directly dependent upon the headword but upon a modifier of the headword. Its relationship to the rest of the group is one of submodification:

```
      D  O   H        SM
She | is | a better hurdler [[than I am]].
```

(The *than* clause is dependent upon *better*.)

```
      SM M  M H   SM
I | have | as good a style [[as she has]].
```

(Both *as* and *as she has* depend upon *good;* neither could appear without *good*.)

Exercises

4. Make up finite clauses to act at Q in nominal groups. Use them in sentences.
   a) 5 with *wh-* words at S
   b) 5 with *wh-* words at C
   c) 5 with *wh-* words at A
   d) 2 with *that* at S
   e) 2 with *that* at C
   f) 2 with *than* at A
   g) 2 with *as* at A

5. Rewrite as unmarked clauses all those in Exercise 4 that can be so rewritten.
6. Make a week's observation of the occurrence of unmarked clauses at Q as compared with marked ones.

8.5 NON-FINITE CLAUSES AT Q

In 2.31 (c) the point is made that only verb forms marked for tense are finite, the others are non-finite. Clauses with non-finite verb forms at P may also occur at Q.

In 8.2 (d) there are three examples of verbs at Q: *competing, to watch,* and *sold.* Each can act at H in a VG but on their own when qualifying a noun they are not considered a VG. At least one more VG element would be needed to make them a VG. Likewise, there must be at least one more group other than a VG to make a non-finite clause at Q. In a non-finite clause at Q, the VG may be simple or complex.

a) V^{to} at P:

$$\qquad\qquad P \qquad\qquad C \qquad\qquad A$$
The best man [[to watch | our interests | carefully]] is Gabriel.

$$\qquad\qquad P \qquad C$$
The man [[to fix | that]] is Joe.

$$\qquad\qquad\qquad P \qquad\qquad A$$
The girl [[to be marked | very closely]] is Wilhelmina.

$$\qquad\qquad\qquad P \qquad C \qquad A$$
You're just the one [[to mess | that | up]].

b) V^{g} at P:

$$\qquad\qquad\qquad P \qquad\qquad A$$
The best horse [[competing | last week]] was Starlight.

$$\qquad\qquad P \qquad C$$
The girl [[flying | the glider]] is on her first solo flight.

$$\qquad\qquad\qquad P \qquad\qquad C \qquad\qquad A$$
The men [[swimming | Cook Strait | last year]] met strong currents.

In each of the examples above it would be possible to expand the non-finite clause into *wh-* marked clauses by inserting a *wh-* word and an auxiliary:

The best horse *which was* competing ...

c) V^{n} at P:

$$\qquad\qquad P \qquad A$$
The last car [[sold | at the auction]] was mine.

$$\qquad\qquad P \qquad\qquad A$$
The man [[caught | by the police]] is very dangerous.

$$\qquad\qquad A \qquad\qquad P \qquad\qquad C$$
The girl [[recently | elected | head prefect]] is very popular.

These clauses, like those in (b), can be expanded into *wh-* marked clauses. Like *wh-* marked clauses these V^n clauses can be Q, as in the examples above, or they can form a dependent element of a sentence as in:

α –   β   – α

The man, < < securely pinned by the arms > >, was dragged away. Here the commas mark off a dependent clause which is *not* part of the NG *the man*. The angle brackets < < .... > > indicate an inserted clause.

Exercise

7. Make up three non-finite clauses with V^{to} at P, three with V^g at P, and three with V^n at P. Incorporate these into NG's at Q and complete the sentences.
8. In the following sentences (i) identify all the nominal groups and prepositional groups and (ii) analyse in detail all those that are qualified.
    a) The mill which is being built in the South Auckland district is expected to start production next year.
    b) A new extracting method was developed, which completely by-passed the old pig-iron stage.
    c) The sand that is converted to pellets of sponge-iron has been previously washed.
    d) Britain's application to join the Common Market in 1963 was blocked by General de Gaulle, who exercised his right to say 'no'.
    e) The main question of the future of the lamb trade with Japan is price.
    f) The diagram accompanying the article shows the main points to watch in an exhibition bird.
    g) The way down was the way out for us all.
    h) I can think of nothing better to do.
    i) I watched the captain, cheered by thousands, as he made his way to the pavilion beyond.
    j) In 1963 several Anglican bishops in South Africa made statements condemning the apartheid policies of the government.

Chapter 9

Nominal Group (IV)
Other Classes at H

9.0   In addition to nouns, various other word classes may act at H in nominal groups (including prepositional groups) as may be seen in the examples below:

This is the book *I* mentioned.
It really is *mine, you* know.
I don't lend *it* to *anybody*.
She wrote *several*.
Many are *hard* to get.
Nobody here knows the early *ones*.
It is quite *something* for *me* to have *five*.
But *these* are not much *good*.
The *best, which* are very *complex*, were written later.
Her *writing* of poetry improved too.
It became more *condensed* and less *wordy*.
Of women writers *she* is the *one whom I* most admire.

Many of the words in italics are pronouns; others are items that commonly appear at D or O or E, or are verb forms or are *wh*-words.

9.1 PRONOUNS

9.11 The characteristics of pronouns were discussed in 2.2. Look again at the examples in 2.24. Do the pronouns in the second sentence of (i) and of (ii) substitute for nouns? *He* replaces *the elderly man* but only *man* is a noun; *the elderly man* is a nominal group. So the pronoun is not really a pro-noun at all but a pro-NG. Even *Jim* is a simple NG with a proper noun at H. We retain the word pronoun, however, because of its long use, but it should be clearly understood that its function is to substitute for a nominal group, whether simple or complex.

9.12 Study the pronouns in italics below. Note the possibilities of M and Q, and the forms used at S, at C, and at A.

> *You* two at the back, come here!
> It was *I* who was caught.
> Surely it's not *me he* wants.
> It's *us,* I guess.
> *We* who are about to die salute *you.*
> *He* punished *us* who had never said a word.
> Just look at *him* with his kewpie curl.
> *We* both vented our resentment.
> *She* pushed *him* away from *her.*
> *She* hugged *herself.*
> *He* kicked *himself.*
> *She* thought wicked thoughts to *herself.*

At H, pronouns may have Q but very seldom M.

Pronouns at S are I-type, at C are me-type, and at H in a prepositional group are me-type.

In current English the I-type is normally used only when it is clearly S. In most other cases the me-type is preferred. In certain formal registers, however, the I-type is found following a subject and a form of the verb *be:*

> It was *I.*
> No, it is not *she.*

More frequent, however, are:

> It was *me.*
> No, it is not *her.*

The myself-type pronouns have a person and number concord with S whether they are at Q or are at C or A.

9.13   *Mine* are no good. Where are *yours?*
Oh, I lost *mine,* but I've got *his.*
Look you two, for goodness' sake use *ours.*
You are both good friends of *mine.*

Mine-type pronouns may act at S and at C with no change of form. They may occur also at H in a pG. A referent has to be supplied from the context.

9.2   WH- WORDS AND THAT

9.21   Notice when *who* and *whom* occur in the sentences below:

i) I wonder *who* is arriving now.
ii) The man, *who* claimed to be a reporter, asked for an interview.
iii) The person *to whom* he wished to speak was my mother.
iv) She wanted to know *who* he had come *from.*
v) He said that his editor, *whom* she knew well, had asked him to call.
vi) 'So! The man *who* I see before me is a reporter,' I thought to myself.

In the examples above the italicised *wh-* words are all at H of an NG or a pG. In (i) and (ii) the groups are at S, in (iii) and (iv) at A, and in (v) and (vi) at C.

The form *who,* the I-type, is obligatory when at S, and *whom,* the me-type, is obligatory at H of a continuous prepositional group. At C, and in discontinous prepositional groups both forms are found. However, in certain formal registers *whom* is usual in both these cases.

The following transformations may help in understanding the forms selected at C and at A in formal registers:

i) The man whom I saw was a reporter.

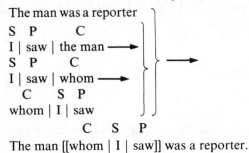

The man was a reporter
```
S   P       C
I | saw | the man  ⟶
S   P       C
I | saw | whom  ⟶
    C   S  P
whom | I | saw
```
              C   S   P
The man [[whom | I | saw]] was a reporter.

ii) Elizabeth knew from whom Bingley had come.

Elizabeth knew the man

```
     S              P              A
Bingley | had come | from the man  ⟶
     S              P              A
Bingley | had come | from whom  ⟶
        A            S         P
from whom | Bingley | had come
```

⟶

```
                          A         S          P
Elizabeth knew the man [[from whom | Bingley | had come]] ⟶
                    A         S        P
Elizabeth knew [[from whom | Bingley | had come]].
```

9.22 WHICH occurs at H in NG's and pG's:

I looked at a pocket *which* bulged rather.

I whipped out the pistol *which* I spotted there.

He was in a position *from which* he could not retreat.

He looked glumly at the pocket (*which*) I had taken the pistol *from*.

A gender distinction exists between *who* and *which*, *who* being used after words that refer to humans, and *which* after words that refer to non-humans. However, in the case of animals, particularly pets, *who* is often used, e.g.,

Our alsatian, *who* is quite a member of the family, sleeps on the divan.

9.23 WHAT occurs at H in NG's and, less commonly, in pG's:

No one can tell *what* happened to the 'Joyita'.

Several people saw *what* neglect did for it.

I don't know from *what* you could have got that idea.

9.24 WHO cannot be modified but can be qualified by a word, frequently *else,* and by a prepositional group:

Goodness knows *who* else was there.

No one has been told *who* of those named will be chosen to play in the last test.

When the NG is at C and its H is qualified by *else, who* is more usual than *whom:*

They insisted on knowing *who* else he had stopped from entering.

When the NG is at C and its H is qualified by a prepositional group *which* is more usual than *who* or *whom*:

> Jones wanted to be told then and there *which* of the players Bates had selected.

In this last example *which* is a *wh-* word at H, as the full NG would read *which one* or *which ones*. This can be more clearly seen in the next example:

> I can't make up my mind *which* of these to take.

What can also be qualified but not modified:

> No one can make out *what* on earth can have happened to her.
> Nor can anyone suggest *what* else we should have done.

9.25   The characteristics of *wh-* words at H apply equally to *wh-ever* words and to *wh-* words in questions. A few examples will serve to illustrate this:

> *Whoever* else could it be?
> *Who* ⎫
> *Whom* ⎬ did Elizabeth see when she looked up?
> *Whoever* will she marry now?
> *Which* of the boys took her out last night?
> *Whatever* else could she do?

9.26   THAT can occur at H in nominal groups at S and at C, and in discontinuous prepositional groups:

> I was aware of an object *that* protruded from his pocket.
> The pistol *that* I removed was loaded.
> The boy *that* I spoke *to* was never seen again.

The gender distinction noted in 9.22 does not apply to *that*.

Exercise

1. a) Make up 5 sentences using *who* at S in its clause and 5 using *whom* at C in its clause.
   b) Show by means of transformations how the *wh-* forms at S and at C have been chosen.

9.3   ITEMS FROM D WHICH CAN OCCUR AT H

> I had *several*.
> *Half* of them got broken.
> *This* is the least damaged one.

Most are quite irreplaceable.
Harry's were Spodeware too.
All of his were buried in solid boxes.
Few were even cracked.
We lost *much* of what we had.
Little was ever recovered.
The wars were disastrous for *many*.
Compensation was awarded to *both* of us.
We have all had *enough* of war.
But *such* is life, I guess.

Most of these items may be qualified, especially by prepositional groups, but few of them may be modified. The NG's of which these items are H can occur at S or C or A in the clause.

Not all the items listed under D can be used in this way, e.g., *my*, whose head form is mine-type. The word *other* when used at H may become a count noun with the appropriate range of forms and some modifiers.

All the items from D which occur at H imply a lexical item from the context. In the first nine examples above, that item is 'Spodeware'. The items in italics refer to sets of china made in the Spode factory.

9.31   A small set of determiners has an H-marked form:

someone	somebody	something
no-one	nobody	nothing
everyone	everybody	everything

These words have the forms of a singular count noun, e.g., *someone*, *someone's*, and when their NG is at S have a singular verb concord. With *everyone* and *everybody* this concord may, but does not have to, include any pronoun referring to H:

Everyone is eating his dinner quickly.
When everybody has finished I'll clear their plates away.

Exercise

2. a) Select six words listed under D (7.23). Make them H of an NG, using each NG at S, at C, and at A. The NG may be altered in its items at Q if any.
    b) List the items at D which cannot act at H of an NG.
    c) Use noun forms of *other* in sentences.
    d) To what extent can any of these forms be modified?

9.4   ITEMS FROM O WHICH CAN OCCUR AT H

As with the items from D, all the O position items which occur at H usually imply some lexical item in the context.

>Eleanor and Ebenezer were *last* in the three-legged race.
>There was no prize for *second*.
>The *first* to finish were Wilhelmina and William.
>I saw all *twenty* of the yachts leaving.
>Only *six* of them finished the course.
>*Five* capsized.
>*Dozens* of crew members came in exhausted.
>Difficult conditions often bring out the *best* in people.
>Of many sports climbing is, in my opinion, the *finest*.
>Of our mountains the *highest* are not always the *hardest* to climb.
>The rocks are *easiest* to climb when at their *clearest*.
>The presence of ice on the rocks makes them *greasier*.
>So the *clearer* they are, the *better* for climbing.

In all the examples above, the words in italics are at H of an NG.

The word *one,* like *other,* can take on noun forms. At H in an NG it can be quite extensively modified and qualified. It also acts at H simply as a numeral, e.g., *One* is enough, thank you.

Exercise

3. a) What noun forms can *fifth* and *hundred* have?
   b) Using *fifth* and *hundred* at H of NG's, explore in sentences what items can occur at M and at Q when the NG is at S, at C, and at A.
   c) Set out the possible noun forms of *one.* Using *one* at H in various NG's demonstrate its characteristics as a count noun.
   d) Use the comparative form of an adjective to show (i) its possibilities of modification and qualification when H of an NG and (ii) the clause elements such NG's can occur in.
   e) Repeat Exercise (d) using the superlative form of an adjective.

9.5   ITEMS FROM E WHICH CAN OCCUR AT H

>It's the *rich* that get the pleasure.
>It's the *poor* that get the blame.
>Life can be just as *difficult* for the *wealthy*.
>The responsibility can be *great* and the hours *long*.
>But conditions are usually *comfortable* and the work is *clean* not *dirty*.
>You might be the most beautiful girl but you are also the most *useless*.
>I thought the *English* very *hospitable*.

I do like landscape which looks thoroughly *English*.

My interest in the landscape was not only *aesthetic* but also *geographical*.

Notice the different structures with *most:*

the most beautiful girl   —   D SM E H
the most useless   —   D O H

Exercise

4. a) When items from E1 and E2 are at H of NG's what modification and qualification is (i) necessary (ii) possible, when the NG is at S, at C, at A?
   b) What noun forms are available for *yellow* when at H of an NG? How does it fit into the count/mass subclasses?
   c) Repeat Exercise (a) using first an adjective of nationality then another item from E at H.

9.6   STRUCTURAL ITEMS AT H

There is a small set of verbs which at S can usually only have *it*. In these examples *it* has no referent:

It is raining.

It had been snowing.

For further uses of *it* see Chapter 19 (also for *there*).

9.7   VERBS AT H

Verbs can only occur at H of a nominal group if they are modified by usual NG modifiers. Items at Q are optional. In the following examples the verbs in italics are H of NG's:

Her *sewing* is beautifully neat.

I do envy her her *sewing*.

On the whole our team's *tackling* is poor.

Stewart's *tackling* of Jones was brilliant.

I don't trust Lee's *tackling*.

Stewart made quite a name for himself by vigorous *tackling*.

However, in the two sentences immediately below, the word *sewing* is H of a simple verbal group, first at S then at C:

Sewing is a useful skill.

I appreciate *sewing*.

Exercise

5. Make up 15 NG's with verbs at H. Use five at S, five at C, and five at A.

9.8   CLAUSES AT H

Clauses can only occur at H of a nominal group if they are modified by NG modifiers. The only verb form possible at P in the clause is the -ing form:

His [[mowing | the lawn | on Sunday]] is a darned nuisance.

This tree diagrams as

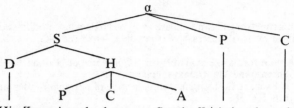

His [[mowing the lawn on Sunday]] | is | a darned nuisance.

Two other examples are:

Their [[signing away his rights]] was unjustified.
Jake's [[retaliating by murder]] was even less justified.

Exercise

6. Make up five clauses to occur at H of an NG. Use them in sentences and tree diagram the sentences.

Chapter 10

The Structure of the Verbal Group

10.0   The basic structure is the same as that of other groups – $M_n H Q_n$. H is usually represented by a main verb; if there is no main verb sometimes an auxiliary stands in:

```
            H
She | can work.
          H
She | can.
```

There may be more than one item occurring at M:

```
      M   H
She has worked.
      M    M      H
She has been working.
       M    M    M      H
She would have been working.
      could
      might
      etc.
        M    M    M    H
He may have been shot.
He      has  been shot.
He           was  shot.
```

10.1   AUXILIARY VERBS

10.11   All the items occurring at M in the examples above are **auxiliary** verbs, (see 2.34). There are twelve in all, some of them with other forms capable of carrying out the special duties of auxiliaries. Here is the complete list:

be	to be, is, are, am, was, were, being, been
have	to have, has, had, having
do	does, did
will	would
shall	should
can	could
may	might
must	
ought	
dare	
need	
used	(This does not pattern as a complete auxiliary, see 10.45)

10.12   Of this group, all except *have, be* and *do* are known as **modal** auxiliaries, used for making certain kinds of structures and statements. *Have, be* and *do* are **non-modal** auxiliaries, though *do* is more of a 'filler', or stand-in verb. Their particular functions will be referred to later in this chapter.

Exercise

1. Consider the forms above, compare them with the forms of a main verb, such as *take* or *love,* and note the differences; list the forms that are lacking in some of the auxiliaries.
2. Would it be sensible to call *ought* a one-form verb? How may forms does *be* possess?
3. Some of these verbs live a double life; they can appear as main verbs. Which are they?

10.2   SEQUENCE OF AUXILIARIES

10.21   Consider the verbs in the italicised VG's below and place them in five columns labelled a., b., c., d., and H, according to the sequence patterns you are able to discover. In each group the final verb will go under H. Forms of the verb *be* may appear in more than one column according to the form of the verb which follows *be* in the group. Start with the longer VG's.

He *did*n't *speak* to me because, at the time, he *might have been being watched.*

In fact, I was sure that he *was being watched.*

If he *had spoken* to me, we *might have been caught.*

Already we *had been warned.*

Both of us *would have been sent* to jail for life.

If an agent *had been shadowing* him, both of us *could have fallen* into their net.

He *must have been eluding* them for days.

Having been pursued for so long, he *must be feeling* the strain.

10.22 Set out below is a sequence table with all the auxiliaries divided into four sub-classes according to the order in which they can occur.

modals   TO HAVE-   TO BE-   TO BE-
         PERFECTIVE   CONTINUOUS   PASSIVE
                  SEE 10.72

a.	b.	c.	d.	H
must	have	is	is	drive
can	has	am	am	to drive
could	had	are	are	driving
may	to have	was	was	driven
might	having	were	were	
will		been	been	
would		be	be	
shall		to be	to be	
should		*always foll. by V³*	being	
need				
dare				
ought				
used				
am ⎫				
is ⎬ *used before V to in b, c or d*				
are ⎪				
was ⎪				
were ⎭				
do				
does				
did				

Items in column b. can be preceded only by items in a. (but not every item in b. by every item in a.); items in c. by those in b., and so on. An example or two will make this clear:

a.	b.	c.	d.	H
He should				drive
He may	have	been		driving
He	has	been		driving
He		was		driving
He		is	being	driven
He	has		been	driven
He			was	driven
He is			to be	driven
He ought				to drive

Exercise

4. Using the table and the examples above, work out the complete sequence possibilities in three separate tables:
   a) with V_g^o at H.
   b) with V_g^g at H.
   c) with V^n at H.

   Pay particular attention to columns c. and d. and the forms at H that these columns select. Start each table with *She* and use *see* at H.

10.3   ITEMS AT a.

When you have constructed these tables, you should have found that there are certain sequence patterns depending, for instance, upon which particular auxiliary of sub-class a. you have chosen. Further, *must* down to *should* pattern in the same way. But the others show some variations. All the auxiliaries in column a., except those which can have an s-form (i.e., the forms of *be* and *do*) are **modal** auxiliaries.

10.31   NEED, DARE. As auxiliary verbs they drop *-s* in the present tense. They are used only for negation and inversion, and only in the present tense:

> She daren't look.
> They needn't come today.
> Need he reply?
> She needn't have been working.
> He daren't be seen in such a place.

But with *-s* restored they also have a life as main verbs:

> No one needs me.
> Chichester dares the Horn.

10.32 OUGHT, USED, BE. These three select V^{to} where the *must* set select V^{o}:

> I ought to hit the ball harder.
> I ought to have hit the ball harder.

> I used to hit the ball harder.
> The ball used to be hit harder.

> I am to hit the ball harder.
> The ball is to be hit harder.

10.33 DO. Very selective indeed is *do*; it bypasses all members of columns a., b., c., d., and chooses at H one faithful follower, V^{o}:

> I do try harder than you.
> Does he try harder than you?
> I didn't try harder than you.

10.34 MAY, CAN. *May* is often interchangeable with *can*:

> Can I come in?   May I come in?

But where we say 'I can't come in', we do not as a rule say 'I mayn't come in'; usually it is 'I may not come in'.

10.35 SHALL, WILL. The normal unstressed speech form of both is *'ll*:

> We'll be there.   It'll be lovely.

Notice the variation in pronunciation in these two examples. But where there is contrastive stress the weak form *'ll* gives place to the full form:

> I won't go.   Oh yes, you will.

In other examples, there may be a certain fluidity:

> Will you go?   I certainly shall not (shan't).
>   I certainly will not (won't).

Which form do you use?

In fact *shall* is comparatively rare except in questions beginning *Shall I,* and when it is almost equivalent to *be* + V^{to}:

> He shall have a reward for that.
> You shall have an application properly made out.

Exercise

5. Refer to the table at 10.22 and work out satisfactory sequences for the

following groups. Follow the patterning at the end of 10.22, and use forms of *show* at H.

They were	He may .....
He could be	I have .....
We had been	They had .....
We do	I shall have .....
He needn't	We might be .....
He will be	He is .....
He might have been	I am .....
He ought	We used .....
He ought to be	They did .....

6. Now refer to table at 2.31 and write down the correct V symbols for the H column.

10.4   CHARACTERISTICS OF AUXILIARIES

There are four of these, which distinguish them from main verbs.

10.41   They have negative forms:

>   I can't do it; he isn't going; he won't stay.

These can be paired off with affirmative forms:

>   I can do it; he is going; he will stay.

Contrast with

>   I tell you; *I telln't you.

Such a negative form is impossible.

10.42   In question clauses where a **discontinuous** verbal group occurs, the auxiliary stands first:

>   Has <the match> started?
>   Are <the girls> going?
>   Can <we> do that?
>   Will <you> help me?

All these follow, in the clause structure, the formula P— S —P.
Note: a) In the VG's in

>   *Has* the man a match?
>   *Is* the girl a leader?

Has and *is* are at H, and they pattern as main verbs.

   b) There is a descriptive convention involved here. P— S —P means there is only one predicator, but that it is represented by a discontinuous verbal group.
Compare the following:

>   M   H
>   The match | has started.

```
M                    H
```
Has <the match> started?

In the latter the NG intervenes, and thus breaks the continuity of the VG.

However, subject insertion is involved in some clauses which are not questions:

```
        P–    S    –P
```
No sooner | had <I> arrived | than we left.

```
        P–    S    –P
```
Hardly | had <I> taken | my seat when the concert began.

There is discontinuity; and although the auxiliary does not stand first in the sentence, it is still first in the VG.

10.43   The third demand on auxiliaries is made by the tendency to avoid repeating a main verb. This is a very common conversational pattern:

> You must behave yourself, and so must we all.
> Can you beat that? Yes, I can.

Notice that the main verbs *behave* and *beat* are not repeated, but the auxiliary is.

A similar routine is followed in the response to questions:

> May I go now? You may.
> Will he do this? He will.
> You enjoyed yourself yesterday? I did.

In the third example, notice that the question is asked merely by tone of voice, and the auxiliary in the answer is a form of *do*. Remember further, that the auxiliary standing alone acts at H:

```
              H
```
I | did.

The following is a schoolgirl's paraphrase of *2 Kings, II* 23-24:

> And Elisha said, 'You rude children, if you call me a bald-head again, I'll send for a she-bear to eat you up.' And they *did,* and he *did,* and she *did.*

Exercise

7. Consider the following:
   > I think he could, you know.
   > Yes, but will he?
   > He might. Of course, he needn't if he doesn't want to.
   > Well, I think he should.
   > Yes, perhaps it's something he ought to do.
   > I agree he must.

This clutter of auxiliaries is nonsense unless you have heard the opening sentence, which is, 'Can he do this linguistics course?'
Make up a similar dialogue using auxiliaries.

10.44 Finally, auxiliaries may be used for insistence in certain situations. *Do* is one that functions frequently in this way:

> You don't like me at all.
> Yes I *do*, I *love* you.

(This is a more strongly stressed *do* than the one in 10.43.)

> You don't really love me.
> I *do* love you, I tell you.

(where insistence occurs after negation)

Do is not the only way of being insistent:

> Do you honestly?
> Of course I love you.

Here *of course* expressed the insistence.

With other auxiliaries this use of *do* does not obtain:

> I *have* seen you with Mary; don't deny it. (not **did have*)
> You *were* out with Mary. (not **did be*)
> You *will* try to stop it, won't you? (not **do will*)

Similarly,

> We *can* win this match (even if they are bigger).
> You really *must* see that picture.

10.45 There are doubtful points about some auxiliaries. *Used* for instance wavers between auxiliary and main verb status. It occurs with negation and subject insertion:

> He usedn't to do that.
> Used he to do that?

In speech, there is some variation, according to the speaker's choice:

> I usedn't to do that.
> I used not to do that.
> I didn't use to do that.
> Used I to do that?
> Did I use to do that?

In two of these examples, it is the main verb. Which are they? And which form do you normally use?

As an auxiliary *used* has no present tense forms, and notice that the final *d* is pronounced as 't'. When, however, it is used as a main verb the *d* is pronounced 'd':

I used all the material you brought.

10.5   BE, HAVE, DO, AS MAIN VERBS

10.51   BE.

S	P	C
My lover	is	a sailor.
My lover	was	seasick.

Be is a special case. It is the only nine-form verb; it is the only verb with three present tense forms:

I *am*, he *is*, we *are*

Further it is the only verb with two preterite forms:

I *was*, you *were*

Been and *being* share no similarity in their form with these.
This is all wildly irregular when compared with the paradigm of a main verb, e.g., *walk*.

10.52   HAVE.

Have too, can behave normally as a main verb, though in questions people vary in their usage. Do you say 'Have you a match?' or 'Do you have a match?' or 'Have you got a match?' In the first two examples *have* is a main verb, in the third, an auxiliary. But in assertions *have* is frequently a main verb:

My friend | has | a pretty daughter.

Its C is not clearly either C^E or C^I (no passive, no concord). There are slight irregularities in its paradigm too:

I have – he has (not **haves*)
he had (not **haved*)

When *have* patterns the same way as the auxiliaries *ought, used, be,* it is then an auxiliary. Otherwise we consider it a catenative verb (see 21.41). The two cases are exemplified in the pairs of sentences below:

i) Has he to work this evening?
Does he have to work this evening?
ii) He hasn't to work this evening.
He doesn't have to work this evening.

10.53   Do. *Do* as a main verb behaves quite normally, except for

I do – He does (not *'doos')

      S   P   C   A

These boys | do | their English homework | well.

10.6   TENSE

There are only two tenses, *present* and *past,* which are marked by differences in form. For the present tense, V^o and V^s are regularly used, for the past tense V^d:

I talk – he talks – we talked

There is no form change in English verbs to record future time. *I shall love* has, for instance, nothing parallel to the form changes in *J'aimerai*. In traditional grammars, *shall* and *will* were taken as markers of the future:

I'll be seeing you.

But these auxiliaries have other functions, and there are other ways of indicating futurity. For instance, in

He could be doing this *soon.*

I'm going *tomorrow.*

the adverb and particle act as markers of the future.

10.7   ASPECT

In addition to tense, English has two **aspects** – the **perfective** aspect, and the **progressive** aspect.

10.71   PERFECTIVE ASPECT. VG's containing forms of *have* + V^n are perfective; they are said to be marked for perfective aspect:

He has gone   present perfective

He had gone   past perfective

When certain of the modal auxiliaries are added, we have

He may have gone   present modal perfective

He might have gone   past modal perfective

10.72   PROGRESSIVE [CONTINUOUS] ASPECT. VG's containing forms of *be* + V^g are progressive; they are said to be marked for progressive aspect. The pattern runs as follows:

He is going   present progressive

He was going   past progressive

He may be going	present modal progressive
He might be going	past modal progressive
He may have been going	present modal perfective progressive
He might have been going	past modal perfective progressive

Exercise

8. Name the tenses, and aspects, if any, in the following:
   a) He might have been running.
   b) He may do it.
   c) I am listening.
   d) You have been working.
   e) He could have been shooting.
   f) He works well.
   g) He may be running.
9. Using the verb *show* at H and *Peter* at S, make up an example of the following VG's:
   a) past perfective progressive
   b) present perfective
   c) present modal progressive
   d) present progressive
   e) present modal perfective
   f) present perfective progressive
   g) past modal perfective progressive

10.8   VOICE

Voice is a term used to describe the system by which it is possible to choose a form of VG marked as **passive**:

> It has been decided.
>
> We were interrupted.

The transformation between the VG unmarked for voice (i.e., the group without $be + V^n$) and the passive (i.e., the group with $be + V^n$), can be worked out from the following examples:

> NG1   +   VG   +   NG2 ⟶
> The coach | trained | the boy.

> NG2 +   VG   + by + NG1
> The boy | was trained | by the coach.

In this type, NG1 may be used as above or may simply disappear:

> NG2 +   VG   + by + NG1 ⟶
> The boy | was trained | by the coach.
> NG2 +   VG
> The boy | was trained.

10.81   Either of the NG's at C in the structure SPC^EC^E may be transformed into S in a corresponding passive structure:

NG1 + VG + NG2 + NG3 $\longrightarrow$
John | sent | Mary | a book.

NG2   + VG   + NG3   + (NG1)
Mary | was sent | a book | (by John).

  or   NG3 +   VG   + (NG2) + (NG1)
    A book | was sent | (Mary) | (by John).

10.82   In the VG's followed by C^EC^I, a slightly different pattern is seen:

    NG1   + VG   + NG2 + NG3 $\longrightarrow$
  The queen | made | him | a knight.

NG2 +   VG   +   NG3 + (by + NG1)
He | was made | a knight | (by the queen).

Note that C^I, *a knight*, stays in the transformation. (This is the 'retained' object of traditional grammar).

10.83   A variant form of the passive transformation is seen in the following examples:

  i) The wing-threequarter promptly dropped on the ball. $\longrightarrow$
    The ball was promptly dropped on (by the wing-threequarter).
 ii) Queen Elizabeth slept in this bed. $\longrightarrow$
    This bed has been slept in by Queen Elizabeth.
iii) People broke into that house. $\longrightarrow$
    That house has been broken into.

10.84   The VG pattern in the passive goes like this:

The boy is trained	present passive
was trained	past passive
may be trained	present modal passive
might be trained	past modal passive
may have been trained	present modal perfective passive
might have been trained	past modal perfective passive
is being trained	present progressive passive
was being trained	past progressive passive

10.85   In scientific and official varieties of English the passive voice is often used without *by* + NG in order to preserve anonymity:

    Unfortunately, the conditions laid down in the circular have been abused, so that serious difficulties in sorting have been experienced by the Post Office. Documents which are folded and then fastened with a gummed sticker vary in size and shape; handling is therefore slowed up in mail-rooms. Moreover, different styles of folding are adopted and addresses are sometimes written so high that they tend to be obscured by the date-stamp. Because of all this, sorting of such mail is greatly retarded.

VG's unmarked for passive have traditionally been called *active*.

Exercise

10. Use the following, first in VG's not marked for passive, then in the passive transform, if one exists:
    taste, dream, speed, stop, fall, lay, dress, write, leave, seem.
11. Work out the tense, aspect, and voice descriptions of the following VG's:
    a) He may have been killed.
    b) The prisoner had been sentenced.
    c) They were being starved.
    d) He could have been hurt by the falling branch.
    e) The enemy may be surrounded.
    f) Passports were demanded.
    g) The job should be finished.
    h) Crops might be grown on this land.
12. Using the verb *show* at H, and *the boy* at S, make up the following VG's:
    a) present modal passive
    b) past perfective progressive
    c) present modal perfective
    d) past progressive
    e) present passive
    f) past modal perfective passive
    g) present perfective

Chapter 11

Subclasses of the Finite Verb

11.1 ANOTHER FORM CLASSIFICATION

In addition to the classification of verbs according to the number of forms (2.3), other classifications are available. There is, for instance, the division exemplified between *swim, dig,* and *hope, walk.* (2.31, 2.32). To some extent, this corresponds to the traditional distinction between strong and weak verbs. Five-form verbs like *walk* (but not *dig*) comprise an open set; all other verbs belong to closed sets.

Exercise

1. Give the V^d and V^n forms of the following:
   get, forbid, hang, bleed, heave, strew, lie, lay, stroke, stink, drive. Some of these have two V^d or two V^n forms.
2. In verbs that have two V^n forms, only one is normally used in an NG. An example is:
   The ships were all sunk in the typhoon.
   We had tea in the sunken garden.
   Examine the circumstances in which the following are used:
   struck, stricken
   melted, molten
   shaved, shaven
   sheared, shorn
   Can you think of similar pairs?

11.2 A STRUCTURAL CLASSIFICATION

Another method of classifying verbs may be developed by examining the way they are used in the clause structures (4.5). The following terms are used to describe the different clause structures:

Structure	*Term for clause structure*
S P ⎫ S P A ⎭	**Intransitive**
S P C^E ⎫ S P C^E A ⎭	**Transitive**
S P C^I	**Equational**
S P C^E C^I ⎫ S P C^E C^E ⎭	**Double-complement**

Observe that the terms are related to the complements of the structures. When a verb occurs in an intransitive structure it is used intransitively; when a verb occurs in a transitive structure it is used transitively; when it occurs in an equational structure, it is used equationally; when it occurs in a double-complement structure, it is doubly complemented.

Exercise

3. How have the verbs been used in the following?
    a) The bloodhound can smell well.
    b) He smelt the cake and it smelt good.
    c) His mother made me an apple pie.
    d) The children made a sandcastle at the beach.
    e) She knitted me a pullover, and that made me a happy man.
    f) After the accident, his broken bones knitted well.
    g) He is a pillar of the community.
    h) John looks stupid and indeed is stupid.
    i) He is here.
    j) The halfback looked quick.
    k) The halfback looked quickly to see where his opponent was.
    l) The paratrooper looked hard.

11.21   Thus verbs can be classified according to the type of structure in which they occur; some verbs occur regularly in a given structure, and can therefore be named after the structure, e.g.,

> *arrive* – intransitive   *chase* – transitive

On the other hand some verbs may occur normally in more than one structure:

> They *watched* the exhibition.
> Thousands of people *watched* the fight.
> The boys *watched* from behind the bushes.
> *Watch,* and see what happens.

It is obvious from these examples that *watch* can be used transitively or intransitively, and therefore it cannot be classified solely as either transitive or intransitive.

11.22   In some clause structures, there is an obligatory adjunct (see 4.51, patterns II and VII). In both these structures only a small number of verbs occur.

11.23   We shall therefore use two criteria to classify verbs into subclasses:
a) The kinds of complement and adjunct they require,
b) The normalcy of these requirements: i.e., regularly, sometimes, not usually.

These points can be seen in the table below.

SUBCLASSES OF THE FINITE VERB

1 LETTER	2 MODEL	3 A	4 C	5 C^E	6 C^I	7 $C^E C^E$	8 $C^E C^I$
R	arrive	÷	—	—	—	—	—
T	be	÷ (⏞+)	÷	—	÷	—	—
U	become	÷	+	—	+	—	—
V	chase	÷	+	+	—	—	—
W	put	+	+	+	—	—	—
X	taste	÷	+	÷	÷	—	—
Y	give	÷	+	÷	—	÷	—
Z	elect	÷	+	+	—	—	÷

The table shows the patterning of verbs with their followers, either adjuncts or different kinds of complement, all of which have already been explained.

The symbols in columns 3 to 8 mean:

+ = regularly   ÷ = sometimes   — = not usually

11.3 READING THE TABLE

11.31 Start with column 1; read across the page from left to right. The columns labelled LETTER and MODEL indicate the class of verb being considered, e.g., verbs similar to *arrive* will have its characteristics. Column three, providing for A only, shows the symbol ÷ for *arrive,* thus allowing for the two possibilities:

    He | has arrived.   S P

    He | has arrived | by taxi.   S P A

Column four (labelled C for complement) shows a — for intransitive verbs like *arrive*. The symbol indicates that it is not usual for such verbs to have a complement. We can say

    He | arrived | with his luggage   S P A

but not

    *He | arrived | the luggage.   S P C

11.32 The remaining columns provide particular information about the kind of C the members of a class require if they require C at all. If they occur with an extensive complement, or an intensive complement, or with a double complement, columns five, six, seven and eight show this. If column four (C) shows a — then all the following columns also show a —. Obviously, if a verb does not occur with C, then it will not occur with the more specific kinds of C. Intransitive verbs of the *arrive* type thus do not normally progress beyond column three. The rest of the table may be interpreted similarly.

Exercises

4. Take any other row in the table, and state what information it gives you about the model verb.
5. Which model do the following verbs follow?
   cause, seem, place, bequeath, feel, come, teach, see, appear, consider, review.

11.4 SUBCLASSES R–Z

We will now consider the members of subclasses R to Z in greater detail.

11.41 SUBCLASS R. Some other members of this class are *go, come, grin*. These verbs show a – in the complement column. The interpretation of the – as 'not usually' rather than 'never' allows for such exceptions as:

He came a cropper.
He grinned a horrible grin.

11.42   SUBCLASS T. *Be* is the main member of subclass T. It is, however, frequently used. As the table indicates, it is regularly followed either by C^I or A or sometimes both. *Remain* and *stay* also belong here:

He is angry.	He remained an Englishman.
He is in the garden.	He stayed at his post.
He was angry today.	He remained angry all day.

Exceptional uses are:

God is.   (no C or A)   Few problems remain.
I think; therefore I am.
Is he?

11.43   SUBCLASS U. Some other members of this subclass are *seem, look, appear*. Exceptional cases are more frequent than with subclass T. Examples of exceptional cases are:

Look!
He seems in a good humour.
A tram appeared.

11.44   SUBCLASS V. Some other members are *see, chase, hit, break,* and so on. As the table indicates, these verbs regularly take a C^E and sometimes an A, but there are exceptional uses:

Do you understand? Yes, I think I see.   (no C^E)
Dawn broke as we were coming home from the ball.

Many verbs are freely used both transitively and intransitively, such as *know, think, play:*

The children are playing outside.
He plays the violin deplorably.

11.45   SUBCLASS W. There are few verbs in this subclass. Among them are *put, place* which regularly require both C and A. This A is normally one of place:

He put his hat on the table.
She placed her arm on his shoulder.

This class is small, but its members occur frequently.

11.46 SUBCLASS X. Verbs such as *feel, hurt, smell, taste* (verbs of the senses) can have C^E or C^I – that is, they may be used transitively or equationally:

> She felt his pulse.
> He felt a fool.
> I tasted the cake.
> It tasted delightful.

11.47 SUBCLASS Y. Verbs like *give, owe, tell, teach*, sometimes take C^E C^E, sometimes C^E only:

> We shall give him the works.
> A fire gives heat.
> He owes me sixpence.
> He owes money to the Tax Department.

(When there is only one C^E an adjunct regularly occurs.)

Teach seems to be a special case. One can say:

He teaches all day.	S P A
He teaches French.	S P C^E
He teaches me.	S P C^E
He teaches me French.	S P C^{E1} C^{E2}

11.48 SUBCLASS Z. Verbs such as *appoint, elect, nominate* must have C^E, and may have $C^E C^I$:

> The cabinet elected him.
> The cabinet elected him leader.

11.49 There are some verbs such as *make* and *choose* which belong to both Y and Z. It should be noticed that though we have listed eight subclasses of verbs, these are only a small number of the classes theoretically possible. There are five major characteristics available: A, C^I, C^E, $C^E C^E$, $C^E C^I$; each of these can be $+$, $\div$, $-$. This gives a total of $3^5 = 243$ possible subclasses. Not all of these are found. Those that are presented here are, however, important ones.

Exercises

6. Make up a fresh subclass with model *behave*, and list its characteristics.

7. Work out the C and A for these clauses. Classify the verbs according to the table, if you can.

He called me a fool.
He called me a taxi.
He called a taxi.
He grew tired.
He grew good crops.
The publishers will send us a nice cheque.
They were standing near us.
She could not stand that fellow.
She sells seashells on the seashore.
The goods sold cheaply.

I don't suffer fools gladly.
He fell asleep.
He fell a victim.
He arrived wet.
He sold me a pup.

11.5   ITEMS AT C AND A

The class of item at C and A is worth some consideration.

11.51 C^E is usually represented by a noun-, or pronoun-headed group:

He gave her the book.

C^I is usually represented by noun-, or pronoun-, or adjective-headed groups:

He is his own worst enemy.
He is sick.
That's him.
He hurt himself.
We thought her a beauty/beautiful.

But some subclass U verbs like *weigh* and *cost* usually have a nominal group headed by a noun, best regarded perhaps as C^I:

It cost a great deal.
It weighs five pounds.

Other kinds of NG are rather rare:

It weighs heavy upon me.   S P C^I A
It cost him dear.   S P C^E C^I

11.52   Optional adjuncts have many possibilities. Obligatory adjuncts (i.e., those with classes T and W) are restricted to prepositional groups and adverbial groups whose H is not represented by *-ly* marked adverbs:

He is in trouble.
He is away.
He put the plate on the shelf.
He put the dog outside.

Using Grammar

12.0   In one sense the title of this chapter is misleading – it suggests there *must* be a practical application of the work we have done so far. This is not necessarily so: the main end of the study of grammar is the understanding of the phenomenon of language. Just as the pure sciences describe chemicals, marine life, vegetation and so on, primarily to gain insight into these phenomena, so too, grammar provides an insight into its particular area of language. But just as there are practical applications of chemistry or botany, so we can use our knowledge of grammar in a practical way.

We shall look at several uses in this chapter:

a) Grammar can be of help in commenting on language appropriate to different registers; grammar can provide a terminology which enables language to be discussed; such discussion can be helpful outside as well as inside the classroom (12.1).

b) Grammar can analyse and sometimes resolve ambiguities (12.2).

c) Grammar can help in describing and comparing styles and registers (12.3).

d) Grammar can help elucidate meaning, especially in complicated prose and poetry, by making clear the relationships of the parts (12.4).

12.1   USED APPROPRIATELY

We use different registers in writing and speech and make further distinctions of register according to the circumstances and the range of language available to the user. Thus 'Good morning,' 'Morning', 'Hello', 'G'day', 'Hi', illustrate differences in register. We often wish to adjust our register to the one we know (or feel) is appropriate.

Grammar is not the only aspect of language involved here: word-selection and voice expression are important.

In spoken English and informal written English the following is very common:

Major Johnson was the man they gave the award to.

In formal written English these are generally preferred:

Major Johnson was the man to whom they gave the award.

Major Johnson was the man whom they gave the award to.

Grammar can help point out these distinctions.

In the sentence *He ate the banana quick* analysis will show

S   P   C   A

He | ate | the banana | quick.

Grammar enables us to comment: '*Quick* is not normally used as an adjunct in formal registers. The adverb form (*quickly*) would be expected here.'

12.2   EXPLAINING AMBIGUITIES

Some ambiguities can be analysed by using grammar:

i) The headline *Food tastes of ancient Romans:*

M H   Q

either Food tastes [of ancient Romans].

S   P   A

or   Food | tastes | of ancient Romans.

ii) I found him a useful ally:

S   P C^E C^E

either I | found | him | a useful ally.

S   P C^E C^I

or   I | found | him | a useful ally.

iii) The headline *Extra late night:*

either   E   E   H   the night is extra and late,

or   SM   E   H   the night is extra late.

The last example shows how the expansion of the truncated forms clarifies the possible grammatical structures.

Note: Ambiguity is not always grammatical; sometimes it is semantic (*Go ask the butcher if he's got any brains.*) or phonological (*Which won? Which one?*).

Exercise

1. Indicate the ambiguities in these examples; sometimes clause divisions, sometimes group divisions, will be more helpful.
   a) Constable disarms man with shotgun.
   b) A recent jazz festival.
   c) Girls plump for marriage.
   d) Five acres of best growing peat land.
   e) Fire alarms generally sound.
   f) Call me a taxi.

12.3   DISTINGUISHING STYLES AND REGISTERS

Grammar can also be used to help show language difference between passages from different styles and registers. Such passages, of course, vary in a number of ways; in word selection, balance, and rhythm as well as in grammar. One readily measurable aspect of different passages is the structure of the NG's. The use of simple or complex NG's and the structure of complex NG's will give factors of comparison.

In the extracts which follow, the NG's (excluding pG's) have been analysed into D, O, E, N, H, Q, and the proportion of modifiers and qualifiers related to H. These samples are too small to be statistically valid but they serve to show the process.

  D   O   N   N   H
i) *The [fifty-five foot] fisheries patrol launch* was now running satis-

                      H   N   H
factorily, said *Commodore B. E. Turner, district superintendent [for*

        Q   Q
the Marine Department] [in Auckland].

       H   H
ii) Mix *cornflower* and *sugar* to smooth cream with a little milk. Heat

  H   Q   E   H
rest [of milk] with butter and salt. Add *mixed cornflour*, boil for three
minutes. Pour into wetted mould to set.

      D   E   E   H   D   O   H   Q
iii) *The little white horse* was *the smallest animal [on the Roundabout*

                              D   H   Q
[at the Fun Fair [at the seaside]]]. There were *all sorts [of animals]* on

                H   H   H   E   E   H   SM D
the Roundabout; *bears, lions, tigers, big brown horses* and *even a*

        H   D   O   E   H
giraffe, but *only one little white horse.*

From this we can see the structure of the NG's is:

	(i)	(ii)	(iii)
D	1	0	5
O	1	0	2
E	0	1	6
N	3	0	0
H	3	4	9
Q	2	1	2
Total non-H	7	2	15
Total H	3	4	9
Total elements	10	6	24

This table enables us to note that the newspaper style of (i) is marked in its NG's by a dominance of items at N (in this case all nouns), while the recipe (ii) in its NG's shows a total absence of N items and a very sparing use of E items. The children's story is remarkable for the comparatively large number of E items in proportion to the number of H's. They are, however, very simple ones: three are colour, three size adjectives.

These specimens are of course extremely short ones and it would be wrong to draw statistical conclusions from these figures. Samples of sufficient length, however, can be compared in a large number of interesting ways, e.g.,

$$\frac{H}{\text{total elements}} \quad \frac{E}{\text{total}} \quad \frac{N}{\text{total}} \quad \frac{Q}{\text{total}}$$

These proportions, conveniently expressed as percentages, can be used to demonstrate significant differences between various kinds of English.

12.31 The following very simple table shows the proportion of words in NG's to the total number of words:

	(i)	(ii)	(iii)
Words in NG's	16	7	35
Total words	21	33	43
	76%	21%	81%

Even this coarse analysis shows that extracts (i) and (iii) make great use of NG's to carry the statement whereas the recipe (ii) uses 'bare' nouns and relies on other methods to carry the meaning.

12.32 Differences in the use of nominal groups are only some of the ways whereby passages vary in their grammar. Here are some of the other grammatical features which are often used differently in passages:

a) The complexity of sentence structure. Some writers tend to use mainly simple sentences; others, complex ones.

b) The kind of relationships between clauses in complex sentences. Some writers tend to use mainly linkage; others, mainly bondage; others again mix the two.

c) The sequence of dependent and independent clauses. Some writers tend to place dependent clauses first, or insert them in the independent clauses, rather than place them last.

d) The use of clauses as clause or group elements. Some writers place many clauses at Q in NG's; others do so infrequently.

e) The use of adjuncts. Some writers use many prepositional groups as adjuncts in a clause; others do so infrequently.

f) The sequence of clause elements. Some writers, particularly in verse, place the clause elements in unusual sequence. The complement may be placed first, or the adjunct (often represented by a prepositional group) moved from its expected position. Other writers make little use of unusual sequence.

12.4   CLARIFYING MEANING

Grammar can help us extract the meaning from any passage. Usually the passages which require such help are quite involved and grammar assists in following the line of thought by indicating the relationships.

a) And the congregation seemed to watch with its own eyes while the voice consumed him, until he was nothing and they were nothing and there was not even a voice but instead their hearts were speaking to one another in chanting measures beyond the need for words, so that when he came to rest against the reading desk, his monkey face lifted and his whole attitude that of a serene, tortured crucifix that transcended its shabbiness and insignificance and made it of no moment, a long moaning expulsion of breath rose from them, and a woman's single soprano: 'Yes, Jesus!'

WILLIAM FAULKNER, *The Sound and the Fury*

In a sentence as complex as this it is necessary to have a thorough grasp of the relationships of the different clauses. The thread of meaning partly depends upon noticing, consciously or unconsciously, the clues to the clause relationships. What follows is a demonstration of how grammar can assist in bringing these relationships and clues to our attention, and thus make us aware of the path by which we normally travel unconsciously to the meaning. The method used is to show step by step how the sentence expands from its initial simplicity to its final complexity.

i) *And the congregation seemed to watch with its own eyes* ||
This can be represented by α. It is the independent clause in the sentence.

ii) *And the congregation seemed to watch with its own eyes* || *while the voice consumed him* ||
Represented by α β; β is made dependent by *while*.

iii) *And the congregation seemed to watch with its own eyes* || *while the voice consumed him* || *until he was nothing* || *and they were nothing* || *and there was not even a voice* || *but instead their hearts were speaking to one another in chanting measures beyond the need for words* ||
Represented by α β γ &γ &γ &γ; γ is made dependent by the particle *until*, which all four linked clauses share; the clauses are linked by *and* and *but instead*.

iv) *... so that* − − − − − *a long moaning expulsion of breath rose from them,* || *and a woman's single soprano: 'Yes, Jesus!'*
The clauses examined up to this stage are represented by α β γ &γ &γ &γ δ− −δ &δ. The *so that* clause is discontinuous. It is made dependent by *so that*. The following clause is linked by *and* and also shares *rose* as P.

v) At this point we will go back to consider the clauses inserted in the *so that* clause
  so that <<*when he came to rest against the reading desk* ||
Represented by δ− ε; ε is marked as dependent upon the *so that* clause by *when*.

vi) *so that* <<*when he came to rest against the reading desk,* || *his monkey face lifted,* || *and his whole attitude that of a serene, tortured crucifix ...*>>
Represented by δ− ε ζ &ζ. (ζ is Zeta.)
These two clauses are linked to each other by *and;* they are marked as dependent. The first is a non-finite clause, the second a predicatorless clause. They may be considered as elliptical transforms of *with his monkey face lifted and his whole attitude that of a serene, tortured*

crucifix. This makes it clear why they cannot be taken as the continuations of *so that.* For while it might seem plausible to read *so that . . . his monkey face lifted,* the following linked clause would be very odd, and there would be no way of explaining the relationships of the final two clauses to the rest of the sentence. The only plausible explanation for the latter is that they are continuations of *so that.* vii) The last two clauses to be added are the linked clauses after *crucifix:*

> *. . . when he came to rest against the reading desk, || his monkey face lifted|| and his whole attitude that of a serene, tortured crucifix [[that transcended its shabbiness and insignificance || and made it of no moment,]] . . .* ε ζ & ζ [[β &β]]

The square brackets indicate that these linked clauses qualify *crucifix.* Unlike the other clauses they are not direct constituents of the sentence, but provide an expansion for an NG. The first is marked as dependent by *that* which is also shared by the second; they are linked to each other by this sharing and by *and.*

Notice that these clauses that qualify are not given the next letter of the Greek alphabet after ζ. The series just concluded with ζ is a series of clauses which represent sentence elements. But the series of clauses now being started is a fresh one; it is a series of clauses that qualify a particular noun. Since these are the first and only clauses in this new series they are represented by β and &β.

Apart from its general complexity, the main difficulty in this sentence is caused by the insertion of a number of clauses into a discontinuous clause. Not only is one part of this clause widely separated from its other part but at first reading it is possible to take a non-finite clause as the second part. However the subsequent difficulty of explaining the relationships of following clauses leads to this possibility being dropped.

Another complexity was created by the use of clauses to expand an NG. This differs from the main way in which clauses are used in this sentence, which is that they are added by linkage or dependence so as to expand the sentence. The use of clauses in NG's is not a prominent feature of this sentence. However in sentences where this use of clauses is a major feature, it is important to pick out the main outline of the sentence first, before turning to consider clauses used to expand NG's.

It is not always necessary to look at all the clause relationships as we have done above. A more compressed approach would restrict the use of grammar to only those particular parts of a text that are causing difficulty. Obviously in the sentence just discussed it is the part starting with *so that* that is likely to require attention. It is in such a part that methods of grammatical analysis can most fruitfully be used to explain and solve problems of understanding.

b) Either to disenthrone the King of Heav'n
    We war, if war be best, or to regain
    Our own right lost: him to unthrone we then
    May hope, when everlasting fate shall yield
    To fickle chance, and chaos judge the strife:
    The former vain to hope argues as vain
    The latter.

JOHN MILTON, Paradise Lost

This time the comment will be restricted to those sections of this sentence which display unusual sequence.

The sequence of clauses in the first part is unusual:

$$\beta$$
Either to disenthrone the King of Heav'n ||

$$\alpha \qquad\qquad \beta \qquad\qquad\qquad \&\beta$$
We war, || if war be best, || or to regain

Our own right lost:

Linked non-finite clauses are not usually separated as they are here. What we would have expected in non-verse would be:

We war, if war be best, either to disenthrone the King of Heav'n or to regain our own right lost.

The sequence of words in the final NG is also unusual. *Lost* would be expected as a modifier rather than as a qualifier.

In the next section the complement *him* precedes its predicator *to unthrone* and, in turn, these elements are placed first instead of immediately following *May hope*. The more usual sequence in modern English prose would be:

we then may hope to unthrone him. . .

The grammar of the final clause contains three unusual features. The subject is *The former vain to hope* which has M H Q structure. The clause which qualifies *former* is elliptical: in a fuller form it could be 'which | it | is | vain | to hope | for.' *Argues,* which is the predicator, here has a complement *the latter.* It is thus used transitively whereas in modern English it is usually used intransitively, e.g.,

He argued for keeping the old house.

He argued against the proposal.

He argued the case.

Finally, the prepositional group at A is placed before the complement rather than after it. In modern English therefore the non-verse equivalent might be:

S   P

The former [[which it would be vain to hope for]] | argues | the

  C   A

latter | as vain.

Understanding the grammatical relationships does not provide the only requirement for understanding the meaning of the passage but without it the latter is hardly possible.

Exercises

2. Look carefully at the grammar of each stanza in the following poem. Describe in detail the grammatical parallels between the three stanzas.

Long-Legged Fly

That civilisation may not sink,
Its great battle lost,
Quiet the dog, tether the pony
To a distant post;
Our master Caesar is in the tent
Where the maps are spread,
His eyes fixed upon nothing,
A hand under his head.
Like a long-legged fly upon the stream
His mind moves upon silence.

That the topless towers be burnt
And men recall that face,
Move most gently if move you must
In this lonely place.
She thinks, part woman, three parts a child,
That nobody looks; her feet
Practise a tinker shuffle
Picked up on a street.
Like a long-legged fly upon the stream
Her mind moves upon silence.

That girls at puberty may find
The first Adam in their thought,
Shut the door of the Pope's chapel,
Keep those children out.
There on that scaffolding reclines
Michael Angelo.
With no more sound than the mice make
His hand moves to and fro.
Like a long-legged fly upon the stream
His mind moves upon silence.

W. B. YEATS

3. Compare the grammar of the following passages. Observe as many grammatical differences as you can and, where possible, provide statistical information to show the extent of the differences:

a) WILLIAM GOLDING *The Lord of the Flies*

Smoke was rising here and there among the creepers that festooned the dead or dying trees. As they watched, a flash of fire appeared at the root of one wisp, and then the smoke thickened. Small flames stirred at the bole of a tree and crawled away through leaves and brushwood, dividing and increasing. One patch touched a tree trunk and scrambled up like a bright squirrel. The smoke increased, sifted, rolled outwards. The squirrel leapt on wings of the wind and clung to another standing tree, eating downwards. Beneath the dark canopy of leaves and smoke the fire laid hold on the forest and began to gnaw. Acres of black and yellow smoke rolled steadily towards the sea. At the sight of the flames and the irresistible course of the fire, the boys broke into shrill, excited cheering. The flames, as though they were a kind of wild life, crept as a jaguar creeps on its belly towards a line of birch-like saplings that fledged an outcrop of the pink rock. They flapped at the first of the trees, and the branches grew a brief foliage of fire. The heart of flame leapt nimbly across the gap between the trees and then went swinging and flaring along the whole row of them. Beneath the capering boys a quarter of a mile square of forest was savage with smoke and flame. The separate noises of the fire merged into a drum-roll that seemed to shake the mountain.

b) DYLAN THOMAS *Under Milk Wood*

The sunny slow lulling afternoon yawns and moons through the dozy town. The sea lolls, laps and idles in, with fishes sleeping in its lap. The meadows still as Sunday, the shut-eye tasselled bulls, the goat-and-daisy dingles, nap happy and lazy. The dumb duck-ponds snooze. Clouds sag and pillow on Llaregyb Hill. Pigs grunt in a wet wallow-bath, and smile as they snort and dream. They dream of the acorned swill of the world, the rooting for pig-fruit, the bag-pipe dugs of the mother sow ... They mud-bask and snout in the pig-loving sun; their tails curl; they rollick and slobber and snore to deep, smug, after-swill sleep. Donkeys angelically drowse on Donkey Down.

Chapter 13

Revision Exercises

CHAPTER 2

1. a) List, with examples, the factors that determine the class of a word.
   b) Accordingly, allocate the word *round* in the following to its class:
      i) He was knocked out in the second round.
      ii) The merry-go-round goes round and round.
      iii) He's just a square peg in a round hole.
      iv) Round the rugged rocks the ragged rascal ran.
      v) The milkman's round was not an easy one.

2. Write short explanatory notes on the following technical terms, and give examples.

   finite, apostrophe form, bound morpheme, complex group, determiner.

3. Explain the term *closed set*. Give three classes or sub-classes of words which form closed sets.

4. Write in a column the verb forms in the following (omit auxiliaries). Then opposite each write the form names and their symbols.

   'What do you mean by that?' said Mr Sikes, looking up in a surly manner. 'What I say, Bill,' replied the lady.
   'Nobody here knows anything about you,' reasoned Fagin, 'so it'll work all right. Stop a minute – carry that basket in one hand – it looks more respectable. No one would suspect a girl who is carrying a basket and is going shopping.'
   'I won't go!' said Nancy.
   'Don't talk like that,' growled Bill, "you must go.'
   'Do you take me for a fool, Bill?' replied Nancy, sobbing. 'You ought to know the boy suspects me.'
   'I'd have to be shown that, my girl,' snarled Bill.

5. Pick out the auxiliary verbs in Exercise 4. State the function of each.

6.

Noun	Verb	Adjective	Adverb
beauty	beautify	beautiful	beautifully

Construct a table according to the pattern above, using the words:

fury, terrible, respectably, tidy, comparison, endanger, able, labour, consider, power.

CHAPTER 3

1. Explain what the symbols M, H, and Q mean. What does the formula $M_n H Q_n$ mean?

2. The desert hills cut into the starry sky with dramatic clarity. The night air was dry from the desert. By the roadside, fires would flicker where owners of donkey trains lay camped by their piled loads. The tired donkeys cropped the grass by the roadside contentedly enough. At times a frightened hare would fly in a distracted zigzag in the lights from the truck, and dogs from the little ranches would bark at our passing.

Pick out, in the above piece, the various groups and analyse in terms of M, H, Q.

CHAPTER 4

1. What are the characteristics of S, P and C?

2. Study the following; then pick out the intensive and extensive complements.
   a) We like icecream.
   b) The doctor felt his patient's pulse.
   c) She looks dreadful without her make-up.
   d) Smith was very angry.
   e) These oranges taste good.
   f) He lost his shirt at the races; he can no longer dress himself in his accustomed style.
   g) He seems quite a good fellow.
   h) After the party she felt dreadful.
   i) She tasted the wine very carefully.

3. Write five examples of sentences with C^{E1} and C^{E2}.

4. Write sentences according to the following structures:
   SPAA, APS, AAPS, SPA, SPCA, ASPC, SPAC, ASPA, SP— A —P C.

5. Write sentences according to the following structures:
   SPC^E, $SPC^E C^I$, PA, $SPC^{E1} C^{E2}$.

6. Using the information you have been given in this chapter calculate the number of possible clause structures.

CHAPTER 5

1. Using the following examples, state the characteristics by which you can recognise that a clause is dependent.

He was working well when I looked in. After I had chatted for a while I left the car. This vehicle, which I had bought the previous day, was in reasonably good order. There were one or two defects that I could repair if I had the time.

2. Explain, with examples, the difference between finite and non-finite dependent clauses.

3. a) What are the linking particles? How is linking represented symbolically?
   b) Make up five sentences each containing a dependent clause.

4. Find five examples of sentences linked otherwise than by a particle.

5. Make up sentences according to the following:
   αβ; βα; αβγ; βαβ; αβγδ.

CHAPTERS 6, 7, 8, 9 (THE NOMINAL GROUP)

1. Define count, mass and collective nouns; give examples.

2. a) The jury is/are divided in its/their opinion.
   b) This class is/are attentive.
   c) These classes is/are attentive.
   d) The yolks of eggs is/are white.
   e) The committee was/were unanimous.
   Choose one form at P in the above, and state the reasons for your choice.

3. 'A noun is a naming word'. For what sub-class of nouns is this statement most appropriate? This sub-class has certain characteristics which differentiate it from other sub-classes of nouns. What are they?

4. What is the difference between M and Q? What word classes may appear at D? At O? At E?

5. What items may appear at Q? Give examples. Classify the word *else* in
   No one else can do it.

6. Groups may occur as group elements. Give examples of such groups at N and at H.

7. Explain with examples the difference between these two structures:
   M H [Q] [Q]   M H [Q [Q]]

8. Explain in grammatical terms the difference in structure between these sentences:
   Those boys who have cars are very popular with some girls.
   Those boys, who have cars, are very popular with some girls.

9. What word classes can act at H of an NG? Give an example for each.

CHAPTER 10

1. Explain, with examples, the following technical terms:
   perfective aspect, progressive aspect.

2. What exactly do you understand by the term *voice*? Show how clauses with no passive VG may be transformed into clauses with a passive VG. What marks a VG as passive? In what kinds of writing is the passive quite frequently used? What is the stylistic effect of such a use? Is it possible to justify the consistent use of the passive?

3. Exemplify the special duties of auxiliary verbs.

4. Make up examples of VG's to show the order of occurrence when more than one auxiliary is employed. What does this order depend on?

5. Discuss the uses of the auxiliaries in the following, first grammatically, than semantically.

> I am going to town tomorrow. I might go tomorrow.
> He could be there by now. He may be there by now.
> Will you do this? Of course, I will.
> You shouldn't do that, you know. But I will do it.
> He ought to have succeeded. He should have succeeded.
> He would get up early in summer. He would get up, though I told him not to. Of course, you would have to interrupt.
> Do behave, you naughty child. How do you do?
> He didn't sit down by the fire.

CHAPTER 11

1. Name, and exemplify, the methods of classifying finite verbs.
   There is only one class to which all newly-formed verbs belong; which is it?

2. Describe the structures to which the following terms apply:
   equational, doubly complemented, intransitive.

3. a) Using the information contained in the table, compose sentences to illustrate each model verb.
   b) List up to five verbs for each model wherever possible.

PART TWO

Chapter 14

Adverbial Groups;
Adverbs and Particles

14.1 ADVERBIAL GROUPS

AG's are almost always adjuncts (although as we have seen in 4.4 adjuncts may be AG's, pG's or even NG's). AG's may be simple or complex.

> He proposed *very hesitatingly*.
> She rejected him *quite firmly*.
> *Sadly*, he departed.

14.2 POSITION POSSIBILITIES OF AG'S

AG's can fill different positions within a clause. Three positions are common.

a) They may be *first*. For some AG's this position is obligatory; for instance, linking and binding particles and groups containing *wh*-words.

> I do not know *how* he gets here on time.
> *Why* he doesn't buy a car beats me.
> The bandit, *into whose hands* she fell, treated her with every courtesy.
> *While* robbing her, he apologised continuously *and* regretted the inconvenience he was causing her.
> She was trembling violently, *but* managed to ring the police.

Certain particles which link sentences, however, may be found in other positions (see 22.22).

For AG's other than the types illustrated above, this first position is optional. Contrast or emphasis may be produced by such positioning.

> *Yesterday* the trains were on time but *today* they are late.
> *Never* have we had such confusion.

b) They may *immediately precede* a simple VG or be *inserted* in a complex VG.

> He *usually* makes mistakes in spelling.
> He will *sometimes* find them himself.
> I'm *forever* pointing them out.
> He has *hardly ever* learned a difficult word properly.

Some of the AG's which usually take this position may also occur at first and final position. (The girls go dancing *occasionally*.)
Others which behave similarly are:

almost	just	quite
already	merely	rather
completely	nearly	soon
hardly	only	still
always	never	rarely
seldom	generally	occasionally

c) They may occupy *final* position.

> The baby is talking *well*.
> He is walking *hesitatingly* but cries *incessantly*.
> He is developing *quite quickly*.

14.3   LINKING AND BINDING AG'S

14.31   Linking AG's may link sentences or clauses:
Sentence linkage:

> I have talked for an hour. *Nevertheless*, I will keep going.
> *Indeed*, it is most important that I persuade you.
> We have only scratched the surface, *so far*. *Despite your re-luctance* you must be persuaded by Wittgenstein's theory.   NO

Other AG's of this type are *notwithstanding, moreover, though*.
Clause linkage:

> We walked || *and* we talked.

Other AG's of this type are *but, or, nor*.

Bread and jam — 'and' is sub-modifier (SM).
He did this and he did that — 'and' is AG.

The linking AG is attached to the second linked clause. (See 5.22)

14.32 Binding AG's act as markers of dependence in a dependent clause.

> *While* fishing in the river, || I caught a cold.
> We went to a shop, || *where* we bought some fish.
> We sauntered in || *as if* we didn't know one end of a fish from the other.
> *As soon as* we had bought the fish, || we went home.

14.4   ADVERBS AND PARTICLES

As we have seen, an important use of adverbs and particles is as H in an AG. These words can have other functions, some of which are given below.

14.41   Adverbs and particles as:

a) submodifiers in an NG

> *nearly* all week
> *very nearly* half the team
> a *somewhat* tatty appearance
> a *rather* pleasant spot
> an *absolutely* terrible house

b) modifiers in an NG (usually as N)   SEE 7.55 a)

> the *then* president
> an *outside* toilet
> an *upstairs* lounge
> an *away* game

c) qualifiers in an NG

> the world *outside*
> the shelf *below*

d) modifiers in an AG

> He jogs *rather* breathlessly and pants *quite* excessively.
> He won the marathon *absolutely* unexpectedly.

e) submodifiers in a pG

> He is *completely* in the clear.
> This presentation is *totally* in error.
> His question is *right* to the point.

14.42   Particles as

f) qualifiers in a VG

Despite a severe battering he was unwilling to give *in*.

After the fight he came *to*.

g) linking particles within a group

a black *and* blue bruise

an open *but* rather bloodshot eye

In *and* out her tongue went.

She walked *and* talked just like a real person.

These linking particles are considered to be submodifying elements (SM).

h) prepositions in a pG

below the horizon

inside the dance-hall

Many particles can carry out more than one of these functions.

quite a day	(a	–	submodifier in an NG)
quite quickly	(d	–	modifier in an AG)
the *very* thing	(b	–	modifier in an NG)
very casually	(d	–	modifier in an AG)

Exercises

1. Make up three sentences containing AG's which are obliged to be in first position.
2. Illustrate in sentences of your own the contrasting and emphatic effect of positioning AG's first in a clause.
3. Which of the words listed in 14.2 (b) cannot occur as AG's in the first position? Exclude responses to questions.
4. Use *rather* as M in an AG, SM in an NG, M in an NG.

Chapter 15

More about Groups and Clauses

15.0   In this chapter we shall present answers to these questions:
1. How many of each clause element can occur in any clause structure?
2. What classes of group or what other units can represent the different clause elements?
3. How many groups can occur as a single clause element?

15.1   POSSIBLE NUMBERS OF CLAUSE ELEMENTS

15.11   There is usually only one subject or predicator in any clause. The exceptions are limited. Certain clauses, for instance, may have a second subject if they are introduced by *there* or *it*. Such clauses are discussed in Chapter 19. Likewise, some clauses may have more than one predicator (see Chapter 21). Usually a clause can have only one or two complements. These possibilities for complement were examined in Chapter 4.

15.12 In contrast there is less restriction on the numbers of adjuncts that may occur in clauses. Some clauses have none; others have several. The clauses below illustrate some of the possibilities:
  i) He'll be coming *round the mountain | any time now.*
 ii) Bats can fly *accurately | in darkness.*
iii) Walk *softly.*
 iv) Wait.
  v) *Through the bush, | over the stream, | across the swamp, | up the ridge | and down the valley* rode the hunters, *with the fever of the chase in every man's blood.*

15.2   REPRESENTATION OF CLAUSE ELEMENTS

15.21   The subject of a clause is usually represented by a nominal group:

> *Jim* is a good cricketer.
>
> *The famous bearded cricketer* made his usual century.
>
> *He* scored heavily in every match.

Less usually it may be represented by one of the following:

a) a verbal group

> *Seeing* is believing.
>
> *To escape* would be difficult.
>
> *Stretching* places a strain on my back muscles.
>
> *To be believed* is all I require.

b) a prepositional group

> *In the morning* will be too late.
>
> *For* [[*John* | *to fail* | *now*]] would be a bitter disappointment.
>
> *After Christmas* would be satisfactory.
>
> *Under the door mat* does not make a good hiding place.

c) a clause

> [[*To have sailed a boat single-handed around the world*]] is a great feat.
>
> [[*Whoever made the mess*]] should clear it up.
>
> [[*Who believes me*]] will follow me.
>
> [[*What he says*]] does not concern us.
>
> [[*Speeding over the potholes and corrugations*]] will result in a broken axle.

15.22   The complement likewise is usually represented by a nominal group:

> The girl is *very pretty*. $\quad C^I$
>
> That dress suits *you*. $\quad C^E$
>
> The workmen elected *him* | *their delegate*. $\quad C^E \quad C^I$
>
> Naturally they gave *him* | *their support*. $\quad C^E \quad C^E$
>
> In time, therefore, he became | *a very good leader*. $\quad C^I$

Less usually, a complement is represented by

a) a verbal group:

His main interest in life is *surfing*.
His aim is *to learn*.

This last example should be distinguished from the following, which comprises a single verbal group with *is* as an auxiliary (see Chapter 10):

S   AUX. P   C
He | is to leave | the prison.

The difference can be demonstrated by comparing the following transformations:

i) His aim is to learn. ⟶
   To learn is his aim.

ii) He is to leave the prison. ⟶
not *To leave the prison is he.

Only when *is* is not an auxiliary can the following V^{to} form become the subject of a corresponding clause.

b) a clause at C :-

The problem is [[*how to stand on a board*]].
But his name is [[*what I don't know*]].
No one knows [[*where he has got to*]].
Shoot [[*whoever is there*]].
His hobbies are [[*drinking beer* || *and standing in the sun*]].

rank-shifted element at C.

non finite verb clauses.

15.23 The predicator is represented only by a verbal group:

Halt!
You *may have been* here before.
I *am running* this show.
Don't argue with me.
You *will be interrogated* later.

15.24 The adjuncts may be represented

a) by adverbial groups:

She swims *fast*.
She practises *very hard*.
Recently she broke the world record.

b) by prepositional groups:

An encyclopaedia salesman came *to the house*.
The man saw the dog *in the garden*.

With remarkable fluency, he developed his usual line of patter.
My father was not impressed *by this insinuation.*
The canvasser departed *with a flea in his ear.*

c) less usually, by nominal groups:

The previous day he caught a trout.
But he caught nothing *last night.*
The sun shone *passionless* on the dead boy.
NOT ADJUNCT? *Sadder and wiser,* he put his broken tackle away.

Notice that the last group has two H items.

d) occasionally, by verbal groups:

David, *smiling,* turned to his friends.
Having stopped, we ate our lunch.
He rose to the surface *gasping.*

(*But in* He rose to the surface gasping for breath
gasping for breath is a dependent clause. See Chapter 18).

Exercise

1. Write out and classify the adjuncts in the following:
    a) We were nattering quietly one day in the private bar.
    b) Suddenly, with a deafening bang, a bottle of champagne exploded.
    c) The barman, with a look of gloom on his saturnine countenance, gazed sombrely at the resultant mess. Carrying the dustpan in his hand, he walked to the broom cupboard.
    d) Close on the heels of the retreating army, the Scots charged, horse, foot and artillery.
    e) Day in, day out, the hammers thudded maddeningly, and the hooters blared in sympathy.

15.25 In 15.21 and 15.22 we have seen that clauses occur as group elements. Earlier in this grammar it has been stated that normally clauses represent sentence elements, alpha, beta, gamma, and so on. Sentences have been analysed into clauses and clauses into groups. However, what we have been looking at above are the instances where clauses occur as elements of a clause, filling positions in the clause which would usually be filled by nominal groups. Clauses such as these are **rankshifted** clauses. The term is meant to indicate that the clauses do not represent sentence elements on the first rank but elements of a lower rank in the scale of morpheme, word, group, clause, sentence. Rankshifted clauses are also found as elements of the group. For instance, it has been shown (see 8.4, 8.5) that clauses frequently occur as Q element in a nominal group. These also are rankshifted clauses. The difference between a rankshifted clause and one which represents a sentence element is demonstrated in the following examples:

    M   H   Q
a) The letter [[which he gave me]] was posted last week.

   Here the *wh*- marked clause depends directly upon the headword *letter*. In the sentence, *letter* is the only word to which it is directly related. Though the elements of a group are usually represented by words, in this instance, the Q element is represented by a clause. This clause is rankshifted.

Now contrast example (a) with the following:

b) The letter was posted last week, || which was too late.
   The apprentice, << who was very skilful with his hands, >> fixed the tap.

   In the first example the *wh*- marked clause is not directly attached to any single word of the preceding clause. Rather, it depends upon the preceding clause as a whole. The sentence consists of two clauses, the second of which is dependent upon the first. The sentence therefore has an alpha beta structure, and the *wh*-marked clause is not rankshifted. In the second example the *wh*-marked clause is marked off by commas to indicate that it is not part of the NG, but dependent on the whole of it. Such a clause acts as β in a sentence. See 8.41.

Exercise

2. In the following sentences classify as rankshifted or not the clauses which are not independent; give the reasons for your decision.
   a) Nearly all the trees which were badly damaged in the hurricane had to be burnt, which was a pity.
   b) The girls, who were armed with hockeysticks, chased the burglar.
   c) The girls who were armed with hockeysticks chased the burglar; the rest stayed inside.
   d) Where once a garden smiled now nothing grows.
   e) Some of the critics assert that this utilisation of the gas is not in the best national interest.
   f) The number of times they have been wrong is just scandalous.
   g) His watching the television so closely affected his eyesight.
   h) Whatever he did was wrong.
   i) Whoever follows that doctrine is bound to end up in trouble.

15.26 Clauses are not the only items which may be rankshifted. Groups also may be rankshifted. The usual rank for groups in a tree diagram is immediately below the rank for clauses. If groups occur at any rank below this they are rankshifted. Prepositional groups, for instance, often occur at the rank below the normal rank for groups. They do so when they represent the Q element of a nominal or prepositional group, e.g.

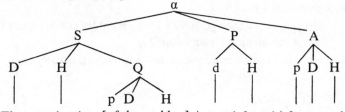

The examination [*of the problem*] | was deferred | for a week.

As is shown in the tree diagram, clause elements (S, P, A) are represented as usual by groups. The adjunct, for example, is a prepositional group. But the nominal group which is subject includes a prepositional group as its qualifier. The structure of this prepositional group (p D H) has to be placed in the tree diagram in a rank lower than that at which group structures normally appear. This prepositional group therefore is rankshifted.

Consider now the following examples where the italicised groups are rankshifted:

> The tempting aroma [*of grilling steak*] was wafted through the open doorway.
> In the distance Beau Geste could see the Arab [*in the scarlet burnous*].
> It was indeed the man [*from Ironbark*].
> Bernstein prefers music [*by Mendelssohn*].

All these prepositional groups depend upon a single noun as their headword. They are not dependent directly upon the rest of the clause.

Contrast the examples above with those following, where the prepositional groups are not rankshifted:

> The spider waited *in his web* | *for prospective customers.*
> Several flies still droned *around the web.*
> Suspicion had obviously developed *in their attitude.*

In none of these examples does the prepositional group depend upon the head of another group, whether nominal or prepositional; it depends more widely on all the other elements of the clause. Such groups therefore are adjuncts of their clauses. They are not rankshifted.

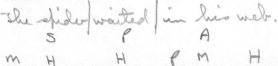

15.27   Not all rankshift is as simple as the possibility demonstrated above. Rankshift can be repeated several times in the same sentence. Consider, for example, the following sentence where a (rankshifted) clause acts as a qualifier of a (rankshifted) group which qualifies in a prepositional group:

He | sniffed | thoughtfully | at the scent [of the dry grass [[he | was crunching | under foot]]].

The adjunct in this sentence has the following structure:

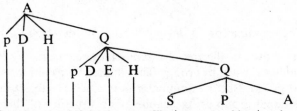

... | at the scent [of the dry grass [[he | was crunching | under foot]]]

Rankshifted items can be shown either by a tree diagram (as above) or, more simply, by using the square brackets, e.g.,

He got desperate in his search [for possible handholds [down the rocky sides [of the shaft]]].

The brackets show clearly how each rankshifted pG is inset within the other, like a series of Chinese boxes. The most deeply inset group is *of the shaft,* the next most deeply inset group is *down the rocky sides of the shaft;* the next is *for possible handholds . . . shaft.*

It is useful to refer to degrees of rankshift. The *first degree* rankshift here is indicated by the outside pair of single square brackets:

. . . in his search [for possible handholds down the rocky sides of the shaft].

The *second degree* rankshift is indicated by the pair of brackets next inside these:

. . . in his search [for possible handholds [down the rocky sides of the shaft]].

The *third degree* rankshift is indicated by the innermost pair of brackets:

. . . in his search [for possible handholds [down the rocky sides [of the shaft]]].

Notice that the scope of the left hand bracket is not limited until the right hand member of its pair is reached. The bracket between *search* and *for* applies till after *shaft*. It does not end at the bracket between *handholds* and *down*.

15.28   The units most often rankshifted are clauses and groups. Sometimes, however, a series of clauses, whether linked or dependent, is found. Since more than one clause is rankshifted these may be regarded as rankshifted sentences. The following examples serve to demonstrate some of the possibilities:

a) The human tendencies [[to prize certitude || and fear knowledge, || to indulge emotion at the expense of reason]] were probably always as strong as now.

In this example, as the bracketing shows, there is a series of linked clauses, all rankshifted since they qualify *tendencies*. This is expressed in a tree diagram in the following way:

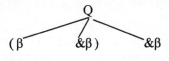

b) The difficulty is [[that we can't have anything to eat || till we find a tin-opener]].

Here the two rankshifted clauses, the second of which depends upon the first, are complement to *is*. This would be shown in the tree diagram as

C
/ \
β   γ

(α = alpha signifies indep. clause.)

These examples will have to suffice to indicate the variety of ways in which rankshift may occur. When English is complicated it often turns out that rankshift is responsible. Individual writers vary considerably in the extent to which they use rankshift. There are both advantages and disadvantages in its use. Excessive use may lead to an impairing of ready understanding; too little use may lead to an effect of naivety.

Exercises

3. Construct tree diagrams for the following sentences, developing the diagram only to the extent required to show how the rankshifted items fit into the sentence:
   a) What he calls himself now is a mystery.
   b) All boys with blue eyes will receive a prize.
   c) The one that got away was a beauty.

d) John brought the station waggon round from where he had found it.

e) Helen looked up from her inspection of the sides of the shaft.

4. Identify all the rankshifted items in the following passage by enclosing them in square brackets:

> At the time I'm speaking of we were living in one of those cramped houses which were all the Council had been able to afford. That they failed to provide anything better was no fault of theirs, nor did we blame them for doing no better. We thought our lot had improved; after all, we had moved from where we were all shut in by crumbling tenements to where we could at least see the distant hills. Moreover, whatever we did and wherever we went was our own business. Well, what I was going to tell you was that no one knew how we were going to shift all our gear – you know how everyone collects rubbish as time goes on. The truck we'd borrowed from Jim's uncle wouldn't go, which was a confounded nuisance.

15.3   POSSIBLE NUMBER OF GROUPS AS CLAUSE ELEMENTS

15.31   The subject and complement may be represented by one or more groups. When there are several NG's representing a single subject or complement they may be linked or apposed.

a) **linked**

  i) All over town *hearty goodnights | and tender farewells* were being exchanged.

 ii) If *the political labels, | the social origins | and the personal opinions of individuals* are forgotten, continuity becomes more striking than change.   SHARED ELEMENT,

iii) *These two uses for the land, | the material | and the spiritual,* may come in conflict, and often do.

 iv) *Stagnation | and an absence of progress* followed from this policy.

  v) *His emphasis upon moral excellence, | his enmity to alcohol, | his passion for cleanliness. for the land and for farming* were all to be fulfilled by a new generation.

In these examples the italicised groups comprise the subjects of their clauses. In each case there are two or more NG's, whether simple or complex, linked together. The linkage may be by particle (e.g., *and*); but, more subtly, it may be by sharing of an element. In (ii), for example, *of individuals,* which occurs as qualifier in the third nominal group, is shared by the two preceding NG's. In (iii) the NG's, *the material* and *and the spiritual,* which are linked by the particle, are together linked to the preceding NG by sharing *uses for the land.*

In a tree diagram, linked nominal groups can be shown thus:

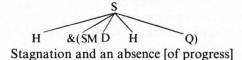

Stagnation and an absence [of progress]

where the round brackets show how the group elements are to be grouped and the & sign placed outside the lefthand bracket indicates the linkage relationship. If a tree diagram is not required, the same relationships may be symbolised as S (NG &NG) where the complex symbol is to be interpreted as meaning that a subject is represented by two linked NG's. Likewise example (iii) could be shown as S (NG &(NG &NG)) where the internal brackets show that the second and third NG's are linked to one another and then together linked to the preceding NG.

These examples of linked NG's as clause elements should be contrasted with the following examples, where there is a single NG with linked head elements:

i) The town | was | hot, dry and dusty.

                                        M   H   SM

ii) The rejected lover | looked | extremely disappointed and dis-
    H
gruntled.

   H   SM H

iii) Kettles and cats | purr | in the kitchen.

In these examples there is no reason for considering the items to be heads of different NG's but only linked heads of the same NG. In example (ii) the fact that *extremely* modifies both *disappointed* and *disgruntled* can be made explicit, if required, by bracketing: M(H &H).

b) **apposed**

i) *Our manager,* | *Mr Papados,* will help you.

ii) The sheriff interviewed *Wild Bill,* | *the bad man of the prairie.*

iii) *The question* [[*whether he should stay*]] must be decided at once.

iv) His latest proposal is this: [[*that hedgehogs should be used as combs*]].

In examples (i) and (ii), nominal groups are apposed in the subject and complement respectively. <u>Apposition</u> differs from linkage because in the former relationship

– both NG's have the same referent,
– both NG's are alternative in the structure – either might be deleted, but not both.

In examples (iii) and (iv) a clause is apposed to an NG in the subject and complement respectively. <u>The rankshifted clause does not qualify the preceding noun, but is in apposition to the group.</u> This can be demonstrated by deleting the NG:

S   P   A

[[Whether he should stay]] | must be decided | at once.

S   P   C

His latest proposal | is | [[that hedgehogs should be used as combs]].

Apposed NG's at S or C may be shown in a tree diagram in the same way as linked NG's, except that instead of &, the sign = is used to indicate apposition:

S

(D   H)   =H

Our manager, Mr Papados

This may be shown (except in tree diagrams) as S (NG =NG): Example (iii) above would appear as S (NG =β).

Exercise

5. Tree diagram the linked NG's in example (ii) above; and provide an alternative symbolisation of example (iii).

15.32 The predicator is usually represented by a single verbal group. Instances like the following where verbal groups represent different predicator elements are described in Chapter 21:

He *wants* | *to be chosen* for the team.
They *have decided* | *not to select* him.

Often, however, a series of linked verbs may occur. Such linked verbs are considered not as the heads of separate simple verbal groups but as linked heads of one complex group:

P

M   H   SM   H

She | *has washed and combed* | her hair.

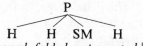

She | *ironed, folded and counted* | the washing.

Some writers frequently use linked verbs. Read through the following passage and pick out all the instances of linked verbs in a single predicator:

> The sunny slow lulling afternoon yawns and moons through the dozy town. The sea lolls, laps and idles in, with fishes sleeping in its lap . . . Clouds sag and pillow on Llaregyb Hill. Pigs grunt in a wet wallow-bath, and smile as they snort and dream . . . They mud-bask and snort in the pig-loving sun; their tails curl; they rollick and slobber and snore to deep, smug, after-swill sleep.

> (DYLAN THOMAS, *Under Milkwood*)

Contrast the examples above of linked verbs at P, and the following examples of linked clauses:

He fell, || and broke his arm.

He stopped, || and listened to the noise.

In these examples, the first verb has no relationship with the final C or A.

15.33 The adjunct may be represented by one or more adverbial or prepositional groups. If there are more than one they may be linked or apposed, or both:

a) **linked**

 i) The chairman squashed the suggestion *very abruptly* | *and quite finally*.

 ii) The band marched *down the hill* | *and over the bridge* till they came to the village green.

 iii) *By intermarriage,* | *by a common education of an exclusively European type,* | *by a shedding of specifically native habits,* the smaller race will eventually be absorbed into the more numerous.

 iv) This situation of amity was only reached after a decade of vigorous controversy, *from the end of the war* | *to the start of the depression.*

In (i) two AG's are linked. In (ii), (iii) and (iv) pG's are linked.

Notice that the agency of the linkage may vary. In (ii) the particle *and* specifically links. In (iii) it is the repetition of *by* which links. In (iv), the particles *from* and *to* are paired.

Linked pG's or AG's are shown in clause structure by a single A symbol. Their representation in tree diagrams follows the same lines as that for linked NG's at S or C. When not in a tree diagram example (iii) could be shown as A (pG &pG &pG). Contrast the examples above with the following:

The burglar's drill bit into the safe door *smoothly and noiselessly*.

Swiftly and unexpectedly retribution followed.

In these examples the linked adverbs are linked heads in a single adverbial group at A:

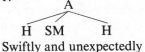

Swiftly and unexpectedly

b) apposed

We live *here* | *in Oban.*

The guide led the way *back* | *to the cave entrance.*

The pioneers looked *out* | *across the magnificent plain.*

The apposed groups are alternatives, one being more specific than the other. All these examples can be shown informally as A (AG =pG).

Linked and apposed groups form part of a single adjunct. Such instances must be distinguished from the following, where the groups represent different adjuncts since they are neither linked nor apposed:

```
      A        S     P       A
Suddenly, | Jim | laughed | aloud.
```

```
          S              P              A
The thirsty explorer | looked | across the treeless plains | to-
          A
wards a dry horizon.
```

Such instances must in turn be distinguished from an example such as the following, where all the prepositional groups except the first are rankshifted:

Shrill Irish voices | screamed | for help [from all the Saints [in the calendar]].

c) **Linkage** and **apposition** of groups at A may be combined as in the following example:

> Working conditions and wage levels must be guarded *by other means, by arbitration and by political pressure.*

The relationships here are shown in this symbolisation: A (pG =(pG &pG)). The internal bracketing shows that the second and third pG's are linked and together apposed to the first.

Exercise

6. Analyse the role of linkage and apposition in the following passage; distinguish their occurrence between clauses, groups and words.

> His blood flowed out from his white side and clotted on the sand – a dark question mark draining out his life. Over him his father, huge and dark and bearded, who had just cut down his own son in mortal combat, knelt weeping. His sword and shield were cast away. He held the boy's drooping head upon his arm. Silently and in sorrow the warriors turned away in twos and threes and went back to their tents. The sun went down and their campfires came out and glowed upon the plain. They left the father in the growing darkness weeping for his son. Soon the Host of Heaven shone passionless upon the dead boy and the strong man undone by grief.
>
> F. D. OMMANNEY. The House in the Park.

Chapter 16

I ran across to see him

adverb particle (no noun cf. below ✻)

He/came across/the bridge.
/P/
H *(particle)*

Particled Verbs

He came [across the bridge.]
A *(S)* *H*

16.0   We saw in 3.28 that a verbal group can have a Q:

    H   Q

I | ran across | a friend.

This possibility is now to be examined further. It is often difficult to separate such cases from apparently similar ones where a particle following a verb belongs to a prepositional group which occupies the element A.

The fact of the difference between the two is illustrated by an ambiguous notice which once hung in a chemist's window:

We dispense with care

which was meant to be

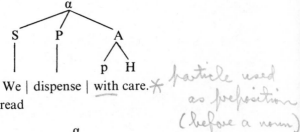

We | dispense | with care. ✻ *particle used as preposition (before a noun)*

but which might be read

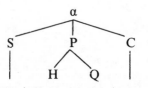

We | dispense with | care.

16.1   POSSIBILITY OF Q IN A VG

The possible occasions where Q occurs in a verbal group are illustrated by the following clauses (under X), each of which is paired with a clause (under Y) which, though apparently similar, does not contain a Q.

X (particle is Q)	Y (particle is not Q)
i) Our petrol gave out.	The sun came out.
ii) (a) Susan ran the car in.	Marion brought the pudding in.
(b) Susan ran in the car.	Marion brought in the pudding.
iii) Barbara looked after her father.	Jennifer trotted after her sister.

(handwritten marginal note: ? where did ... she bring ... the pudding ... ∴ A.)

It will be seen that in both columns X and Y the cases ii (a) and (b) are synonymous; the difference in the word order is a stylistic one. If we try replacing the NG in ii(a) and ii(b) by a pronoun, the results are identical in both cases.

ii) Susan ran it in.	Marion brought it in.
(*not* ran in it)	(*not* brought in it)

Structures ii(b) and iii, which are superficially similar, can always be distinguished in this way.

The composition of the three pairs of clauses before the structural differences between columns X and Y have been resolved is as given below. [ii(a) is taken as representative also of ii(b), which can be transformed to it. A similar transformation applied to iii would not produce an acceptable result.]

i) NG + verb + particle
ii) NG + verb + NG + particle
iii) NG + verb + particle + NG

Remembering that a pG consists of a preposition followed by an NG, we can see that the differences between X and Y can be expressed as follows:

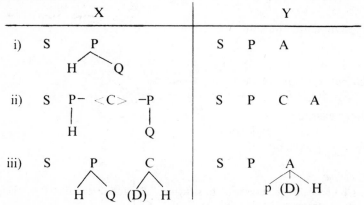

Although many cases can be quite easily distinguished, such as those given above, difficulty can arise as to whether a certain clause belongs to column X or column Y.

It is true that the cases in X (where the particle is Q in a VG) tend to contain verbal groups which can be replaced by a simple verb (*looked after – nursed; gave in – yielded*); and that the VG's with a Q often have a metaphorical component in their meaning. But the distinctions so far mentioned are very difficult to use as tests.

16.2   TESTS FOR PRESENCE OF Q IN A VG

One test which can be applied follows from the fact that with the column Y structure the particle can often be replaced by another, the resulting clause having a slight but *comparable* difference in meaning. To use a case (iii) example:

> The dog turned into a wood.
> The dog turned through a wood.
> The dog turned beside a wood.

But with *The frog turned into a prince* nothing like that can be done.

However this is often a cumbersome test to apply. On the whole, tests which involve transformation are the most reliable, and the three cases will now be examined by this method.

16.21   CASE (i). If the particle can be transferred to the beginning of the clause so that the result is acceptable (even if slightly unusual) English, the particle is to be treated as A:

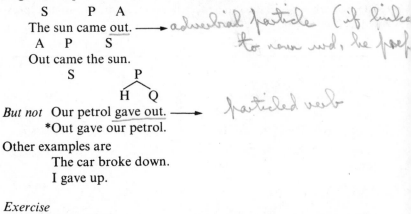

>   S   P   A
> The sun came out. ⟶ adverbial particle (if linked
>   A   P   S   to noun wd, be prep
> Out came the sun.
>   S   P
>   H Q
> *But not* Our petrol gave out. ⟶ particled verb
>   *Out gave our petrol.

Other examples are

>   The car broke down.
>   I gave up.

Exercise

1. Compose three clauses with the structure P and three with S P A, where
   A is represented by a particle.
          H Q

16.22 CASE (ii). A similar test can be applied here; again the particle is placed at the beginning of the clause:

> Marion brought the pudding in.}
> Marion brought in the pudding.} ⟶
> In Marion brought the pudding.

> Marion brought it in. ⟶
> In Marion brought it.

> He tossed his cap up.}
> *or* He tossed up his cap.} ⟶
> Up he tossed his cap.

> He flung down the gauntlet.}
> *or* He flung the gauntlet down.} ⟶
> Down he flung the gauntlet.

In these examples the structure is therefore S P C A (or S P A C), transforming to A S P C.

But the following clauses will not permit of such transformation:

> Susan ran the car in.}
> *or* Susan ran in the car.} ⟶
> *In Susan ran the car.

> Susan ran it in. ⟶
> *In Susan ran it.

Where the S consists of a complex NG it may be difficult to decide if the transform is acceptable. If so, one can try whether replacing the NG by a pronoun will make the decision easier. Thus,

> Marion brought in the pudding.

transforms tolerably to

> In Marion brought the pudding.

But in considering

> Our old family servant brought in the pudding

there is some doubt about the acceptability of the transformed clause:

> In our old family servant brought . . .

If, however, we replace *our old family servant* by *she:*

> In she brought . . .

the result is certainly acceptable.

Contrast the following, where even the replacement of the NG by a pronoun does not produce an acceptable transform:

The awkward member brought up a difficult question.

*Up he brought a difficult question.

Exercise

2. Classify the following as belonging to Class (ii) X, or Y, or to neither:
    a) I looked up an old friend.
    b) He was running over some songs.
    c) His sister was making up her face.
    d) She put the telephone down.
    e) She had made it up with her boyfriend.
    f) My mother sent in a block of ice-cream.
    g) We thought up some good ideas for the party.
    h) Deborah wrote out the invitations.
    i) I dropped them in the letter-box.
    j) The gendarmes run them in.

16.23   CASE (iii). First it should be remembered that case (iii) can always be distinguished from case (ii) by changing the non-subject NG, if noun-headed, into a pronoun. Consider the following:

The rabbit sent in a little bill. ⟶

The rabbit sent it in.

The particle now follows *it* and the case is (ii).

Alice fell down a rabbit-hole. ⟶

Alice fell down it.

not *Alice fell it down.

The particle precedes *it* and the case is (iii).

Which cases do the following belong to?

He ran down the hill.

He ran down the Government.

In case (iii) the difference between the clauses which belong to column X, and which have the structure

$$\begin{array}{ccc} S & P & C \\ & H \diagup \diagdown Q & \end{array}$$

and those which belong to column Y and have the structure

$$\begin{array}{ccc} S & P & A \\ & & p \cdots H \end{array}$$

is not always easy to decide.

There are two tests. First, not only the particle, but also its following NG (which forms with it a potential pG), can be tried out at the beginning of the clause. In the following examples the transformation is successful and the transferable material can be regarded as a pG appearing at A.

(Y) Jennifer trotted after her sister. ⟶
After her sister trotted Jennifer.

Alice fell down a rabbit-hole. ⟶
\Down a rabbit-hole\ fell Alice.

The cow jumped over the moon. ⟶
Over the moon jumped the cow.

In the following cases the transformation is not successful, and the structure is therefore   S   P   C

H   Q

(X) Barbara looked after her father. ⟶
*After her father looked Barbara.

He was running over his songs. ⟶
*Over his songs he was running.

The second test, which is less conclusive, consists of replacing the NG following the particle by a *wh-* word and seeing if the result is acceptable:

(Y)   Her sister, behind whom Jennifer trotted.
A rabbit hole down which Alice fell.
The moon over which the cow jumped.

but (X) * Her father after whom Barbara looked.
* His songs over which he was running.

In doubtful cases it is better to describe the structure as P A. An example of a doubtful case is

I was looking for the pencil.

For a pencil I looked is doubtfully English, although *The pencil for which I was looking* is quite acceptable. The structure of *I was looking for the pencil* is therefore S P A.

16.24 Observe that the operation of transforming a clause into the passive does not constitute a satisfactory test. A few of the clauses in case (iii) which would belong to column Y do not provide satisfactory transforms:

*A rabbit hole was fallen down by Alice
but *The moon was jumped over by the cow* is possible.

The possibility of passive transformation does not in fact reveal anything about the distinction for which we have been looking in this chapter, but is concerned with a 'delicate' distinction between two very similar P A structures.

In case (ii) both X and Y structures can be made passive:

The pudding was brought in by Marion.

The car was run in by Susan.

In case (i), of course, passive transformations are out of the question.

16.3   THE PARTICLED VERB

16.31   The combination of verb plus particle as found in the examples under column X, where the particle forms Q in a VG, may be called a **particled verb.** In case (i) the particled verb is intransitive; in cases (ii) and (iii) it is transitive. In case (ii) it is potentially discontinuous.

Particled verbs are an important feature of English and often correspond to simple verbs in other languages. They do occur however, in some other Germanic languages; their use in the Scandinavian languages is particularly close to that of English.

16.32   Some particled verbs contain complex particles:

I will not put *up with* this behaviour.

The time-honoured but unacceptable transformation of this [second test for case (iii)] results in:

*This is behaviour up with which I will not put.

The first test would have given

*Up with this behaviour I will not put.

Exercises

3. Provide three examples of the structure   S $\underset{H \quad Q}{P}$ C   and three of the

structure S P A where A is represented by a pG.
4. Provide tree diagrams for:
   a) Pat ran in the egg and spoon race.
   b) We worked up a lot of enthusiasm for her.
   c) She did away with her husband.
   d) This is behaviour which I will not put up with.
5. Extract the particled verbs in the following passage and classify them as case (i), (ii) or (iii):
   Louise made out she had dreamed up a perfect way of getting out of clearing up our rooms, but by the time we had worked through all the

bright ideas she trotted out we came to the conclusion we would have been better off facing up to the job and getting it over. When Father came in and we were still trying to put it off he gave us a dressing-down. After he stormed out we got steamed up and told Louise where to get off.

What can you pick up from this about the set-up when people go in for the particled verb in a big way?

6. Go on with the above story and see how many particled verbs you can think of. Do not give up till you have worked in at least four. You could lead off by setting down how Louise answered back.

16.33 Most of the particled verbs so far discussed have a frequently-used verb as their head: *come, put, take, set*. There is often more than one particle which will act as Q:

The new pilot *took over;* the plane *took off.*

There is another group of particled verbs, however, involving verbs which are less common and which take one particle only. There is less modification of meaning of the verb at H than in the instances previously examined, but the particle is still closely attached to the verb.

Examples for consideration are:

Her unsuitable makeup *detracted from* her appearance.

(*From her appearance her unsuitable makeup detracted.)

They *dispensed with* formality.

I shall *abide by* your decision.

He expected me to *connive at* his attempt.

In Rome we *complied with* Roman law.

Compared with *put, take, set* these are rather rare and learned verbs. In these examples they are followed by particles. Are they to be regarded as particled verbs? We can try changing the position of the verb + particle + NG, but because the verbs are less common it becomes more difficult to say if the transform is acceptable, e.g.,

With formality they dispensed.

Hardly, yet it is not easy to assert that

By your decision I will abide

With Roman laws we complied

are impossible.

In the latter sentence there is the complication that *comply* can exist on its own. This suggests that *with* is separable and that it therefore begins an A and is not itself a Q. One can moreover say

We complied with Roman laws *and with* Roman customs.

and, rather more doubtfully,

We dispensed with shoes and with jackets.

Whereas one cannot say

   *Barbara looked after her father and after her mother.

Therefore, it is not reasonable to treat these two types on the same footing. If we remove the *with* from *dispense with* or the *from* from *detract from* we are still left with what is recognisably the same verb but in an incomplete form. If we remove the *after* from *look after* we are left with *look* which is not recognisable as the same verb.

It is perhaps not wise to press for a decision in the case of these **uniquely particled** verbs. Where there is no possible variation of parts a truly grammatical description of an item cannot be expected. If a decision one way or the other is required, for example for purposes of statistical analysis, it may be said that these verbs adhere so closely to their particles that together they are to be regarded as H Q. There are perhaps a few exceptions, such as *comply with;* since *comply* can (in the same sense) exist on its own, the structure of *we complied with Roman laws* is S P A.

Superficially ambiguous cases may arise:

   We decided on the boat.

There are two possible underlying structures here. *Decide* and *decide on* are two different verbs, the latter having H Q structure.

16.34   In the example involving *Her unsuitable makeup,* notice the noun *makeup,* derived from a particled verb. Compare *breakdown, breakthrough, takeover, writeoff.* This has become such a frequent pattern for noun formation that there is often no familiar corresponding verb: *fallout, frameup, teach-in.*

Exercises

   7. With what particles do *vie, devolve, commiserate* and *inveigh* combine?
   8. Compose four sentences containing uniquely particled verbs not yet mentioned.
   9. List six more nouns derived from particled verbs.
   10. How would you comment on an expression like *He is a ton-up rider*?

Chapter 17

Dependent Clauses (I)
Finite

17.0   Clauses may be independent:

> I agree.
> I'll come.

or dependent:

> I agree *if you do.*
> I'll come *when I'm ready.*

Dependent clauses may be **finite** or **non-finite.** The dependent clauses above are finite.

> *Opening the door cautiously,* I saw the burglar.

The example here is non-finite. This chapter deals with the dependent clauses which are finite.

17.1   THE FINITE DEPENDENT CLAUSE

17.11   It is obvious that there are some clauses which are not usually independent, although they can be so as answers to questions:

> When will you stop kicking your sister? *When she stops kicking me.*

Usually these are dependent sentence elements, but they may also be clause or group elements:

a) Sentence element

>   β   α
> Where he lives || there is a big new housing settlement.

b) Clause element

>   S   P   C   A
> [[Where he lives]] | is | quite unknown | to us.

c) Group element

S   P   C

The place [[where he lives]] | is not | very fashionable.

17.12   Finite dependent clauses are of various kinds:

i) Miss Smith, *who arrived late,* had just received a proposal.
ii) It was from young Mr Murgatroyd, *which was a great surprise to all of us.*
iii) He left *as I came in.*
iv) *After the conference was over,* she told us all about it.
v) *Before I start,* push the door shut.
vi) *If you like me,* say so.
vii) *However coldly you answer me,* I will never look at another girl.
viii) We doubt *whether he really put it like that.*
ix) We can't think *why he wants to marry her.*
x) *Had I realised his intentions,* I would have warned him.
xi) *Clever though he is,* he cannot do the impossible.
xii) *Whatever he does,* he will be in the wrong.
xiii) She said *that we must come to the wedding.*
xiv) I suppose *we'll have to express our enthusiasm.*
xv) Cats, *when they are thwarted,* often exercise their claws.

The dependent clauses in the sentences above may be classified according to the manner in which their dependence is marked: the features that indicate dependence are often associated with the predicator and adjunct elements.

These clauses may be:

a) Particle marked
b) Sequence marked
c) *Wh- ever* marked
d) *That* marked
e) *Wh-* marked
f) Unmarked.

Note: For the purposes of this chapter *dependent* includes the idea of *interdependent.* In (viii), (ix), (xiii) and (xiv) the italicised clauses are strictly speaking *interdependent items.*

Exercise

1. Before going on, try to classify the examples above according to the features which mark their dependence.

17.2   PARTICLE MARKED

17.21   Particle marked dependent clauses have a binding adverbial group as an adjunct; such groups include *after, before, while, though, as, whether.*

Many of them have already been listed (see 5.12). The occurrence of any of these in a clause marks that clause as dependent. Such particles usually introduce the clause:

β   α

While he was walking, || John eyed the pretty girls.

α−   β   −α

John, < <while he was walking,> > eyed the pretty girls.

α   β

John eyed the pretty girls || while he was walking.

Thus the particle marked dependent clause may precede or follow the independent clause or be inserted in it.

17.22   Such clauses usually occur as sentence elements, as we see in most of the sentences above (or as in this one just written). Sometimes, however, they occur as dependent elements in other units:

D   H   Q

Come to my room the moment [[after you have finished work]].

Here the dependent clause acts as Q to the NG.

[[After I finish work]] | will be too late.

Here the dependent clause is itself a clause element, acting as S to P.

17.23   Dependent clauses marked by particles *than* and *as . . . as* are worth special attention; they differ from other particle marked clauses in not usually occurring as sentence elements, but only as rankshifted clauses. *Than* marked clauses occur as qualifiers in groups that also contain comparatives or items such as *rather, other :*

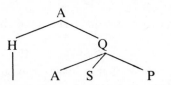

They played | harder [[than | we | had expected]].

The game was | harder [[than we had expected]].

We found the game | harder [[than we had expected]].

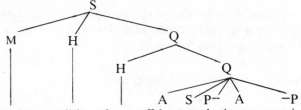

Playing conditions [worse [[than we had ever experienced]]] made it difficult for us to do our best.

A   S   P

They certainly played better [[than we (did)]].

This elliptical structure contrasts with instances when *than* is a preposition:

Indeed our opponents played a great deal better [than us].

17.24   An *as* marked clause at Q requires a previous *as* or *so* as a submodifier:

SM   D   H   Q

There | are | as many opinions [[as there are men]].

Fill in the application form as completely [[as you can]].

She is not so/as stupid [[as she seems]].

Note: Only in negative statements is a choice possible between *so* and *as*.

Exercises

2. Make up examples of *than* marked clauses: one with *rather*, one with *other*, and one with a comparative.
3. Make up further sentences using *as* marked clauses at Q.

17.3   SEQUENCE MARKED

17.31   Examine the following sentences:

P−   S   −P   A

Had <she> arrived sooner, || she might have prevented the proposal.

P−   S   −P   A

Should <the course of true love> run smooth, || they'll be married tomorrow.

　　P　　　　　S　　　　　　　C
Were | that course of action | possible, || her father would not hesitate to act.

Note: The verbs *had, should, were* precede the subject, giving sequences P− S −P or PS. Further, *had* and *were* are the only forms of *have* and *be* that occur in this pattern. *Were* is used, even though S is singular.

17.32　In some dependent clauses, sequence marking and particle marking are combined:

　　　　C　　　　　A　　　S　　P
Impossible | though | it | seems, || an elephant has been mislaid.

　　　　　　　　　　　　C　　　A　　S　　　　P
I really dislike icecream, || absurd | as | it | may appear.

This pattern normally occurs only with *though* and *as*.

Exercise

4. Make up clauses of this pattern opening with *indifferent, terrible, delightful, complicated, strange.*

17.4　WH- EVER MARKED

Some clauses are marked as dependent by such items as *whoever, whatever, wherever, whichever, whatsoever, whosoever, however.* They may be found as sentence and clause elements. When the *wh- ever* clause is a sentence element, the *wh- ever* item can occur at S, C, or A:

　　　S
Whoever | is responsible, || the matter will not end here.

　　　C
Whichever | he chooses, || we know that the decision will be a wise one.

　　　A
Whenever | he comes, || he causes trouble.

The *wh- ever* clause can also be a clause element:

　　　　　S　　　　　　　P
[[Whoever did this]] | will be punished.

It can also be a group element:

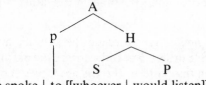

He spoke | to [[whoever | would listen]].

Exercise

5. Make sentences using *whatsoever, wherever, whenever, whichever,* as elements in dependent clauses. Indicate which element of the dependent clause the *wh- ever* item represents.

17.5   WH- MARKED

$\alpha-$ β $-\alpha$
17.51   Mr Smith, < <who is our friend, > > spoke harshly to me.
α β
I took no notice of his remark, || which did not please him.

These clauses are elements of the sentence. They are usually marked off in written English by commas. These two sentences provide examples of what are referred to as **non-defining** clauses. For earlier examples see 8.41 and 15.25.

17.52   The *wh-* clause can also occur as an element of a clause:
S   A   P   C
Mr Smith | then | realised | [[who I was]].

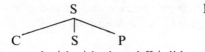

[[What remarks | he | had made]] | did not matter.

17.53   *Wh-* clauses are frequently found at Q in NG's or pG's:
H   Q
Boys [[who have long hair]] are popular with some girls.

They may be described as **defining** clauses. For further examples see 8.41.

17.6   THAT MARKED

That marked clauses occur as clause and group elements.

17.61 CLAUSE ELEMENTS. *That* marked clauses may be subject or complement in their clause.

a) as S:

$$S$$

[[That the Browns will enjoy their dinner]] | is quite likely.

[[That they will relax afterwards]] | can be safely predicted.

In sentences such as these the *that* is A in its clause.

b) as C:

When they occur as complement, *that* marked clauses may be C^I (after equational verbs), C^E (after transitive verbs), or C^{E2} (after double complemented verbs):

$$C^I$$

The truth | is | [[that they enjoy a good dinner]].

$$C^E$$

Don't forget | [[that the Browns are coming to dinner]].

$$C^E$$

I | believe | [[that the Queen herself is coming]].

$$C^{E1} \qquad\qquad\qquad\qquad C^{E2}$$

No doubt | they | will tell | us | at the last minute | [[that they cannot come]].

Most verbs that may be followed by a *that* marked clause are regularly used transitively:

He knew that they had been told of the arrangement.

He knew the truth of the matter.

He knew it.

Some verbs which are not usually followed by a noun-headed NG as C may nevertheless have a *that* marked clause as C: *say, think, hope*. These often have *so* as a C, and sometimes *that*:

Did he say so/that?

'I hope so.

Tell often takes both C^{E1} and C^{E2}. A *that* marked clause after *tell* is usually C^{E2}.

$$C^{E1} \qquad\qquad C^{E2}$$

She told him [[that she was leaving him]].

Other verbs may have this structure with a *that* marked clause, though elsewhere they would be followed by C^E + pG:

He convinced me of it.

He convinced me that he was sincere.

Persuade acts similarly.

Some intransitive verbs may be followed by a *that* marked clause at C, although elsewhere they take a pG at A:

He complained about the heat.
He complained that it was hot.

The case for regarding the *that* marked clause as a complement of verbs such as *convince, persuade, complain* is therefore not strong. However, as with the others, their *that* marked clauses are analysed as C to reduce complication.

17.62 GROUP ELEMENT. *That* marked clauses occur as qualifier in NG's and pG's. The *that* may be S, C, or A in its clause.

I've never seen people [[that enjoy their food so much]].

Here *that* is S in its clause.

The reason [[that she gave]] is inadequate.

Here *that* is C in its clause.

They appreciated the trouble [[that | their hosts | had gone | to]].

Here *that* is part of a discontinuous pG.

That marked clauses may occur as qualifier in a group that is already rankshifted:

He has one [of the finest horses [[that we have ever seen]]].

Notice here that the *that* marked clause is Q in a pG which itself qualifies the head item *one; that* is C in the dependent clause.

That marked clauses often occur at Q after superlatives and *only,* and after such items as *day, year, time, rate, reason, fact, place, anything, now* and so on:

H   Q
Now [[that you've arrived]] we can get on with the business.
Everywhere [[that we go]] we find some trace of him.

Note that after *fact, that* introduces a clause which is appositional rather than dependent:

The fact [[that he agreed]] was surprising.

A transformation is possible in such examples:

The fact that he agreed was surprising. ⟶
{ The fact was surprising.
{ That he agreed was surprising.

Exercise

6. Make a tree diagram of *He has one of the finest horses that we have ever seen.*

17.63   *That* is often used with *so :*

A

She cut the pudding | so [[that | everyone | got | a sixpence]].

M   H   Q

He ran | so hard [[that he was exhausted]].

M H   Q

The dancer was | so fat [[that she could only cavort clumsily
around the stage]].

Exercise

7. Show by means of a tree diagram at which element the *that* clause occurs in
   the following:
   a) The excuse he gave for his lateness was that he was not early.
   b) Do you remember the time that you fell into the pond?
   c) The heat was so great that the butter melted.
   d) The reason that Jim offered was not acceptable.
   e) I've heard of people that believe the moon is made of green cheese.
   f) That careless driving was the cause of the accident has not been proved.
   g) I cannot remember everything that you said.

17.7   UNMARKED

17.71   Unmarked clauses are alternative to *that* marked clauses
except at S of another clause and when *that* is S of its own clause:

They thought they would be sick.

They thought that they would be sick.

The reason she gave was inadequate.

The reason that she gave was inadequate.

They appreciate the trouble their hosts had gone to.

They appreciate the trouble that their hosts had gone to.

Contrast the following, where the (inter)dependent clause must be
marked by *that :*

That the Browns will enjoy their dinner is quite likely.

This is a problem that will not worry us.

17.72   When *that* does not occur, the clause may not contain any
particular feature which marks it as dependent or rankshifted.
Rather, it may be its particular context which makes it so:

S   P   C

i) He | knew | [[the train would be late]].

ii) The station master says [[the train will be late]].

iii) The excuse [[he gave]] was quite absurd.

<pre>
                        S   P   A
</pre>

iv) The other people [[he | spoke | to]] paid no attention.

These examples have in common that they are not marked by any of the features listed previously. It is in this sense that they are unmarked. However there may be some other feature which indicates that they are dependent or rankshifted. In (i) it is the use of *would*, in (iii) the absence of a C, and in (iv) the absence of an NG after *to*. In (ii) it is only its context which makes *the train will be late* rankshifted.

Chapter 18

Dependent Clauses (II)
Non-finite

18.0   Non-finite clauses are those whose predicator element consists of a non-finite verbal group. Such verbal groups are those in which the first verb in sequence is

V^g *as in* || seeing | the boys ||
or V^{to} *as in* || to see | the boys ||
or V^n *as in* || seen | by the boys ||
or V^o *as in* || see | the boys ||

The most frequently used non-finite clauses are those with V^g and V^{to}; V^n is found less frequently, while the use of a non-finite clause with V^o is quite restricted.

18.1   CHARACTERISTICS

18.11   Non-finite clauses are usually dependent elements of sentences. Occasionally they occur as independent sentence elements:

      P   A

To return | to the subject. (We'll now consider the remaining
   implications of group dynamics . . .)

This independent use particularly applies to responses to questions:

                    P   C   A

(What are you doing?) Minding my own business, Sir.

18.12   Non-finite clauses do not usually have a subject but there are some patterns in which they do.

a) With S

       S   P   C

There | being | no objection, || the meeting proceeded to its next business.

       S   P

All things | considered, || we should reach the top in another hour.

b) Without S

       P   C

Not being | very ill, || John got out of bed.

       P   C

To amuse | himself, || he switched on the television.

                        P   C

He fell asleep || watching | it.

18.13   Non-finite clauses are sometimes marked as dependent by the occurrence of a binding particle or *wh-* item:

a) With a binding particle or *wh-* item

      A   P   C

While | watching | television, || John fell asleep.

      A   P   C

When | closing | the cupboard, || be careful not to jam your fingers.

b) Without a binding particle or *wh-* item

       P   C

Watching | television, || John became sleepy.

        A   P   A

Thoroughly | bored | by the programme, || he could no longer keep his eyes open.

18.14   Non-finite clauses can occur as sentence, clause, or group elements. Their normal occurrence is as sentence elements; but they often occur also as elements in groups or clauses.

a) as an element of a sentence – see examples in 18.12 and 18.13.

b) as an element of a clause

                    S

          P   C

[[Climbing | the Khumbu icefall]] required all their skill.

c) as an element of a group

D   H   Q
| | P⌒C

The girl [[flying the glider]] is just sixteen.

18.15   When non-finite clauses occur as sentence elements they can precede, interrupt, or follow independent clauses:

β
Seeing the ball drop, || Paul ran forward || to catch it.

α—   β   —α   β
Paul, << seeing the ball drop, >> ran forward || to catch it.

α   β   β
Paul ran forward || to catch the ball, || seeing it drop.

The next sections provide a more detailed consideration of the different types of non-finite clause.

18.2   NON-FINITE CLAUSES WITH V^g AT P

18.21   As A Sentence Element. Non-finite V^g clauses occur as sentence elements with or without S:

S   P
The butter | being finished, || the cullers had to use deer fat for cooking.

P   C
Being | tired, || they went to bed early.

Being tired presupposes *they,* the S from α. When a V^g clause has no explicit S, there is an implicit S, which is the S of the independent clause.

18.22   As A Clause Element

a) at S

S   P   C
[[Being | tired]] | is | no excuse.

b) at C

S   P   C
[[What I dislike most]] | is | [[darning smelly old socks]].

This is the only way, or almost the only way, such a clause can occur at C.

Examples such as the following are discussed in Chapter 21.

```
S   P     P          C
```
I | hate | darning | smelly old socks.

18.23   AS A GROUP ELEMENT

a) at Q in an NG

```
   D   H                Q
```
The worm [[galloping across the road]] | was in mortal danger.

b) at H in an NG

```
                        D          H
```
We | appreciate | your [[writing to us]].

```
     D          H
```
Cynthia's [[passing her exams]] is most welcome news.

c) at H in a pG. The non-finite clause may or may not have an S.

   i) with S

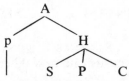

Indeed | you | 're | right | about [[there being no time]].

I don't worry | about [[people [like him] making money]].

   ii) without S

In [[making his pile]] | he provides a livelihood for thousands
   of people.

One boy was paid two dollars| for [[mowing his lawns]].

Exercises

1. Provide two further examples of non-finite clauses with V^g at P parallel to those under 18.2.
2. Tree diagram the examples in these sections: 18.22 (b), 18.23 (b) and the three undiagrammed sentences in 18.23 (c).

18.3   NON-FINITE CLAUSES WITH V^{to} AT P

18.31   AS A SENTENCE ELEMENT.

To get to the zoo || you need to catch the bus at the next stop.

You will have to hurry || to catch this bus.

18.32 As a Clause Element

a) at S

   [[To steal | the money]] | was going | too far.

   [[To <actually> kick | your opponent]] | is | unforgivable.

b) at C

   The problem | is | [[to provide | an adequate outlet | for animal instincts]].

18.33 As a Group Element

a) at Q in an NG

   The place [[to see elephants in large numbers]] | is | the Ruaha valley.

This structure occurs frequently after *too :*

   Our cat | is getting | too lazy [[to bother about [[catching mice]]]].

   He | is | too fat [[to do up his boots]].

b) at H in a pG

The preposition in these cases is *for*. The non-finite clause has an S :

   We | waited | for [[the bomb to go off]].

   For [[Ebenezer | to attempt | to defuse | it]] | was asking | for disaster.

In the second example a pG is S of the clause; at H in the pG is a non-finite clause.

18.4 NON-FINITE CLAUSES WITH V^n AT P

18.41 As a Sentence Element. The clauses here may or may not have an S.

a) with S

   | S | P | A |

   The Queen | shown | to the royal box, || the curtain rose on the first performance.

b) without S

   | | P | A |

   The Queen, <<watched | by a huge crowd,>> drove past to the world première

18.42 As a Group Element

a) at Q in an NG

The last play [[written by Albee]] | was <highly> praised | by the critics.

Politicians | usually | appeal | to prejudices [[built up by their own propaganda]].

b) at H in a pG

With [[his jersey | ripped | off his back]] | the winger | dived | half-naked | for the line.

18.5   NON-FINITE CLAUSES WITH V^o AT P

The use of the V^o non-finite clause as a dependent clause is rare, though the use of such clauses as independent clauses is common enough (see 21.32). The following example shows a V^o non-finite clause:

```
          S                P            C
```
[[What this book does]] | is | [[destroy the reputations [of a number [of respectable people]]]].

Exercises

3. In the following extract, pick out the non-finite clauses. State in each instance whether the verb is V^g, V^{to}, V^o, or V^n, and also the element each non-finite clause represents.

   I put up at the old inn, and went down to look at the sea; staggering along the street, strewn with sand and seaweed; afraid of falling slates and tiles, and holding by people I met, at angry corners. Coming near the beach, I saw, not only boatmen, but half the people of the town, lurking behind buildings; some, now and then braving the fury of the storm to look away to sea, and blown sheer out of their course in trying to get zigzag back. Joining these groups, I found bewailing women whose husbands were away in fishing boats. Grizzled old sailors were among the people, shaking their heads as they looked from water to sky, and muttering one to another; ship owners, excited and uneasy; children, huddling together, and peering into older faces; even stout mariners, disturbed and anxious, levelling their glasses at the sea.

   CHARLES DICKENS, *David Copperfield*.

4. In a prose text you are studying find examples of non-finite clauses, and indicate in each instance what element it represents.

18.6   PREDICATORLESS CLAUSES

18.61   Some dependent clauses have no predicator. Examine the italicised clauses in the following sentences:

   Although not fully fit, the team played a good game of lacrosse.

   If in doubt, get in touch with your nearest police station immediately.

The items italicised must be considered clauses because they consist of at least two groups, and dependent clauses because they are optional and contain a binding particle (*although, if*). In order to determine the relationships between the group elements of these dependent clauses, it is necessary to compare them with a fuller version of each. It is assumed that the predicatorless clause is an elliptical version of a predicated one and that the groups in the predicatorless clause represent the same clause elements as their equivalents in the fuller version. Thus corresponding to

Although | not fully fit.

is the predicated clause ·

Å   S   P C^I

Although | the team | was | not fully fit.

On the assumption mentioned above, the groups in the predicatorless clause represent the following elements:

A C^I

Although | not fully fit.

Likewise, by referring to the corresponding fuller version

A   S   P   A

If | you | are | in doubt

it is possible to describe the structure of the second predicatorless clause as

A   A

If | in doubt.

Notice that in neither of these instances is the assumed predicator the same as that in the independent clause.

In both these instances the predicatorless clauses are dependent elements in the sentence. The important feature of their structure is the binding particle.

18.62 Predicatorless clauses are also found as elements of groups. Examine the following sentences:

It's quiet with [[the children away]].

With [[all its passengers | asleep]] | the train rolled through the night.

With [[plenty of work and overtime | until about a month ago]], little anxiety was expressed about the economic situation.

The items introduced by *with* have the form of a prepositional group. But instead of the usual noun as head, they have a predicatorless clause. All this can be represented in a tree diagram.

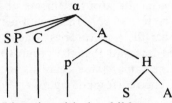

It's quiet with the children away

That these clauses are best analysed in this way may be seen from the transformation:

It's quiet with this situation. }
The children are away.   } ⟶

It's quiet with the children away.

With can also have a non-finite clause as its head as the following examples show:

With *the children sitting on each other's knees,* we were able to squeeze everyone into the car.

The ship finally left port, with *cars stacked high on its deck*.

Exercises

5. Make up three sentences with predicatorless clauses as dependent sentence elements.
6. Make up three pG's with predicatorless clauses as H, and use them in sentences.
7. Tree diagram *With all its passengers asleep, the train rolled through the night*.

Chapter 19

Apposed Subject Clauses

19.0   Most clauses have only one subject, but there are occasions where two subjects occur in the same clause. Such occasions arise with the use of *it* or *there*.

19.1   There are three main uses for *it* as a subject:
a) As a non-referring subject:
   It was raining.
where *it* is supplied to fill out the clause structure but has no referent.
b) As a referring subject:
   The paper was wet. *It* had been lying on the grass.
where *it* has a definite reference to *the paper*.
c) As a substitute subject:
   i) [[To stay in bed on a wet Sunday morning]] is pleasant.
   ii) *It* is pleasant [[to stay in bed on a wet Sunday morning]].
Sentences like the last one present some difficulty of structure. The problem is to decide whether the clause for which *it* substitutes is a sentence element or a clause element. *To stay in bed on a wet Sunday morning* is S in example (i); it is replaced by *it* in (ii) and placed at the end of the sentence. Thus these items are in apposition. The structural analysis is therefore

It | is | pleasant | [[to stay | in bed | on a wet Sunday morning]]
When *it* replaces an item at S and that item is written in a later place in the clause, an **apposed subject** clause is created. The *it* is the **substitute** subject and the second subject is the **appositional** subject, symbolised as =S.

19.2   APPOSITIONAL SUBJECTS WITH it

19.21   The following sentences illustrate the range of items that can occur as appositional subject:

  i) It is not a matter of indifference *whether you come or not.*
 ii) It would have been more accurate *to have said no.*
iii) It is not apparent till the very end *that this is a preliminary report.*
 iv) In some extracts, it is difficult for the reader *to locate the true issue.*
  v) It was always possible *for the two loyalties to conflict.*

In these examples the appositional subject can replace *it* without requiring any alteration in order to be able to do so. The only special point to note is that (iv) and (v) are superficially similar but in (iv) the prepositional group with *for* qualifies *difficult.*

The tree diagram analysis of (v) is:

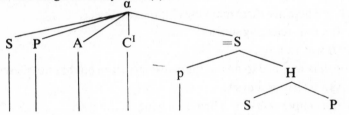

It | was | always | possible | for [[the two loyalties | to conflict.]]

Exercise

1. Underline the appositional subjects in the following sentences:
    a) It is still problematic whether New Zealand can avoid a shortage of doctors within the next five years.
    b) If action is to be taken, it is apparent that the issues should be laid bare in this way.
    c) It is convenient to categorise such information under suitable headings.
    d) It's nice letting your hair down now and then.
    e) It was kind of you to come.
    f) Theoretically it would be possible to have four different levels of readership.

19.22   Not all appositional subjects are as easy to locate as those in the preceding section. The examples below illustrate possibilities which are less easy to analyse:

  i) It was a pity *you failed to score.*
 ii) It's when I'm in *that I haven't the foggiest idea what time it is.*
iii) It was not a revolution *that endangered the British connexion.*
 iv) It is these and other matters *which I would like to discuss now.*
  v) And you've no idea how confusing it is *all the things being alive.*

vi) *Why I made all them noises,* it was because of the draught.

vii) It is far better *to observe consistency of style* than to try to write at different levels, sometimes explaining what you feel to be obscure, sometimes not.

viii) It would be possible for reports of this type to be headed in a different way.

ix) It turned out that he was born in Glasgow.

x) Now it may well be that they will arrive too late.

In (i) the appositional subject is an unmarked clause. The corresponding single subject clause is

That you failed to score was a pity.

Example (i) therefore can be seen as a transform of

It was a pity that you failed to score.

(ii) is an apposed subject clause but in the corresponding single subject clause, *that* is replaced by *when:*

[[When I haven't the foggiest idea what time it is]] | is | [[when I'm in]].

In the corresponding single subject clause of (iii), *that* is replaced by *what:*

[[What endangered the British connexion]] | was not | a revolution.

In (v) the appositional subject is a non-finite clause with its own subject. The corresponding clause, derived by transformation, confirms however that this example is also an apposed subject clause:

And you've no idea how confusing it is [[all the things being alive.]] ⟶

And you've no idea how confusing | [[all the things being alive]] | is.

Example (vi) is interesting because it illustrates a further development of apposed subject clauses in certain types of spoken English. The following transformations show the process:

$$\quad\quad\quad\quad\quad\quad\quad\quad S \quad\quad\quad\quad\quad\quad\quad P \quad\quad\quad\quad C$$
[[Why I made all them noises]] | was | [[because of the draught]]. ⟶

$$S \quad P \quad\quad\quad\quad\quad C^1 \quad\quad\quad\quad\quad\quad\quad\quad\quad\quad =S$$
It | was | [[because of the draught]] | [[that I made all them noises]]. ⟶

$$\quad\quad\quad\quad\quad\quad =S \quad\quad\quad\quad\quad\quad S \quad\quad P \quad\quad C^1$$
[[Why I made all them noises | , it | was | [[because of the draught]].

Example (vii) is of interest because it is relatively complicated, though there is no problem in locating the appositional subject, as the following transformation shows:

> It | is | far better [[*to observe consistency of style*]] [[than to try to write at different levels, || sometimes explaining [[what you feel to be obscure]], || sometimes not]]. ⟶
>
> [[*To observe consistency of style*]] | is | far better [[than to try to write at different levels, || sometimes explaining [[what you feel to be obscure]], || sometimes not]].

The structural organization of the first sentence is partially shown in the following tree diagram:

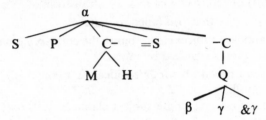

Example (viii) is interesting because it illustrates the ambiguity of apposed subject clauses with a pG introduced by *for*. There are alternative transformations:

> It would be possible for reports of this type to be headed in different way. ⟶
>
> { For reports of this type to be headed in a different way would be possible.
>
> { To be headed in a different way would be possible for reports of this type.

There does not seem to be much to choose between these possibilities. Either of the following analyses would therefore be acceptable:

> S   P   C   =S
> It | would be | possible | for [[reports of this type to be headed in a different way]].
>
> S   P   C
> It | would be | possible [for reports of this type] | [[to be headed
>   =S
> in a different way]].

The analysis of examples (ix) and (x) as apposed subject clauses is not as certain as that for the others. In favour of analysing them in this way is the apparent appositional relationship between *it* and the *that* marked clause. But against it is the fact that there are no corresponding transforms:

*That he was born in Glasgow turned out.

*Now that they will arrive too late may well be.

On balance, however, the apposed subject analysis is preferred in this text:

S   P   =S

It | turned out | [[that he was born in Glasgow]].

   A   S   P   =S

Now | it | may well be [[that they will arrive too late]].

Exercises

2. For each of the following sentences write out the version of the appositional subject which would be present in a corresponding single subject clause:
   a) It is the second sentence of the original which falls to pieces.
   b) It was because we thought we needed his experience that we did so.
   c) It is a good kick in the pants that he needs.
   d) It is telling the truth that matters.
   e) It is the last sentence which destroys the meaning.
3. Provide tree diagrams for the last two sentences of Exercise 2.
4. Transform the following sentences into apposed subject clauses:
   a) What they have done with the booty is anybody's guess.
   b) That you have made a mistake is quite obvious.
   c) What should be discussed is the second theorem.
   d) To act in this way would be absurd.
   e) To make a statistical report interesting takes more than a few coloured trimmings.

19.23 A further kind of apposed subject clause may be observed in the following sentences:

It was John *who answered the door.*

It was really him *who won·the competition.*

It was Mary *who ate all the cakes.*

Superficially it might seem as if the *wh-* marked clauses qualify the preceding proper noun or pronoun. Against this, however, is the fact that proper nouns and pronouns do not usually have qualifying clauses. The following transformations indicate that these clauses are apposed subject clauses:

i) The one *who answered the door* was John. ⟶
   It was John *who answered the door.*

ii) The one *who won the competition* was really him. ⟶
   It was really him *who won the competition.*

iii) The one *who ate all the cakes* was Mary. ⟶
   It was Mary *who ate all the cakes.*

The last sentence, which is typical, can be analysed as follows:

$$S \quad P \quad C \qquad\qquad =S$$

It | was | Mary | [[who ate all the cake]].

In these transformations only Q of the original subject is retained as an appositional subject.

19.24   This use of *it* as a substitute subject may also be paralleled by its use as a substitute complement:

He made it clear *that his intentions were good.*

The *that* clause is apposed to *it*. *Make* can be followed by $C^E C^I$ as in:

He made his intentions clear.

But when a clause is C^E the result is awkward:

$$S \quad P \qquad\qquad C^E \qquad\qquad\qquad C^I$$

He | made | [[that his intentions were good]] | clear.

There are two corresponding passives:

It was made clear by him that his intentions were good.

That his intentions were good was made clear by him.

Another type of appositional complement is the non-finite clause:

$$C^E \quad C^I \qquad\quad =C^E$$

I think it wrong | [[to do this]].

Notice the exceptional structure:

$$S \quad P \quad C \qquad =C$$

I | take | it | you have a pass.

He took it that there was no objection.

This *it*, which introduces an interdependent clause, seems to be limited to the verb *take*.

Exercise

5. Analyse the clause structures of the following sentences:
    a) They thought it strange that the meeting had not been arranged earlier.
    b) We consider it unwise to proceed with the plan any further.
    c) However, the committee deemed it expedient to continue the project.

19.3   THERE AS A SUBSTITUTE SUBJECT

19.31   Consider the use of *there* in the following sentences:

i) Is *there* any reason why we should wait any longer?

ii) *There* is one criterion you should remember.

iii) *There* has not always been an absence of legal discrimination.

iv) In each of the paragraphs *there* are two main statements.

v) Of course *there* is always a tendency for a flush of sympathy to break out for the losers of any battle.

vi) *There* is something wrong.

In these sentences *there* does not have any definite reference, but occurs in the usual subject position. However, unlike the usual subject it does not agree in number with the verbal group. This is the prerogative of the nominal group which follows the verbal group. *There* enters the same kind of transformation as *it* does; it can be replaced by an item recurring later in the clause:

There is something wrong. ⟶

Something is wrong.

To describe the process in reverse, the original subject is displaced from its normal position which is then filled by *there*. Such *there* clauses will therefore be treated as apposed subject clauses. The clause structure of (vi) would be

S   P   =S   C^1

There | is | something | wrong.

The appositional subject agrees in number with the verbal group.

Most of these apposed subject clauses do not have an acceptable corresponding clause such as (vi) has. The equivalent corresponding clause for (iii) would be:

*An absence of legal discrimination has not always been.

This makes it clear in fact that *there* is used as a substitute subject in such instances precisely because *be* requires another group to follow it. Placing *there* first enables the otherwise empty position after *be* to be filled by the appositional subject.

Sometimes the appositional subject is inserted in the verbal group in the apposed subject clause:

S   P   A

Three boys | are sitting | on the fence. ⟶

S   P−   =S   −P   A

There | are <three boys> sitting | on the fence.

In this transformation the original subject *three boys* is inserted within the VG and becomes the appositional subject; *there* is introduced as the substitute subject.

Exercises

6. Make up four sentences with *there* as substitute subject.
7. Discuss the use of *it* in the following newspaper examples:
   a) That may be a general New Zealand attitude, but it is apparently not universal.
   b) It is ironic that most of the troubles were centred in territories formerly British.
   c) It was only after they started that the communists stepped in to exploit them.
8. Analyse the use of *it* and *there* in the following:
   The children were not asleep. It was most annoying. It was obvious that something had upset them. There was James wide awake and Mildred out of bed in her bare feet and it was almost eleven, and there they were all talking. What was the matter? It was that horrid skull again. There was not much use doing anything about it now. It was foolish of her really to bother. She should not have put the skull there; well, it was no use crying over spilt milk; after all, there are more ways of killing a cat than choking it with cream.

(Adapted from VIRGINIA WOOLF, *To The Lighthouse*.)

The Mood System — *Signals ways of indicating statements, questions & commands in written language.*

20.0 The clause which is obligatory in a sentence is the *independent* clause. For the purpose of this chapter we take an independent clause as being of the normal pattern, with a subject and predicator, and perhaps a complement and adjuncts. This rules out such examples as –

> *Tut, Tut!*
> *Coffee?*
> When will you be finished? *Any time now.*

20.1 COMPLEMENTATION SYSTEM

Some of the structures of independent clauses or simple sentences have already been examined, (see 4.5). Those structures examined earlier illustrated the possible ways of using a complement in a clause. There are not many choices available:

a) Intransitive (with no C)
b) Equational (with C^I) — *C identical with subject*
c) Transitive (with C^E)
d) Doubly complemented (with C C)

When, as in this case, only a few possibilities are available, the set of possibilities is called a **system.** This particular system is the **complementation** system. It applies to all clauses.

20.2   MOOD SYSTEM — *arrangement of words.*

20.21   There is another system which applies mainly to independent clauses. This is the mood system, which describes the possible sequences of subject and predicator in a clause. There are three such possibilities.

a) Straightforward sequence, i.e.,   S   P
        S   P
    The girl | has knitted | a scarf.

b) Inserted sequence, i.e.,   P–   S   –P
    P–   S   –P
    Has <the girl> knitted | a scarf?

c) Inverted sequence, i.e.,   P   S
                P   S
    In the garden | stood | the fatal apple tree.
    P   S *in apposition*
    Is | there | a doctor | in the house?

[margin notes:] cf. old grammar / subjunctive / imperative / interrogative / —using meaning / instead of / sequence.

20.22   The mood system is an important clause system in English because it is used to establish differences in meaning, mainly in independent clauses. In dependent clauses variations of the S P sequence are usually employed for stylistic purposes only. In independent clauses, however, straightforward sequence is regularly used in statements or affirmations, whereas inserted sequence is regularly used in questions. We have used 'regularly' here because the connexion between meaning and the mood system is by no means simple. The rest of this chapter demonstrates the nature of this connexion.

20.3   STRAIGHTFORWARD SEQUENCE

20.31   AFFIRMATIONS. Affirmative clauses with straightforward sequence provide the great bulk of continuous written English:
    Julia has captured the burglar.   S   P

20.32   EXCLAMATIONS. These are usually marked by *what* or *how*.
a) *What* or *how* as M in the complement:
    What courage Julia showed!
    How terrified the burglar was!
(Of course the place in sequence of C is here unusual.)

b) *What a* as M in the subject:

What a long time will pass before he burgles again!

What a surprise awaited him at the end of his efforts!

c) *How* as M in the adjunct:

How hard the burglar pleaded with her!

How triumphantly Julia held him!

20.33 WH – QUESTIONS. These occur with *wh-* words as S or as M in an NG at S. Not all *wh-* words can be used here.   *Straight-forward sequence.*

What aroused Julia?

Who sent for the police?

Whose judo throw took the burglar by surprise?

What hold finally overpowered him?

Which elbow was dislocated?

Exercise

1 Provide additional instances for each different type of clause shown above.

20.4   INSERTED SEQUENCE

20.41 AFFIRMATIONS. Affirmative clauses with P– S –P sequence are known as **restrictive** clauses:

   A   P⁻   S   –P

Seldom had <Sarah> sung so sweetly.   *restrictive use of affirmation*

Never has an audience been so enchanted.

Rarely did an accompanist show such sensitivity.

Not only did we have an evening of unalloyed pleasure, but an experience of unusual quality.

As these examples show, restrictive clauses are marked by an initial adjunct such as *seldom, never, rarely, not only, neither, nor.* Insertion cannot happen however when the VG is simple:

Rarely is he accurate in his predictions.

Occasionally, particularly in poetry, adjuncts other than those above precede inverted sequence:

Rightly are they called pigs.

Sometimes, again more frequently in poetry, inserted sequence may be initiated by a complement:

Not many singers have we heard capable of this range.

20.42   WH- QUESTIONS. In these questions the *wh-* words occur in groups at C or A.

a) At C:

> Who did he beat at chess?
> Whom did he beat at chess?

(How often is *whom* used in this structure?)

> What are you going to do next?
> Which pawn should I take now?
> What move did Sarapu recommend?
> Whose gambit are you using here?

b) At A:

> How did your knight get there?
> When is black going to castle?
> Where can I hide my king?
> From whom did you learn this opening?
> With what piece should I cover my rook?

These patterns in the last two examples are more formal than:

> Who did you learn this opening from?
> What piece should I cover my rook with?

20.43   YES/NO QUESTIONS. These are questions to which the regular response is *yes* or *no*. They are marked as questions by the use of the inserted order:

> Are you coming quietly?
> Will you hit me if I don't?
> Did you leave the loot behind?

Exercise

2. Provide additional examples of the kinds of clauses in 20.42 and 20.43. Find examples for 20.41 in poetry.

20.5   INVERTED SEQUENCE

20.51   AFFIRMATIONS. Affirmative clauses with P S sequence usually have an adjunct preceding the predicator:

> Lightly stepped Sir Bedivere.
> From the lake rose an arm, clothed in white samite.
> Up goes Meads for the ball.
> And out goes the ball again to touch.

20.52 EXCLAMATIONS. These occur in this sequence only with auxiliaries and as responses to previous affirmations or questions. It is sometimes difficult to decide whether particular instances are exclamations or questions. The auxiliary carries a strong stress in speech.

> Oh, won't I just!
> Did you indeed!
> Have they then!

20.53 QUESTIONS. a) Yes/no questions occur in inverted sequence when the verb is an auxiliary in a simple VG:

> Is she?
> Has he?
> Must she?
> Will he?
> Did they?

b) *Wh-* words in groups at C or at A:

> Who is your friend?   — inversion of, 20.33
> Who are your friends?   — agreement C + V in number
>   — C usually no agreement

(Notice in these examples that the second NG agrees in number with P and so is subject.)

> When is the party?
> How is Bill?

Exercise

3. a) Find further instances of affirmative clauses with inverted sequence in poetry and radio or TV sports commentaries.
   b) Provide further examples for 20.53 (b).

Chapter 21

The Predication System

21.0 In the previous chapter we have seen that a system is concerned with the small number of ways in which a particular feature occurs. The possibilities for a complement in the clause structure were described in the complementation system; the possible sequences of S and P were described in the mood system. In this chapter we will describe how many predicators may occur in clauses. There are only three main possibilities and these make up the **predication** system.

21.1 Read the following list of independent clauses:

   i) John.
  ii) On Tuesday.
 iii) John told a lie.
 iv) The furniture was saved from the fire.
  v) She was anxious to please.
 vi) He was easy to please.
 vii) Anton wanted to help Norman.
viii) Noel tried to get home.
 ix) He asked Bill to help Jim.
  x) Bill helped Jim plant the cabbages.
 xi) Norman saw Bill injured in the accident.
xii) He saw Jim planting the cabbages.

There are, in this list, clauses

a) with no predicator – **predicatorless**
b) with one predicator – **single-predicated**
c) with more than one predicator – **multi-predicated.**

The following sections examine these possibilities in greater detail.

21.2 PREDICATORLESS CLAUSES

Examples occur in (i) and (ii) above. Such clauses are not frequent in formal written English, but are quite common in spoken English and in written approximations to spoken English. For example:

Mick (eluding him):	This bag's very familiar.
Davies:	What do you mean?
Mick:	Where'd you get it?
Aston (rising, to them):	Scrub it.
Davies:	That's mine.
Mick:	*Whose?*
Davies:	It's mine. Tell him it's mine!
Mick:	*This your bag?*
Davies:	Give me it!
Aston:	Give it to him.
Mick:	*What?* Give him what?
Davies:	*That bloody bag.*

(HAROLD PINTER, *The Caretaker,* Act III.)

In this passage, the italicized items are predicatorless clauses. The structure of such clauses is not immediately obvious; it is necessary to examine also the context. Consider the example *That bloody bag.* If we were to consider this item in isolation, we would decide that it is a complex NG. But we could not decide what sort of clause element it is. We have to look at the previous clause:

$$P \quad C^E \quad C^E$$

Give | him | what?

That bloody bag presupposes *Give him,* so that, like *what* in the clause above, it is a C^E.

Here are the clause structures of two other predicatorless clauses from the passage above:

$$C^I$$

Whose?

$$S \qquad C^I$$

This | your bag?

Exercise

1. Explain why the two examples immediately above are given the indicated clause structure. Is there another possibility for *whose?*

21.3   SINGLE-PREDICATED CLAUSES

21.31   Clauses usually have only one predicator:

John *saw* the fight.
The girl *told* him a lie.

As in these examples, the VG in single-predicated clauses is usually a finite one. Independent clauses with a non-finite VG are infrequent in the formal register. **Imperative** clauses form the major exception.

21.32   IMPERATIVE clauses are marked by a VG whose first verb is in the V^o form:

> *Tell* him *off.*
> *Don't get* too cheeky.
> *Be thinking* about this problem while I'm writing on the blackboard.

Some imperative clauses have an NG to indicate the person being addressed: *Vocative*

> Don't get out of your depth, *friend.*
> Well, stop telling me fibs, *John.*
> Now don't get perky, *son.*

Such NG's usually occur finally, but they may occur elsewhere in a clause:

> *John,* ask him what he wants.
> Now, *son,* don't get perky.
> *Willy,* remind John he is late for his appointment.

These NG's are adjuncts because they are optional, can occur in different positions and do not have number concord with the verbal group. There are, however, some sentences, such as those following, where the NG's can only precede the VG's:

> Heaven help us.
> Thy kingdom come.

The first NG's of these sentences are therefore subjects, though they do not have the usual concord with their VG's.

21.33   Other kinds of non-finite independent clauses are rare in formal English, but may be found frequently in responses to questions in spoken English and in its written approximations:

> A. Can you give me a lift?
> B. Why?
> A. *To get me to the church on time.*

21.4   MULTI-PREDICATED CLAUSES

There are two main kinds, according to the presence or absence of another element intervening between the predicator elements.

21.41 Multi-predicated clauses with no intervening element:

He *helped* | *wash* the dishes.
She *likes* | *to ring* the bell.
He *wants* | *to go* to the pictures.
He *prefers* | *to be visited* by his wife.
She *kept* | *waiting* for Peter.
After being tackled, the boy *let* | *go* the ball.
Old people *enjoy* | *watching* television.

Note carefully the following points:

a) Verbs which can be followed by other verbs in this way are **catenative** verbs.

b) It is possible to have a string of several catenated VG's:

He *intends* | *to help* | *to build* the dam.
She *keeps* | *trying* | *to please* everyone.
I *don't want* | *to have* | *to be forced* | *to begin* | *to try* | *to make* more money.

(This example was first used by the American linguist A. A. Hill.)

c) The catenative verbs may be followed by V^{to}, V^g or V^o forms, but the V^{to} and V^g forms are the most common. There is one verb *get* that catenates with a V^n form:

The children got washed.
The cup got broken.

In such instances *very* cannot submodify the V^n form. When it can, then the form is not a verb form but an *-ed* adjective form as C^I:

He got (very) tired.
They got (very) interested in the nature of the work.

Exercise

2. Look up the derivation of *catenative;* then emulate, if you can, the American example above.

21.42 Catenative verbs may be classified according to the verb form or forms which follow. Some of the main subclasses are:

a) Verbs with V^o

He *let fly* with his boot.
We can *make do* with very little.
He *helped feed* the baby.

Help is also followed by V^{to}, e.g., he *helped to feed* the baby.

b) Verbs with V^{to}

> They *arranged to meet* the plane.
> The girls *refused to disembark*.
> The men *threatened to go* on strike if their wage demands were
>   not met.

Notice that in the following example

> The bus stopped, to pick up passengers.

stopped and *to pick up* occur in different clauses because they are not tightly catenated. Compare the following pairs:

> The bus stopped, to pick up passengers. ⟶
> To pick up passengers, the bus stopped.

> The bus started to pick up passengers. ⟶
> *To pick up passengers the bus started.

c) Verbs with V^g only

> He *finished feeding* the ducks.
> She *kept banging* doors.
> The bus *stopped moving*.

d) Verbs with V^{to} or V^g

> I *like shooting* ducks.
> I *like to shoot* ducks.
> She *loves meddling* in other people's business.
> She *loves to meddle* in other people's business.

Exercises

3. There are not many verbs followed by V^o. How many can you find?
4. List three other verbs followed only by V^{to}.
5. Which of the following verbs are followed by V^g only:
   avoid, enjoy, practise, fancy, mind, consider, hate?
6. Test if *loathe, bear, dislike, begin, cease, continue, start,* belong to the subclass described in (d).
7. What differences of meaning occur when *remember* is followed by V^{to} (catenative) or V^g (part of rankshifted clause)?

21.43 Multi-predicated clauses may have an element intervening between predicators. There are three main structures to be considered.

Structure (a)

> The man is *eager* to please.
> The Prime Minister seemed *anxious* to expedite the legislative
>   programme.
> They will be *happy* to help if they can.

They were *able* to finish the exercise sooner than expected.

In this structure an adjective is followed by a verbal group with a V^{to} verb. Such VG's share the same subject as the first VG. For this reason it does not seem satisfactory to regard such VG's and their accompanying elements (if any) as qualifiers of the adjectives. The analysis adopted here regards each group as a separate element of the clause:

S	P	C^I	P	C^E

The Prime Minister | seemed | anxious | to expedite | the legislative programme.

Structure (b)

> The man is easy to please.
> This piece of music is difficult to play.
> These children are impossible to train.

Superficially these examples are similar to those of structure (a). Nevertheless there are transformations which apply to these examples but not to the earlier ones. Contrast the following:

i) The man is easy to please. ⟶
   It is easy to please the man. ⟶
   To please the man is easy.

ii) The man is eager to please. ⟶
   *It is eager to please the man. ⟶
   *To please the man is eager.

It is apparent that the subject in structure (b) can be transposed as the complement of the second VG. This establishes that in

> The man is easy to please

the man is both subject of *is* and complement of *to please;* its complement relationship with *to please,* which is quite obvious in the transforms, still remains in structure (b). The structure analysis therefore needs to show both these relationships. This is done in the following manner:

S/C	P	C^I	P

The man | is | easy | to please.

The complex symbol S/C is to be read as subject to first P, complement to second P. It does not of course indicate two elements, but one double element.

A further difference between structures (a) and (b) is that only in

(a) may the second P be followed by a complement. It is possible to find

> She is happy to help her friends

but there is no

> *She is easy to please them.

When S/C is represented by a pronoun the relationships with both P's still persist:

> She is easy to please.

The pronoun is of course in the form appropriate for a subject. But in the transforms it adopts the forms appropriate for the complement:

> She is easy to please. ⟶
> It is easy to please her. ⟶
> To please her is easy.

It cannot in structure (b) have simultaneously the forms appropriate for subject and complement. The fact that it is I-type does not here rule it out as a complement. So the analysis will be

> S/C   P C^I P
> She | is | easy | to please.

In each of structures (a) and (b) only limited sets of adjectives may be used as C^I. These sets intersect slightly, with resulting ambiguity as:

> She was sweet to remember.

With some of these adjectives the relationship between them and what follows is clearly interdependence rather than dependence. This particularly applies to adjectives such as *liable, apt, bound, able,* which occur in structure (a).

Exercises

8. Make up four examples of structure (a).
9. Show by transformations that in the following sentences the NG's in italics represent double elements:
   a) *This question* may be difficult to answer.
   b) *All the alternatives suggested* are impossible to remember.
   c) *Kittens* are delightful to watch when they are very young because their antics are so unpredictable.

Structure (c)

> The scouts let *Jack* lead the way.
> The visitors helped *her* wash the dishes.
> The government took *steps* to suppress the rebellion.
> She teaches *deaf children* to read.

> They instructed *a Commission* to investigate the charges.
> You can hear *the love-sick wood pigeons* mooning in bed.
> They noticed *a man* beckoning to them.

The NG's in italics are related to the VG's on either side of them. They are complements of the VG's that precede and subjects of the VG's that follow. The following transformation may help to demonstrate this:

> You can hear the love-sick wood pigeons.
> The love-sick wood pigeons are mooning in bed. } ⟶
> You can hear the love-sick wood pigeons mooning in bed.

The double element analysis used for structure (b) is also useful to indicate the relationships in these clauses. The structure of the last sentence is:

S	P	C/S	P	A

You | can hear | the love-sick wood pigeons | mooning | in bed.

21.44 The second P in this structure may be represented by any of the non-finite verb forms. The verb which represents the first P selects the form of the verb at the following P. Here are some examples of the possibilities:

a) *help* may be followed by V^o or V^{to}:

> He helped them wash the dishes.
> He helped them to wash the dishes.

b) *see* may be followed by V^o or V^g:

> He saw them crash the car.
> He saw them crashing the car.

c) *leave* may be followed by V^{to} or V^g:

> They left their friends standing outside the shop.
> They left their friends to stand outside the shop.

d) *expect* may be followed by V^{to} only:

> He expected them to arrive late.

e) *find* may be followed by V^g only:

> I found him sitting inside.

f) *get* may be followed by V^n:

> They got the tunnel built in record time.

Like *get* is *have*:

> They had the old building pulled down.

The fact that the first verb usually selects the form of its follower provides another reason for considering such sentences as consisting of a single clause.

When the second verb is V^g or V^{10}, the following kind of transformation is usually possible:

<pre>
       S   P   C/S   P   A
i) You | can hear | the love-sick wood pigeons | mooning | in
   bed. ———►
</pre>

<pre>
                    S   P   P   A
   The love-sick wood pigeons | can be heard | mooning | in bed.
</pre>

ii) They instructed a Commission to investigate the charges.———►

A Commission was instructed to investigate the charges.

But notice the following case where this transformation provides an unlikely transform:

I remember him describing his job. ———►

He was remembered describing his job.

Exercise

10. Make up lists of verbs that pattern like *see, expect* and *find* respectively. Be as exhaustive as you can.

21.45   The examples of structure (c) should be contrasted with the following:

Judith asked Jim, *to make sure the answer was correct.*

They appointed a Commission, *to investigate the charges.*

She teaches deaf children, *to amuse herself in her spare time.*

The italicised clauses are dependent clauses. Their subject is not the preceding complement; they share the same subject as the independent clause. They can be placed before the independent clause:

To make sure the answer was correct, Judith asked Jim.

To investigate the charges, they appointed a Commission.

To amuse herself in her spare time, she teaches deaf children.

Exercise

11. Indicate which of the following sentences are multi-predicated clauses and which are α β etc:
    a) The boy sent the book flying across the room.
    b) You need nerves of steel to fly an aeroplane.
    c) You would need to be a genius to make this old car work again.
    d) They watched the blacksmith shoeing a horse.
    e) There should be no need to use force to steam open a letter.

as marked

Beyond the Sentence

22.0   It is usual to assume that grammar stops at the sentence. Grammars generally deal with the patterns of sentences, and of lesser units. The patterns of any larger unit are not usually their concern. The way that sentences are interrelated is considered a matter of stylistics rather than a matter of grammar.

Yet it is not entirely a matter of style. If sentences are placed in a haphazard sequence, the text which they make up will seem nonsense. Consider the following text:

> One line of approach would be to assume that our standard family will not change its demands from year to year. Whoever wants it can have it. Stunned by the blow, the cat collapsed. If the boxers are well-matched, an exciting contest can be safely predicted.

Individually each of these sentences will make sense. But together they do not form an intelligible unit. They are fitted together at random with no attention to the connexions that must be made between sentences in continuous discourse where continuity is vital. Such continuity is not the result of chance. There are various rules which govern it.

Continuity in discourse is usually thought of as being regulated by logic alone. Sentences must occur in some logical arrangement. In general this is true. But logic is not the only consideration that is relevant here. There are also various linguistic devices which may be used to connect sentences with one other so as to provide a continuous and coherent piece of writing. Some of these devices are grammatical; others are lexical.

The study of such connecting devices involves considering a broader span than the individual sentence. It means looking beyond the individual sentence to see how it fits in with its neighbours. Methods of linguistic analysis for this purpose are less developed than, say, for the analysis of a sentence or a clause. Nevertheless it is possible to illustrate how such analysis can be undertaken. And despite problems, such analysis is likely to prove of great value in helping one to understand the characteristics of good writing.

22.1   We can start the study of sentence connexions by looking at the following paragraph (each sentence has been numbered for later reference):

 i) Consider the question of the changes which take place in retail price.
 ii) As every housewife knows, *the price we are asked to pay* bears only the faintest resemblance in many cases to the worth of the article.
 iii) *She* knows, *too,* that for many *commodities* it is more accurate to speak of *prices* rather than *price*.
 iv) *Tomatoes* in one shop may be 5c per pound; the same tomatoes in another shop may be 8c or 10c.
 v) Some people are well enough off to be able to *shop* by *price*.
 vi) *They* like lots of service and servility and are willing to pay for it.
 vii) *Yet,* even if *these sections of the community* are excluded, there still remains a fair variation between one district and another for the same article, things like fish and fruit being notorious in this respect.
 viii) *In addition to this variation in the price of the articles,* we have to recognize that different families have different spending patterns.
 ix) If cheese were made as dear as gold it would not matter one iota to *the family that hates cheese like poison*.
 x) *Conscientious vegetarians* would probably regard it as an excellent thing if the price of meat rose to prohibitive levels.

xi) *Total abstainers* positively loathe the idea of beer and spirits being cheap.

xii) *Non-smokers* love to see the Chancellor raise the money by piling the tax on 'non-essentials' like tobacco.

xiii) It is evident that we shall get nowhere if all *this individuality* is to run riot.

xiv) *It* is far too inconvenient for the statistician.

Each of these sentences after the first has at least one part in italics. This is the part which serves to make a connexion with a preceding sentence. Usually the connexion is with a sentence which immediately precedes it, but not always.

22.2   SENTENCE CONNECTORS

The ways in which the connexions are made fall into several broad categories.

22.21   There are the connexions which are made by third person pronouns. Such pronouns usually presuppose a referent which has already been mentioned in the text or which forms part of the general situation. In (iii), *she* relates its sentence back to *every housewife;* in (vi), *they* relates its particular sentence to *some people;* and in (xiv), *it* relates its sentence back to *if all this individuality is to run riot.*

Exercise

1. Not all pronouns in all their uses serve as sentence connectors. Examine in the paragraph 22.1 those uses of *it* which do not serve as sentence connectors.

22.22   ·There are sentence linkers, whose specific role is to provide connexions between sentences just as other linking particles provide connexions between clauses, and groups, and words. *Too* [in (iii)] and *yet* [in (vii)] have this function. Perhaps one should also include here the pG introduced by *in addition to.* But in any case this group is a sentence linker on other grounds, as we shall see. There are quite a number of particles like *too* and *yet* which serve to link sentences. Some others are: *however, therefore, thus, equally, as well, nevertheless, then, further, moreover, similarly, likewise, though.* These sentence linkers may be placed first in their sentence or in a later place. There are some other items, however, which as sentence linkers occur only in first place. Some of these are *and, but, so, for.*

These items, of course, regularly occur as clause linkers. Some people feel that such linkers should not be used as sentence linkers. Whatever the reasons for this ban, it is a fact of English that even writers of recognized literary merit use such linkers to connect sentences.

Exercises

2. Give further examples of sentence linkers; describe whether they pattern like *and* or like *however*.
3. In the blanks below use as many sentence linkers as possible to provide acceptable connexions between the pairs of sentences:
   a) Two of Wilde's plays were running at the West End of London at the same time, both of them huge successes, and each quite different from the other. ——————— no play in living memory was received by intelligent audiences with such continuous and hilarious laughter as was *Earnest* at every performance.
   b) The train has been delayed by a slip on the line. The Railways Department ——————— does not expect the delay to be a long one.
4. Provide sentences where the following items are (i) used as sentence linkers, (ii) used in any other way: *though, however, equally, then.*

22.23 Certain determiners are used to point to the occurrence of connexions. The most common ones illustrated in the text are the demonstratives as in (vii), (viii) and (xiii), and *the* as in (ii) and (viii). There may however be some doubt about the linking role of *the* in these instances since it also has the role of indicating that its head is qualified. Less ambiguous occurrences of *the* to indicate sentence connexions may be observed when its head is a word such as *latter, former, above, question, problem*:

> At present we cannot decide whether to buy a television set or not. *The problem* may resolve itself in the end without our needing to make a hasty decision.

> Many separate pictures can be made on the same piece of film by slightly rotating the film each time. As long as *the same changes* are made when viewing, *the many different pictures* can be seen separately.

As can be seen from this second example, when *the* is used to indicate a sentence connexion it is often accompanied by a reinforcing modifier such as *same* or *other*.

Other determiners not present in the illustrative paragraph, which frequently imply sentence connexions, are *such* and *another*. Others are personal pronouns: *his, her, its, their*.

22.24 The fourth main way in which sentence connexions are made is by lexical means. This may take the form of repeating the same word (providing identity of meaning). This can be observed in (iii) and (v) where *price* is repeated from (ii); it can be seen in (viii) where *variation* is repeated from (vii). In (v) *shop* is repeated from (iv).

The relation between lexical items may be less direct. Often words are synonyms. *Commodities* in (iii) is similar in meaning to *article* in (ii); *articles* relates (viii) to these earlier sentences.

Lexical items may be related through some other semantic relationship than similarity of meaning. Words are related through inclusion of meaning, that is, the meaning of a word may be included in that of another word. *Tomatoes* in (iv) is included in the category of *commodities* (iii). The meaning relationship of these words can be expressed in a Venn diagram:

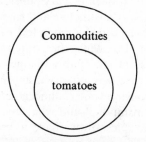

As this diagram shows, the whole of the class of tomatoes is included in the class of commodities, but not vice versa, so the meaning of the latter can be taken to include the meaning of the former.

A different sort of relationship can be observed in certain words that occur in sentences (ix), (x), (xi), (xii). Here the items *the family that hates cheese like poison, total abstainers, conscientious vegetarians,* and *non-smokers* are terms which represent discrete classes since their meanings do not directly overlap. This might be expressed as

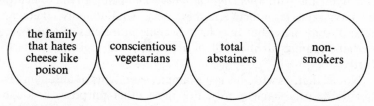

But together these items form the class of *different families* mentioned in (viii). Though the classes are discrete they are in conjunctive relationship with one another; their conjunction forms the

class of *different families*. This relationship can be expressed as

DIFFERENT FAMILIES

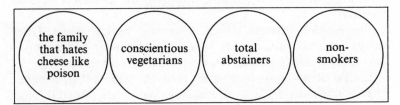

It will be apparent that at this level we are dealing with more subtle relationships of words, but relationships that are just as valid and important to understand as those mentioned earlier. But it is also clear that such relationships vary considerably in their sharpness. What starts out as a distinctive and easy-to-describe relationship at one end tends to become much less easy to distinguish and describe at the other. For while the conjunctive relationship just described may still seem reasonably distinct and easy to comprehend, the following case may not seem as clear. In (xiii) *this* indicates there is a relationship which connects sentences, but what sort of connecting relationship is it and what does it connect? For the answer to the second question we have to reach back to *different families have different spending patterns* in (viii). It is with this item and the sentences which follow it that *this individuality* enters into a relationship. And that relationship is probably one of inclusion.

Likewise there are other relationships between (ix), (x), (xi) and (xii) which are undoubtedly present but which are difficult to pin down. There is, for example, a relationship between *would not matter one iota, would regard it as an excellent thing, loathe,* and *love.* These obviously fall into different sets, with *would regard it as an excellent thing* and *love* forming synonyms; with *loathe* being an antonym, and with *would not matter one iota* being a kind of neutral or unmarked term between these sets. Undoubtedly, there are relationships here, but they have become more elusive and would perhaps require all the skill of a professional logician to clarify further.

Notice that, as with this last example, synonyms or antonyms are not necessarily single words. For most other purposes it is convenient to deal with synonymity and other semantic relationships as if they operated only between words since these provide the most ready instances of these relationships. But as the analysis of the above passage shows, and it is not untypical in this respect, these relationships often hold between items which are larger than words.

Exercises

5. Read the following pairs of sentences and in each case (i) identify the item in the first sentence with which the italicised item has a relationship, and (ii) state the nature of this relationship:
   a) Television and radio messages can be sent over a laser beam. In a recent experiment all seven New York television channels were *relayed* across a room on a shaft of *the strange light*.
   b) In trying to reconstruct the early phases of our culture we rely mostly on sources from the ancient East. *This* is perhaps more true of the history of writing than of any other great cultural achievement.
   c) There are many ways of communicating by means of objects alone. When a person sets up *a pile of stones or a single stone monument on a grave,* he intends *to give expression* to his feelings for the deceased and to perpetuate his memory in the days to come.
6. Discuss the various semantic relationships that occur between the sentences of the following paragraph. Can you arrive at any definite conclusions? The most important system of auditory communication is the spoken language directed to the ear of the person receiving the communication. Language is universal. Within the span of human knowledge there has never existed a group of men who have not possessed a fully developed language.

22.3 GRAMMAR AND MEANING

22.31 It is important to note that the kinds of semantic relationships that we have been observing often receive reinforcement from grammar. The two work in closely with each other, like partners in a tennis match. Items which have to be related in meaning are often given the same place in their sentences and have a similar grammatical function. In (x), (xi) and (xii) *conscientious vegetarians, total abstainers* and *non-smokers* are placed first and are subjects of their respective clauses. This patterning helps to underline the conjunctive relationship of these items.

The reinforcing grammatical patterning of this kind may often involve not just a single element but the patterning of the whole sentence. Though their clauses have a different sequence, sentences (ix) and (x) have an *if*-marked dependent clause and an independent clause. This similarity in sentence patterning helps reinforce the semantic connexions between them.

22.32 Such use of similar grammatical patterns is less frequent in prose than in poetry. In some poems repetition of the same grammatical pattern is one of the most effective means of providing semantic continuity. Consider for example the following sonnet:

> That time of year thou mayst in me behold,
> When yellow leaves, or none, or few, do hang
> Upon those boughs which shake against the cold,
> Bare ruined choirs, where late the sweet birds sang.
> In me thou seest the twilight of such day
> As after sunset fadeth in the west,
> Which by and by black night doth take away,
> Death's second self, that seals up all in rest.
> In me thou seest the glowing of such fire,
> That on the ashes of his youth doth lie,
> As the death-bed whereon it must expire,
> Consum'd with that which it was nourish'd by.
> This thou perceiv'st, which makes thy love more strong,
> To love that well which thou must leave ere long.

(WILLIAM SHAKESPEARE: *Sonnet LXXIII*)

The structure of this poem is clearly defined, partly of course by the verse form which consists of three quatrains and a final couplet. But the verse form provides a relatively superficial structuring. It does not on its own explain the final unity or cohesion of the poem. Nor (by itself) does the meaning of the individual sections of the poem provide an explanation. Leaves shaking on branches in autumn (first quatrain), the last twilight of a day (second quatrain), and a fire almost reduced to ashes (third quatrain), are all distinct and separate phenomena.

It is partly by certain grammatical features that verse form and meaning are drawn together to make the poem a satisfying whole. The quatrains, for instance, start with independent clauses which are almost identical in structure and which share many items:

```
        C              S      P-      A          -P
That time of year | thou | mayst <in me> behold
A       S       P              C
In me | thou | seest | the twilight of such day
A       S       P              C
In me | thou | seest | the glowing of such fire
```

Apart from the difference in sequence in the first, they are identical in clause structure. These independent clauses are in each case followed by a succession of dependent clauses. There are further parallels here between the quatrains; these are easily observable and need not be explained in detail here.

The grammatical parallels between the different quatrains help to direct our attention to the parallelism (but not identity) in their meaning. All these meanings are in conjunctive relationship with one another and each is separately identified with the *me* of the poem. Together they are included in the larger class of things subject to death. This may be represented as

THINGS SUBJECT TO DEATH

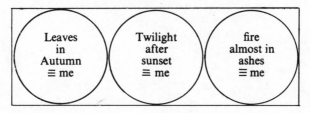

where ≡ is shorthand for 'is identified with'.

The inclusion of these items in a larger class is of course not made explicit in the poem. It does not need to be, but its existence is important for understanding the poem's unity.

Continuity achieved elsewhere in this poem by purely grammatical means should also not be overlooked. For instance the *this* (made prominent by being placed first) links the couplet to all that precedes, since the domain of *this* extends over the three quatrains.

Though the final unity of a poem such as this may at first glance seem an accident, something that just happens, close scrutiny will always show how much it owes to the grammatical structuring usually taken for granted.

Exercise

7. Take any other sonnet by Shakespeare and discuss the various features which help to form it into one continuous whole.

An Outline History of English Grammar and Its Current Developments

Much of the material in this book has developed from the work of linguists in the last forty years. Language studies, however, have been a feature of a number of civilisations over several thousand years and, in a general way, every writer on the subject owes something to the past. Ancient China and India, the early Arab and Graeco-Roman world, each made its contribution.

As with law, philosophy and critical theory, our most direct debt is to the Greeks, whose studies, from the fifth century B.C., have been passed on to us through the Romans, the Middle Ages and the Renaissance. In particular, the work of one of the Greek grammarians, Dionysius Thrax, became a model for the Latin grammarians, of whom Donatus and Priscian became the most prominent.

During the Middle Ages these Latin grammars were widely used. The schoolmen associated grammar and logic, giving priority to logic, assuming that grammar was dependent on logical analysis. A mediaeval concept dividing language into writing, speaking and *thinking* caused a close association of the processes of thought and grammar. And as logic – laws of thought – appeared to be universal, it followed that grammar was universal too; one grammar would do for all languages despite individual word variations. Thus grammar was a field of study for the philosopher. Grammar, rhetoric and logic formed the trivium, the first part of the usual university course.

The emergence of a national spirit in many Western European countries at the end of the Middle Ages was reflected in the attitude they adopted towards their languages. For the twentieth century speaker of English, whose language is understood by more people than any other, it is difficult to understand how optimistic were the opinions expressed about it at a time when it was being spoken in part only of an island on the fringe of the civilized world.

Richard Mulcaster wrote in 1582: 'Whatsoever shall becom of the English state, the English tung cannot prove fairer, then it is at this daie, if it maie please our learned sort to esteme so of it, and to bestow their travell (i.e., labour) upon such a subject, so capable of ornament, so proper to themselves, and the more to be honored, bycause it is their own.' And again, 'I love Rome, but London better. I favor Italie, but England more. I honor the Latin, but I worship the English'.

With similar enthusiasm Charles Butler, in his *English Grammar,* published in 1634, dedicated to Charles I, and described by the author as 'a second Milk for Babes', writes thus:

> The Excellenci of a Language dooeth consist chiefly in three things, [1 Antiqiti, 2 Copious Eleganci, and 3 Generaliti:] for the first the Hebrue, for the second the Greeke, for the third the Latine, for all the English is woorthily honoured . . . For copiousnes, noe marveil if it exceede the Greeke, so happy in composition; seeing it hath woords enou of its own, to expres any conceipt; besides the store of borrowed woords, which by soom change it maketh hir own; and from which . . . wee deduce infinit others.

Not surprisingly Latin provided the chief model for grammars of English. For centuries the Latin language had been what 'grammar' chiefly referred to – whence 'grammar school'. In the fifteenth century *Wakefield First Shepherds' Play* one of the shepherds remarks

> Virgill in his poetré sayde in his verse
> Even thus by gramaré, as I shall reherse.

The others tease him about his learning.

It is often observed that the early English grammarians modelled their description of English so closely on that of Latin that they quite ignored the characteristic differences between the languages. There are indeed instances of this in the grammars of the time: one is the insistence on there being future tenses. Butler, for example, not only adduces a future indicative (indicated indiscriminately by *will* or *shall*), but also a future infinitive, e.g., *to lov heere-after.* But there are also indications of his close observation of the nature of English. The importance of the auxiliaries, called *verbs suppletive, supplements* or *signs,* is stressed. Nouns are said to have two cases only: 'rect' or nominative and 'oblique' or genitive; a comment is added that 'Dhe odher Obliqe cases of dhe Latins, ar supplyed by dhe Rect, eidher with, or without prepositions, as dhe sens shall reqire.'

Although the verb tenses are made to parallel those of Latin, it is interesting that the distinction is made between the *form* of a verb and the *use* to which it is put. Calling the simple form of a verb the rect or right case and that ending in *-ed* the oblique case, Butler then explains that the present tense is formed from the right case and the preterite imperfect from the oblique, and the preterite perfect from the oblique case together with *have.* The theory is not systematically worked out, but interest in the peculiar structure of English is clearly shown.

One of the most influential grammars of the eighteenth century was that of Robert Lowth, later Bishop of London, *A Short Introduction to English Grammar,* 1762. Defining grammar as 'the Art of rightly expressing our thoughts by Words', Lowth not only offers his book for the benefit of those deliberately learning to write English but also applies it to the correction of well-established writers. In a note occupying nearly two pages Lowth censured Addison for writing 'you was' and Pope for writing 'Thou . . . touch'd'. Swift and the Bible translators also come in for criticism. The remarks about 'you was' illustrate, incidentally, that prescriptive grammarians do not always prescribe in vain, as is sometimes supposed.

Heavily prescriptive and reliant on Latin and reason though Lowth is, his capabilities as a grammarian should not be overlooked. Refusing to draw what he considered an unreal distinction (in transitivity) between verb classes exemplified by *sleep* and *walk* he writes, 'However these latter may differ in nature, the Construction of them both is the same; and Grammar is not so much concerned with their real, as with their Grammatical properties'. Lowth, like Butler, lays down only two cases for English nouns – Nominative and Possessive – though in practice he works with three in order to keep nouns parallel with pronouns to which he allots Nominative, Possessive and Objective cases. His comment on gender is apt: 'The English Language, with singular propriety, following nature alone, applies the distinction of Masculine and Feminine only to the names of Animals; all the rest are Neuter'. Lowth gives a good deal of attention to auxiliaries and the meanings they convey; in particular he distinguishes between the uses of *shall* and *will,* remarking that these distinctions were formerly not clearly made. The introductory remarks on the auxiliary verb are much to the point: 'The peculiar force of the several Auxiliaries is to be observed. *Do* and *did* mark the Action itself, or the Time of it, with greater force and distinction. They are also of frequent and almost necessary use in Interrogative and Negative Sentences. They sometimes also supply the place of another Verb, and make the repetition of it, in the same or a subsequent sentence, unnecessary: as,

> "He *loves* not plays;
> As thou *dost,* Antony."   Shakespear, Jul. Caes.'

The chief shortcoming in grammars of this and the following century is their concentration on the word. Some general comments are indeed added by Lowth on complex sentences, but the group, and its relationship to the word and the clause, is neglected, as it was to be for a long time.

An interesting work of this period is *The Rudiments of English Grammar,* by Joseph Priestley, a many-sided scholar and scientist better known for his discoveries of gases, including 'dephlogisticated air', later known as oxygen. Perhaps the most interesting feature of Priestley's linguistic work is his original attitude towards English grammar, expressed in the preface to the third edition (1772). At times his sentences sound as if they were written in this century. Aware of the need to guard against importing too much of the Latin grammar into the English, he writes: 'I own I am surprized to see so much of the distribution, and technical terms of the Latin grammar, retained in the grammar of our tongue; where they are exceedingly aukward, and absolutely superfluous. . . . A little reflection may, I think, suffice to convince any person, that we have no more business with *a future tense* in our language, than we have with the whole system of Latin moods and tenses; because we have no modification of our verbs to correspond to it; and if we had never heard of a future tense in some other language, we should no more have given a particular name to the combination of the verb with the auxiliary *shall* or *will,* than to those that are made with the auxiliaries *do, have, can, must,* or any other.'

His descriptive aim is stressed: 'With respect to our own language, there seems to be a kind of claim upon all who make use of it to do something for its improvement; and the best we can do for this purpose at present, is to exhibit its actual structure, and the varieties with which it is used.'

And in the first sentence of the Grammar proper Priestley seems to be fore-shadowing the approaches both of the structuralists and the generative grammarians of the present day: 'Language is a method of conveying our ideas to the minds of other persons; and the *grammar* of any language is a collection of observations on the structure of it, and a system of rules for the proper use of it.'

Priestley dealt with words under eight Parts of Speech making the significant innovation of excluding the participle but including the adjective; he thus established a scheme which was to remain orthodox for a very long time: noun, adjective, pronoun, verb, adverb, conjunction, preposition, interjection. He also used the term *particle* though not as a major word class.

One of the most popular and influential grammars to be used in schools was that of Lindley Murray. His *English Grammar adapted to the different classes of learners* (1795) was a school grammar, which in the course of fifty editions over fifty years, became the norm for textbooks. (It is not surprising that Nicholas Nickleby found a Murray's grammar on a table in Squeers's parlour.) His book dealt with prosody and spelling as well as grammar – an obvious advantage in the classroom.

The pattern in school grammars remained virtually unchanged through the nineteenth century. C. T. Onions and J. C. Nesfield were the most influential at the turn of the century. Nesfield's *English Grammar Past and Present* established itself in the schools' curricula and in the first decade of this century attained almost Biblical authority. In New Zealand, in 1911, thirty-one out of the thirty-four secondary schools then in existence used a Nesfield grammar in both their highest and lowest forms. Nesfield produced several books adapted to different levels in the schools – *Uses of the Parts of Speech, Manual of English Grammar and Composition, Outline of English Grammar*, etc.

All these school grammars followed the same tradition and were closely related to one another. While there was some disagreement on the exact number and the boundaries of the word classes there was no fundamental opposition of points of view. Grammar was concerned with the word and the sentence. It was common practice for each section of the text to start with a definition which was sometimes based on meaning ('a verb signifies an activity or a being acted on'). Generally the grammars were authoritarian; they were expected to provide unequivocal answers in the same way as a dictionary provides meanings.

The grammars of the Nesfield school have been heavily criticised in recent years and the 'linguistic approach' has received a proportional amount of adulation. Some of this has been carried too far. In an effort to establish themselves, the disciples of the new have sometimes overstated their case and decried the past with undue vehemence. And they have lost sight of the virtues of traditional grammar: it was particularly strong in its approach to the sentence; its weaknesses lay in the inadequacy of its treatments of units smaller than the clause, and in the artificial division of parsing and analysis.

In contrast to the relatively unchanging course of the study of English grammar during the nineteenth century, this period saw a momentous development in other linguistic areas. Its beginnings have been traced to the activities of traders, missionaries and colonisers, who indirectly increased men's knowledge of languages different from those of Europe. In particular, colonisation made known Sanskrit, the classical language of India, which led to highly productive researches into comparative historical linguistics.

In a somewhat similar way, anthropological surveys of the American Indian brought about new linguistic approaches in the twentieth century. From the work of Frank Boas and Edward Sapir and their followers considerable advances were made, notably in the study of the phoneme and the morpheme. The problems met in describing these unfamiliar languages resulted in an increased emphasis on the form and distribution of words in speech. Meaning, as a technique of analysis, began to be mistrusted. From these beginnings came many of the important concepts in modern linguistics.

In the nineteen-thirties several different scholarly disciplines were making contributions to language studies. They were rather diversified and, to a certain extent, carried out independently of each other. Leonard Bloomfield, an American, wove together the different threads of anthropology, psychology, history, dialectology and traditional grammar. His great work, *Language* (1933), consolidated the contributions of the past and provided a firm base for further advances.

In Europe, too, fresh ground had been broken, notably by the Swiss linguist, Ferdinand de Saussure. In the field of English grammar several important publications appeared, in particular those by grammarians in the Netherlands and Scandinavia. The major works are: Etsko Kruisinga, *A Handbook of Present-Day English* 1909-11 (later revised); Hendrik Poutsma, *A Grammar of Late Modern English*, 1st. ed., 1904-26; J. O. H. Jespersen, *A Modern English Grammar on Historical Principles* (7 vols) 1909-49. These scholars were not native speakers of English; their conclusions are based on a large body of written material. The grammars are fully documented, carefully regulated and are works of independent scholarship. They paid considerable attention to the history of the language and were generally conservative in their framework. Meaning was still the main basis of treatment of syntax.

The work of the linguists was accelerated by the Second World War. The need for speakers of non-European languages gave the opportunity for experimentation in approaches to language learning, and the success of new methods had the effect of popularising the work of linguists generally.

In Britain the progress of linguistic (including grammatical) studies has perhaps been relatively more even. Though it has been influenced from time to time by developments elsewhere, these have been assimilated to existing traditions rather than accepted as replacements. Thus, for example, the anthropological and behavioural linguistics of the Americans, Sapir and Bloomfield, with their emphasis on the description of living languages, were not new to British linguists, though many of their principles and procedures were. As early as 1877 in his presidential address to the Philological Society of Great Britain, Henry Sweet, the outstanding British linguist of the nineteenth century, was able to assert that the tendency of British work was 'towards the observation of the phenomena of living languages.'

Sweet himself contributed much towards the development of descriptions of living language. His work both on phonetics and grammar provided the basis for later British linguists. Sweet's fame as a phonetician has spread further than the immediate circle of linguists. Shaw partly based the character of Higgins in *Pygmalion* upon him – thus bringing him to the attention of a wider public.

His contribution to grammar is no less impressive. In *A New English Grammar* (1892) he gave emphasis to those aspects of English grammar which have been re-emphasised more recently. He paid much attention to the features of spoken English, pointing out the role that stress and intonation have in carrying many differences in meaning. He emphasised the role of word order in a language such as English: 'We see, then, that in languages which have both a normal and an exceptional order, the latter is due to a variety of causes, the most important of which is emphasis. In such languages the normal order is grammatical (syntactic), serving to show the grammatical relations between words. The fewer the inflections, the more important this function becomes, but even highly inflected languages observe general principles of syntactic order, however freely they may disregard them in special cases.'

Sweet is only one of a number of scholars who this century have maintained and developed a British or perhaps, more generally, European approach to grammar. This approach has frequently been pragmatic rather than theoretical, turned towards the needs of the foreign learner of English. Writers of grammars for this purpose have been more ready to examine traditional assumptions about how grammars should be written and to include information about the spoken language. Recent examples of such grammars are H. E. Palmer & F. G. Blandford, *A Grammar of Spoken English on a Strictly Phonetic Basis* (1939) and A. S. Hornby, *A Guide to Patterns and Usage in English* (1954).

The most distinctive British contribution to the theory of writing grammars has come from J. R. Firth, first professor of general linguistics at the School of Oriental and African Studies in London. From the first he co-operated with the phonetician, Daniel Jones and the social anthropologist B. Malinowski. Firth's work was distinguished by his insistence that language must be studied in its social contexts: 'Language text must be attributed to participants in some context or situation in order that its modes of meaning may be stated at a series of levels, which taken together form a sort of linguistic spectrum'. Grammar, therefore, according to Firth is just one of the levels of language that are to be looked at.

Firth suggested many fruitful ideas for the development of a complete theory of grammar. His work has been carried on by many of his former students and colleagues, such as M. A. K. Halliday, F. R. Palmer, Randolph Quirk, and R. H. Robins.

CLASS-STRUCTURE GRAMMAR

The theory that has guided the description presented in this text was developed chiefly by Halliday. His theory has several distinctive aspects. Perhaps the most important are these:

1. The insistence that units are ranked above one another in a definite order. Sentences, for example, never consist directly of words, but only of clauses. This insistence upon a definite ranking of units (a rank scale) in the end makes for a simpler description.

2. The insistence that classes must be defined by their role in structure. For Halliday the class NG, is defined by its role as subject and complement of a clause; likewise the class VG, by its role as predicator. He regards the form of a class (its morphology) as being of less significance.

3. The recognition of differences in 'delicacy' of analysis. Some classes and structures are more 'delicate' or more specific than others. For instance, the 'non-finite clause' is more delicate than the 'dependent clause'; and 'V^g non-finite clause' is more delicate again. This notion of delicacy is important as it draws attention to primary similarities first before directing attention to secondary differences.

4. The emphasis upon systems. It is not sufficient in grammars to describe variations in classes or structures. Those which vary in the use of a specific feature must be brought together to show the range of choice that is possible. What range of choice, for example, does English provide in the use of complements? What range of choice does it provide for determiners? These questions are answered by the complementation system and the systems for determiners.

Because Halliday's theory of grammar lays particular emphasis upon categories and scales (rank, delicacy etc.), grammars of particular languages which are guided by it are sometimes known as category-scale grammars. But they are also known as class-structure grammars after two of the major categories of the theory. Since this text has been chiefly guided by this theory, it is an example of a class-structure grammar.

SOME OTHER GRAMMARS

Class-structure grammar is not the only grammar resulting from recent linguistic studies. There have been several other approaches which have differed significantly from that of traditional grammars. One of the first of these was the so-called structural grammar. This kind of grammar grew out of the work of an American linguist, Leonard Bloomfield. The chief characteristic of this approach was a rigid exclusion of considerations of meaning as a method of defining classes. There was a great emphasis on objective discovery procedures which could be applied to find out, for example, what particular class a word belonged to. One of the procedures most emphasised was substitution in a frame. For instance, we can take a sentence *The birds are singing* and substitute other words such as *children, people, crickets* for *birds*. The words which remain unchanged *The . . . . . are singing* provide the frame in which the substitution takes place. The words which can be substituted for *birds* are members of the same class. This frame provides only plural forms. To obtain singular forms a further frame must be added: *The . . . is singing.* By using frames such as the two just illustrated it is possible to produce a set of nouns.

The most extensive use of this procedure may be found in C. C. Fries, *The Structure of English* (1952). He provided frames to enable anyone to derive four major word classes, roughly corresponding to *noun, verb, adjective* and *adverb* classes. He also provided frames to distinguish fifteen minor classes, some of them having only one or two words. In order to emphasise the objective way of deriving these classes, he referred to the major classes by number, and the minor ones by letter. This was a means of circumventing the interference likely to be caused by the traditional word class terminology. There can be no doubt of the merit of this change, but it has not been followed in many other grammars.

As well as an emphasis on procedures, structural grammar developed the technique of **immediate constituent analysis.** This is a technique for cutting a sentence into its immediate constituents. In turn, these constituents are broken into *their* immediate constituents. Eventually, constituents are reached which can not be divided up further. These are the ultimate constituents.

A brief illustration of immediate constituent analysis is provided by the analysis of the following sentence:

The trees were lying on the ground.

The sentence is first broken into its two immediate constituents:

The trees | | were lying on the ground.

Each of these constituents needs to be broken into its constituents. The next cut, therefore, will be

The trees | | were lying | | on the ground.

The next cut will be made to show the constituents of the pG:

The trees | | were lying | | on | | the ground.

The next cuts, to shorten the process, will all be carried out together, giving as a final representation:

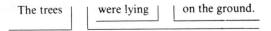

The | | trees | | were | | lying | | on | | the | | ground.

Various graphic conventions are adopted to show where the cuts are made. The convention above is just one of the possibilities. Usually a single cut is made at a time, on the assumption that most structures in English are binary. Most accounts of immediate constituent analysis provide explicit directions for the order in which these cuts are to be made. Further information about the nature of the structures (usually called 'constructions' in such grammars) is given by adding signs to specifically indicate the kind of structure. The most comprehensive grammar based on the principles of immediate constituent analysis is E. Nida, *A Synopsis of English Syntax* (1960).

The aim of structural grammars was to be as concrete and objective as possible. Discovery procedures and immediate constituent analysis were some of the means used to pursue this aim. In addition, an attempt was made as far as possible to indicate all the phonetic clues to grammar. As the main interest of the structuralists was in spoken English, they naturally dealt with the phonetic and phonemic facts of the language before turning to consider the grammar. The priority given to phonology led many linguists to search out the purely phonetic clues to many grammatical distinctions. How were different kinds of unit such as the word, the group and the clause signalled? How were different grammatical classes distinguished in their phonetic features? It was pointed out, for example, that yes/no questions are accompanied by a rise in pitch, while a statement is usually accompanied by a fall. Likewise, a compound such as *blackbird* is distinguished from *black bird* by having a different pattern of stresses. In the compound, the heavy or primary stress occurs with *black*; *bird* is less heavily stressed. But in the adjective + noun sequence, *black* is less heavily stressed than *bird*. Structural grammar has made a valuable contribution to grammatical studies by demonstrating the role that these phonetic features have in signalling important grammatical contrasts. The main examples with this emphasis are G. L. Trager and H. L. Smith Jr., *An Outline of English Structure* (1951), and A. A. Hill, *Introduction to Linguistic Structures* (1958).

Another approach is tagmemics. What gives this approach its name is the unit used as its chief means of description, the tagmeme. This is the name given to the partnership of a slot (place in a structure) and its filler (the particular class occupying that place). A simple illustration is the tagmeme which describes the subject and its class representative. This tagmeme could be written S: NG. Thus the tagmeme is, roughly, a simultaneous class and element representation. Tagmemes themselves may be joined together to form a larger unit. The subject tagmeme, for example, could join with other tagmemes to form a clause. The relationships between tagmemes are explicitly indicated. The clause, *The dogs were barking at the stranger*, would be + S: NG + P: VG ± A: pG. The plus sign before a tagmeme is used to indicate that the tagmeme is obligatory; the ± sign is used to indicate that a tagmeme is optional.

Tagmemics has been used to describe the grammars of many non-European languages. Its development has been associated with the work of the Summer Institute of Linguistics, which prepares missionaries and others for work among peoples whose languages have not previously been recorded, or at least only partly recorded. The essentials of this method are available in B. Elson and V. Pickett, *An Introduction to Morphology and Syntax* (1962).

Recent grammars have been written to serve a variety of purposes: to fulfil the needs of the foreign learner of English, to present the results of researches into little explored areas of English grammar, to provide a grammar explicit enough to be used by a computer, to satisfy the curiosity of the native speaker of English about the organisation of his language. No matter how different they may be in purpose, recent grammars have usually been guided by some explicit theory – a theory that provides a basis for writing grammars not only of English but of other languages as well.

TRANSFORMATIONAL-GENERATIVE GRAMMAR

Probably the most important and certainly the most interesting of all the newer theories of grammatical description is transformational-generative grammar or, for short, TG grammar. TG grammar is largely the brain child of one linguist, Professor Noam Chomsky of the Massachussetts Institute of Technology. His first published book, *Syntactic Structures* (1957) has been the main source for ideas about this method of description. In later books and articles he has contributed further suggestions for its development.

TG grammar has commanded respect from the beginning because of the attention it has paid to many of the theoretical problems underlying the writing of grammatical descriptions. Its theory is both rigorous and self-consistent and when applied to English has provided descriptions of many aspects of grammar which structural grammar did not touch upon. The results of such work have been made accessible in good introductory grammars by Paul Roberts, *English Syntax* (1964), Owen Thomas, *Transformational Grammar and The Teacher of English* (1965), and Ralph Goodman, who contributed a valuable section to Norman C. Stageberg, *An Introductory English Grammar* (1966).

Chomsky has pointed out that a grammar must satisfy various requirements. It must be based upon accurate observation of actual language and also satisfy the native speaker's intuitions about his language. It must for example be able to account for his intuition that active and passive sentences are related to each other, that some sentences are grammatically ambiguous, that some pairs of sentences though alike on the surface are different at a deeper level. Thus Chomsky says that the following pair of sentences

The man was eager to please
The man was easy to please

are alike in their surface grammar but are different in their deep grammar. For Chomsky, the intuition of the native speaker is important and, in finding a place for it, he has indicated that grammar is not perhaps as concrete and physical as it had appeared to be to the structural grammarians.

He also adopted a rather different view on what is meant by analysis, and in fact what a grammar is to be used for. It often seemed in structural grammar that analysis was a matter of cutting a sentence into successively smaller pieces; this is what happens in immediate constituent analysis. Opposing this, Chomsky offered the view that grammar is a set of rules for forming sentences. A grammar produces or generates sentences, hence the term generative. A grammar can only produce sentences if the apparatus that it uses is very precise and explicit, more so than in traditional or structural grammar. Our immediate concern is with the principles of TG grammar rather than with the details of its apparatus. For a detailed view of these you must refer to one of the books listed earlier. But a sketch of such an apparatus can be given.

Let us consider what rules might be required to form the following sentence:

The headlights penetrated the darkness.

This is a sentence of minimal complexity. According to the kind of analysis that would usually be given such a sentence in TG grammar, it is a sentence (S) that consists of a noun phrase (NP) followed by a verb phrase (VP). In turn the noun phrase consists of a determiner (T) and a noun (N); the verbal phrase consists of a transitive verb (Vt) and a noun phrase (NP), and this last NP consists of a determiner and noun. This information can be represented in a tree diagram:

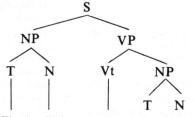

The headlights penetrated the darkness.

So far this is a kind of analysis that is very similar to those used in this book. Such an analysis becomes generative when it is expressed in the form of rules. The analysis above could be expressed in the following rules:

1. S ⟶ NP + VP
2. VP ⟶ Vt + NP
3. NP ⟶ T + N
4. Vt ⟶ penetrated
5. T ⟶ the
6. N ⟶ darkness, headlights

In these rules the arrow means 'is rewritten as'.

Rules such as these which allow for a single symbol at a time to be rewritten or replaced by another symbol or a string of symbols (e.g. T + N) are known as phrase-structure rules. They do not alter a sentence but independently of speaker or hearer may produce a sentence provided that they are applied in the sequence in which they are listed above.

By applying these rules it would be possible to produce the sentence that we wanted. Because N may be either *darkness* or *headlights* they could also produce the following sentence:

The darkness penetrated the headlights.

In fact, by adding further words to the right hand side of rules 4, 5, and 6, they could produce hundreds of sentences. These rules produce relatively simple transitive clauses; by adding rules of the same type it would be possible to produce a vast number of sentences of different kinds. Though it is not possible to demonstrate this point here, even a comparatively small set of rules can be made to produce a vast number of sentences.

It is not simply the fact that TG grammar is a generative grammar that helps to distinguish it from other grammars. Any other grammar, if it is explicit, is at least implicitly generative; it could be used to generate as well as analyse sentences. What helps to make TG grammar different is that it is both explicitly generative and its rules are ordered in a definite sequence.

Chomsky has claimed that structural grammars, if they were made explicit, would all have the form of a phrase-structure grammar; that is, a grammar consisting only of phrase-structure rules. He claims that any grammar of this sort is inadequate. There are some kinds of sentence that cannot be generated by this type of rule, and there are other sentences that can be generated only with difficulty. Phrase-structure rules are adequate for producing relatively simple sentences; more complex sentences are best produced by transformational rules.

As the term implies, a transformational rule has the effect of altering the shape of a sentence – something that a phrase-structure rule does not do. It may change a sentence by adding to it, or deleting part of it, or changing the order of some of its constituents. Thus, for example, a transformational rule may change an active sentence into a passive one, or change a statement into a question. Extensive use of such transformations is made in TG grammars of English in order to generate more complicated sentences. Since this is one of its distinctive features, Chomsky's grammar, as opposed to structural grammar, is aptly called transformational-generative.

The apparatus of TG grammars is strikingly different from those employed in the English grammars that preceded them. What are its origins? One can see tendencies in the work of earlier grammarians. The tendency, for instance, towards a symbolic notation is apparent in Fries, while transformations were employed by Zellig Harris in his work on discourse analysis. But there is not a great deal that immediately leads up to it from within grammar. Influences from outside grammar seem to have been stronger. Chomsky's apparatus is very similar to those which have been used in certain kinds of symbolic logic. It is the axiomatic method, which starts with a single axiom – sentence – and deduces new theorems by applying specific rules. Such an axiomatic method may also be familiar to you through Euclidean geometry.

TG grammar has already proved very fruitful in providing new information about English grammar. And this perhaps is a measure of its value. Not all linguists, however, have fully or even partly accepted its claims. This may be in part due to the sometimes excessive zeal of its advocates in pressing its claims for recognition. But whatever the outcome of the current debate, TG grammar has already made a major impact and, along with other types of grammar, may be expected to make further important contributions to grammatical studies.

ANSWERS

Many of the exercises, particularly in Part One, are merely drills; many others may be done quite easily from the indicated paragraphs. Therefore to avoid needless repetition, full answers are not always given.

CHAPTER 1

1. The reasons are not definitely known but the existence of many languages is certainly concerned with the fact that (i) language is acquired by imitation, which can never be perfect and (ii) human communities are always changing their composition. It would certainly be impossible for political reasons to make everyone speak the same language. Apart from that, it would be very difficult as long as most children are brought up in their parents' houses. Bilingualism is obviously possible on a small scale. To achieve a universal *second* language might not be impossible.

3. Words for 'he or she', 'his or her', 'friend of the same sex', a period of 24 hours as distinct from period of daylight, the two senses of *or* as distinguished by Latin *vel* and *aut*. Note recently introduced *sibling;* note various attempts to create a word meaning 'you' which is clearly plural – you-all, yous, yez, you-people.

4. Not known for certain, but it seems highly likely, since a person's knowledge of the world depends to a great extent on the way his own language has analysed it. Even if he does not use language to think with he uses it to explain his thinking which affects the way someone else understands it.

5. Strictly one cannot quote allophones until a system of phonemes has been drawn up. But the following are generally held to be examples: the 'k' sounds in *kill, cat, cool* are all slightly different; so are the 't' in *top, stop* and the 'r' in *race, trace, very*. Length is different in vowel allophones in *feet, feed*.

6. anti-, quasi-, pseudo-, -monger, -est, -ist, centi-, deka-, -ide (in chemistry).

8. male nurse/nurse, X Girls' Grammar School/X Grammar School, West Virginia/Virginia, Palmerston North/Palmerston, safety matches/matches; you may know better local examples.

11. Subjects under linguistic taboo vary from one language community to another, though some are common to many languages. They also vary over time. Taboo may be complete but is usually partial; the topic may be mentioned in certain circumstances only; some words referring to it are permissible, not others. It often results in substitute words and expressions, which constitute **euphemism.** Examples of such topics are: death, serious illnesses, mental illnesses (many substitute terms which keep being replaced), nakedness, some parts of the body and the clothing associated with them, elimination of bodily wastes, reproduction and associated topics. (Note euphemisms in this list). Under partial taboos are some words relating to sacred subjects. Some communities also taboo the names of supernatural creatures such as elves (substituting 'the good people'), names of animals being hunted, and words which happen to be the same as some person's name.

CHAPTER 2

1. **a)** e.g., scissors **(b)** e.g., mathematics.
2. **a)** conspicui*ty*/*ness;* gesticula*tion;* perspicaci*ty*/*ness;* regenera*tion;* fissipar*ity,* fissipara*tion,* fissipar*ism.* **(b)** See 2.11.
3. Look at form and position.
4. e.g.,He was tied to the post. If ifs and ands were . . .
5. Globnocks, limnickings, commissions, bresdecs, knofpings, dunbers, tafts, seinfeirs, derf, mogs, ashert, poplisses, honks, vindun, rerton, sercentation, urop, lamisation, benters, dobs, splogger, kink, America, New Zealand, crisis, allery, werthums, plallion, monthings. Possibly *auguest.*
6. e.g. electronics, nuclear physics.
7. **a)** See 2.3 **(b)** See 2.3.
8. Five-form verbs.
9. Be-9, have-5, *and so on.*
10. See 2.34.
11. e.g., bad, little.
12. e.g., *-ive, -ent;* e.g., *-ic.*
13. e.g., inaudibly, softly, quietly, noisily, lustily, uproariously.
14. e.g. for*ward,* side*ways,* tailor-*fashion; a*board, *a*loft.
15. Adverbs – steadily, quietly, fairly, asleep, forward.
    Particles – and, across, the, and, a, into, with, on, down, in, of, onto.

CHAPTER 3

1. **a)** The (M) lass (H) with the delicate air (Q). **(b)** Over the field (M M H), the exhausted footballers (M M H). **(c)** Some fifteen shoddy blue teenage dresses (M M M M M H) in the glittering new cornershop (M M M M H). **(d)** Materials (H) of this kind (Q), in sufficient quantity (M M H).
2. **a)** Man, cry **(b)** Man, bread **(c)** We **(d)** We, leaders, group.
3. e.g., Fred swims, is swimming, will be swimming, should have been swimming.
4. **a)** (much more) often (M H) **(b)** Perhaps (H), very politely (M H). **(c)** Most unfortunately (M H). **(d)** Note that *shy,* and *gentlemanly* are adjectives. **(e)** extremely stupidly (M H).
5. quite, rather, extremely, *and so on.*

CHAPTER 4

1. **a)** (i) They (ii) The girls (iii) The sweet young things in our school choir; *and so on.*
2. **a)** have galloped; *and so on.*
3. **a)** smell, taste, look, seem **(b)** became.
4. **a)** e.g., offered, promised, left, lent, bought, played.
   b) e.g., Laura promised her boyfriend the latest pop record. ⟶
       Her boyfriend was promised the latest pop record by Laura.
   c) The latest pop record was promised (to) her boyfriend by Laura.
   d) Laura promised the latest pop record to her boyfriend.
5. **a)** The wicketkeeper | moved | to his left. **(b)** He | dived | high. **(c)** He | held | with apparent ease | a sensational one-handed catch. **(d)** Three young men | were missing | on the moors | in the thick fog. **(e)** The bandit | successfully | dodged | the traffic on the motorway. **(f)** He |

P   C^I A   S   P
was | furious | over his recent failure. **(g)** Not every girl | would con-
              C^E C^I
sider | the speedway | her ideal Saturday night's entertainment. **(h)** Hun-
      S   P   C^{E1} C^{E2} A
dreds of people | sent | Chichester | good wishes | at the start of his
                   A   S   P
lonely voyage. **(i)** In hot, sunny Northland | the emphasis | is | on the
    A
cool, natural and casual look for brides. **(j)** Crew squabbles, . . . Island |
                               S
P   C^{EI} C^{E2}
give | a sensation-loving public | a diet of good red meat.

6. a) The pavlova; **(b)** . . . placed . . . in the ford; *and so on.*

7. a) Pattern I **(b)** IV **(c)** IV **(d)** III **(e)** III **(f)** V **(g)** V **(h)** VII **(i)** IV **(j)** VI **(k)** VII **(l)** III **(m)** II **(n)** IV.

                  H   Q   H M H   Q   M H
8. e.g., **(b)** Much of his writing | is | a record of his experiences. **(g)** The pigs
   H   M   M   H   H
| consider | the other animals | foolish.

CHAPTER 5

1. (ii).

2. and, but (with shared subject), and, either or, or, and (with shared subject), but (with shared subject), nor (with shared predicator), and (with shared subject).

3. a) Two linked clauses **(b)** Three linked clauses **(c)** See last example 5.22 **(d)** Two linked clauses, with one bonded; e.g., They arrived || while we were out || and made themselves a cup of tea. **(e)** Independent clause followed by two bonded clauses linked.

4. e.g., **(e)**

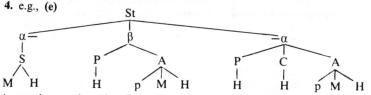

An apple, <<dropping from the tree>> struck| Newton | on the head.

(f)

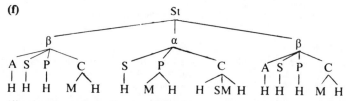

If| we| had| some bacon, || we| could have| bacon and eggs,|| if| we| had| any eggs.

         α   &(β   α
5. a) He lay back || and, tearing open the packet, || placed the last cigarette
                                   &α)
on the window ledge || and began to write . . . surface. **(b)** His lips mur-
       α   &α
murmured the first verses over and over; || then stumbled through half the

verses; || then slipped. **(c)** The light spread upwards from the glass roof,
|| making the theatre seem a festive ark, || anchored among the hulks of
houses, || her frail cables of lanterns looping her to her moorings. **(d)** At
the far end near the street a faint light showed in the darkness || and as he
walked towards it || he became aware of a faint aromatic odour.

CHAPTER 6

1. **a)** dog, fox, hen, *and so on* **(b)** A fox lives here. Foxes live here. The third fox . . . Many foxes . . . *And so on.* **(c)** He bought a few hens. He sold the best hen. He raised many hens. *And so on.* **(d)** e.g., African; Welshman; Highlander; Zulu.
2. **a)** Sheep, fish, *and so on.* **(b)** e.g., Milanese.
3. e.g., The family is/are divided in its/their opinions.
4. **a)** e.g., wheat, flour, mustard. **(b)** I bought some mustard (*not mustards*). Mustard brings out the flavour, but too much mustard is not good for you. **(c)** See 6.21.
5. Mass – a, b, c, e, h; Count – d, f, h, i; either – g.
6. See 6.31.
7. See 6.33.

CHAPTER 7

1. **a)** e.g., All those clever boys; such a charming older brother; our other two new cars. See 7.24. **(b)** e.g., All those clever boys are working well. *All* and *those* occur with plural count nouns *boys,* and are in plural concord with the predicator *are working.*
2. **a)** e.g., The first man | wins the prize.   : **(b)** singular agreement
   Their best clothes | have been pressed. : plural agreement
   The uncut bread | is sold here.   : singular mass agreement
3. e.g., **(a)** The two other very charming small boys (will come too). **(b)** The same three red Irish shawls (were up for sale). See 7.42.
4. grammar, Invercargill, (no instance), laboratory, gunnery.
5. e.g., The air terminal waiting room, a rubbish collection van, a plywood factory hand; a submarine depth gauge, the Cathedral bell tower, a Lowestoft herring trawler.
6. **a)** D O N H **(b)** D SM E N H **(c)** D N N H **(d)** D O N H **(e)** E E E N H **(f)** D D N N N H, *and so on.*

CHAPTER 8

1. **a)** e.g., The bride will wear something old, something new, something borrowed, something blue. **(b)** e.g., The trees yonder (will be destroyed). **(d)** e.g., The first crops harvested.
2. **a)** e.g., a trout nine inches long. **(b)** e.g., the halfback behind the scrum.
3. **a)** e.g. the halfback behind the scrum last week ; the halfback behind the scrum of the Varsity team. **(b)** e.g., the sufferings of the man in the motorcar.
4. **a)** e.g., The fish that was caught last week is now uneatable. **(b)** e.g., The man whom we passed in the street used to be our neighbour. **(c)** e.g., The experience which you were telling me about has done you no harm. **(d)** e.g., The tramping gear that cost so much has been stolen. **(e)** e.g., The books that you bought yesterday are good value.

5. **b)** The man we passed . . . **(c)** The experience you were telling . . . **(e)** The books you bought . . .
6. See 8.43.
7. See 8.5, e.g., The reply *to make in such circumstances* should be obvious.
    The birds *twittering in the trees* keep me awake.
    The debris *left by the storm* has been removed.
8. e.g., **a)** (i) NG's: The mill which is being built in South Auckland district . . . production . . . next year.
    (ii)

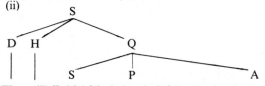

The mill [[which| is being built| in the South Auckland district]].

CHAPTER 9

1. **a)** e.g., The boy who wanted an exeat must see me now.
    The ballerina whom I chose was a beautiful dancer.

        S   P   C   A

   b) e.g., The boy | must see | me | now.

        S   P   C

   The boy | wanted | an exeat.

                S   P   C

   The boy [[who | wanted | an exeat]] must see me now.

   e.g., The ballerina was a beautiful dancer.

      S   P   C

   I | chose | the ballerina

      S   P   C

   I | chose | whom

        C   S   P

   Whom | I | chose

                    C   S   P

   The ballerina [[whom | I | chose]] was a beautiful dancer.

2. **a)** e.g., *Many* failed in this exam. This failure disappointed *many*. It all meant hard work for *many*. **(b)** See 9.3. **(c)** e.g., I saw the others. He put one apple on the table and the other in his mouth. **(d)** See 9.3.
3. **a)** singular and plural. **(b)** e.g., A fifth of the class will receive a marble. He sold a fifth of his farm. He sold it for a fifth of its value. **(c)** one, one's, ones, ones'. I'll take a large one. Those frilly ones over there will do. **(d)** and **(e)** See 9.4.
4. **a)** See 9.5. **(b)** singular and plural forms: e.g. *the rich yellows of these orchids.* It may be count or mass; e.g., *a yellow like this;* mass: *yellow is my favourite colour.* **(c)** Deduce from 9.5.
5. e.g., Her cooking is adventurous. I really go for her cooking. The guests were delighted by her splendid cooking.
6. e.g.,

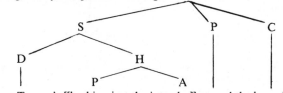

Towser's [[barking | at the intruder]] roused the household.

CHAPTER 10

1. e.g., *take* is a Six-form verb; *love* is Five-form; *can* is Two-form; V^{to}, V^g, V^n, V^s are missing; *and so on.* See 2.3.

2. Yes. Nine.

3. Have, be, do, use, dare, need.

4. e.g., **(a)** V^o at H

	a.	H		
She	must	see	shall	see
	may	see	should	see
	might	see	can	see
	will	see	could	see
	would	see	need	see
			dare	see

5. e.g., They were showing, shown, being shown, to show. He needn't show, be shown, be showing, have shown, have been shown, have been showing.

6. V^g, V^n, V^n, V^{to}, V^o, V^n, V^g, V^n, V^n, V^g, *and so on.*

7. See 10.43.

8. a) past modal perfect progressive **(b)** present modal **(c)** present progressive **(d)** present perfective progressive **(e)** past modal perfective progressive **(f)** present **(g)** present modal progressive.

9. a) Peter had been showing **(b)** has shown **(c)** may be showing **(d)** is showing **(e)** may have shown **(f)** has been showing **(g)** might have been showing.

10. e.g., I taste the soup; the soup is tasted by me.
The tree is falling; *no transform.*
The girl has written a nice letter; a nice letter has been written by the girl.

11 a) present modal perfective passive **(b)** past perfective passive **(c)** past progressive passive **(d)** past modal perfective passive, *and so on.* (N.B. An easy way to work out tense and aspect of passives is to turn them into the active.)

12. a) The boy may be shown **(b)** had been showing **(c)** may have shown **(d)** was showing **(e)** is shown **(f)** might have been shown **(g)** has shown.

CHAPTER 11

1. get-got, V^o and V^n; forbid-forbade, V^d, forbidden, V^n; hang-hanged, hung, V^d and V^n; *and so on.* In U.S. English V^n of *get* is sometimes *gotten.*

2. e.g., drink (drunk, drunken); shrink (shrunk, shrunken).

3. a) intransitive **(b)** transitive **(c)** equational **(d)** double complement **(e)** both are doubly complemented **(f)** intransitive **(g)** equational **(h)** both are equational **(i)** intransitive **(j)** equational **(k)** intransitive, transitive, intransitive **(l)** intransitive and equational; ambiguous.

4. e.g., Row W shows that verbs of this class usually have an adjunct, a complement, C^E type. See table 11.23.

5. *Cause* like *give*; *seem* like *become*; *and so on.* See table 11.23.

6. A plus sign in the first column. Exceptional cases have myself type pronoun as C^I: They behave themselves.

7. e.g.,

He called me a fool.	$C^E C$	⎫
He called me a taxi.	$C^E C^E$	⎬ Subclass (Y + Z)
He called a taxi.	C^E	⎭
He grew tired.	C^I	Subclass X

But note also *Gum trees grow in Australis;* which makes *grow* a special case: $A \div$, $C \div$, $C^E \div$, $C^I \div$.

CHAPTER 12

1. **a)** Constabie | disarms | man with shotgun. OR. Constable | disarms | man | with shotgun. **(b)** A recent jazz festival (a festival of recent jazz). OR A recent jazz festival (a recent festival of jazz). **(c)** Girls | plump | for marriage. OR Girls plump | for marriage. **(d)** Five acres of best growing peat land (best land for growing peat). OR Five acres of best growing peat land (peat land for best growing). **(e)** Fire alarms | generally | sound. OR Fire alarms (are) generally sound. **(f)** Call | me | a taxi. OR Call | me | a taxi.

2. As an indication, note a similarity in structure of the first four lines in each stanza: the imperatives in the third lines, upon which the first two lines depend. These structures are basically similar, but not identical. Verse 1, $\beta \gamma \alpha$ &α; Verse 2, β &$\beta \alpha \beta$; Verse 3, $\beta \alpha$ &α.

3. See 12.3.

CHAPTER 13

The revision exercises given in this chapter can be readily answered by referring to the examples and exercises in the chapter concerned.

CHAPTER 14

1. See 14.2 (a).
2. e.g., He is late today but *usually* he is punctual. In summer we swim, but in winter we play hockey.
3. almost, completely, always, merely, nearly, quite.
4. e.g., She speaks rather quietly. But she is a rather talkative girl. In fact she is often rather garrulous.

CHAPTER 15

1. **a)** *quietly* – AG, *one day* – NG, *in the private bar* – pG. **(b)** *suddenly* – AG, *with a deafening bang* – pG. **(c)** *with a look of gloom on his saturnine countenance, at the resultant mess, in his hand to the broom cupboard* – pG's, *sombrely* – AG. **(d)** *Close on the heels of the retreating army* – pG (with *close* as SM), *horse, foot and artillery* – NG. **(e)** *Day in, day out* – NG, *maddeningly* – AG, *in sympathy* – pG.

2. **a)** *which were badly damaged in the hurricane* – rankshifted, depends upon *trees; which was a pity* – not rankshifted, depends upon rest of sentence. **(b)** Not rankshifted: commas indicate that the *wh-* clause is not part of an NG. **(c)** Rankshifted: depends directly on *girls*. **(d)** Not rankshifted: it can vary its position. **(e)** The *that* marked clause is rankshifted; it is complement to *assert* and therefore a clause element. **(f)** Rankshifted: depends directly on *times*. **(g)** Rankshifted: it is H in an NG. *His* indicates that the clause is part of an NG. **(h)** Rankshifted: it is S in a clause. **(i)** Rankshifted: it is S in a clause.

3. a)

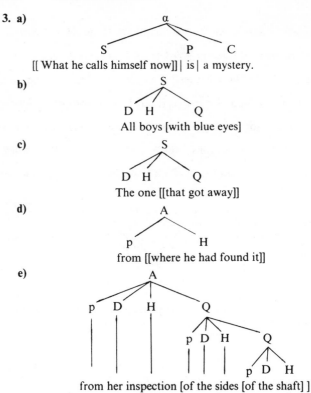

[[What he calls himself now]] | is | a mystery.

b)

All boys [with blue eyes]

c)

The one [[that got away]]

d)

from [[where he had found it]]

e)

from her inspection [of the sides [of the shaft]]

4. [[I'm speaking of]]; [of those cramped houses [[which were all [[the Council had been able to afford]]]]]; [[that they failed to provide anything better]]; [of theirs]; [[doing no better]]; [[our lot had improved]]; [[where we were all . . . tenements]]; [[where . . . hills]]; [[whatever we did || and wherever we went]]; [[what . . . tell you]]; [[that no one knew [[how . . . gear]]]]; [[how everyone . . . || . . . goes on]]; [[we'd borrowed from Jim's uncle]].

5. a)

(E   H) =(D   E   H   Q)
Wild Bill, the bad man of the prairie.

b) S(NG =β) PA.

Note: 15.32. The instances of linked verbs at P in the Thomas passage are *yawns* and *moons; lolls, laps* and *idles; sag* and *pillow; snort* and *dream; mud-bask* and *snort; rollick* and *slobber* and *snore.*

6. 1st Sentence. *His blood flowed . . . and clotted:* linked clauses; *out, from the white side:* apposed groups, A(AG =pG). 2nd. *Huge and dark and bearded:* linked adjectives at Q. Notice that a single adjective would not function in this way. 3rd. *His sword and shield:* linked nouns as heads of S. 5th. *Silently and in sorrow:* linked groups, A (AG &pG); *in twos and* *threes:* linked words, A (p H SM H); *the warriors turned away . . . and went . . . :* linked clauses, α &α; *back to their tents:* linked groups, A (AG =pG). 6th. *The sun went down and their campfires came out and glowed upon the plain:* linked clauses. 8th. *Upon the dead boy and the strong man . . . :* linked groups, A (pG &NG).

CHAPTER 16

1. **a)** e.g., As it was late we turned in. Having received our orders, we took off. The boiler blew up. **(b)** The Norman Knights rode on. He was cramped, so he stepped over. As the door was open, he walked in.
2. **a)** X, **(b)** neither, **(c)** X, **(d)** Y, **(e)** X, **(f)** Y, **(g)** X, **(h)** X, **(i)** neither, **(j)** X.
3. **a)** e.g., I switched off the light. She looked up the answer. The detective saw through the scheme. **(b)** She was talking *to him*. We ran *after the lorry*. He fainted *during the operation*.
4. **a)**

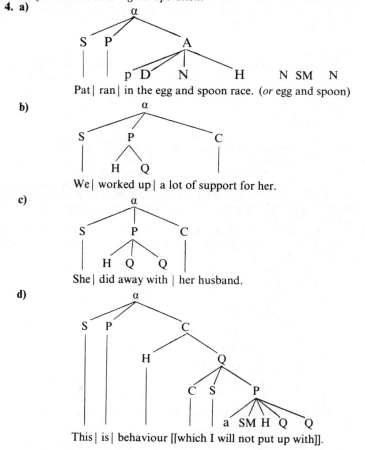

Pat| ran| in the egg and spoon race. (*or* egg and spoon)

b)

We| worked up| a lot of support for her.

c)

She| did away with | her husband.

d)

This| is| behaviour [[which I will not put up with]].

5. *made out* (i), *dreamed up* (ii), *getting out of* (iii), *clearing up* (ii), *trotted out* (ii), *facing up to* (iii), *getting over* (ii), *put off* (ii), (*steamed up,* though it

looks like a particled verb, it occurs in only the one form and therefore is best treated as an -ed adjective form), *get off* (i).

6. e.g., Louise told us to *clear out*. She really *went off*. She accused us of *butting in*. Then she *broke off*, *broke down*, and *broke into* tears. We were, of course, all *broken up*. Louise was explaining how she had fallen in when the telephone *cut off* the conversation. She was still *cut up* when we left.

7. vie *with*, devolve *upon*, commiserate *with*, inveigh *against*.

8. e.g., We inveigled him into the trap. We mediated between the parties. We should not participate in a domestic quarrel.

9. e.g., a proper *washout;* let's go for a *walkabout,* and buy some *takeaways;* just a *pushover;* where is the *pull-through?;* I will give him a good *build-up*.

10. Syntactically *ton-up* is a particled word (consisting of two interdependent morphemes) used as a modifier in an NG. It is probably a transform of (*He has a*) *ton marked up*, i.e. done 100 m.p.h., or possibly implies that he has done *up*wards of 100 m.p.h.

CHAPTER 17

1. *Particle marked* – iii, iv, v, vi, viii, xi. *Sequence marked* – x, xi. *Wh- ever marked* – vii, xii. *That marked* – xiii. *Wh- marked* – i, ii, ix, xv. *unmarked* – xiv.

2. e.g., It was none *other than* Bill who rang up. He was *more* talkative *than* a parrot. He wanted me to go to the dance, but I would *rather* stay home *than* go with him.

3. The dance was just *as* enjoyable *as* I had hoped. The band was not *so* noisy *as* I had feared. And my dress was quite *as* daring *as* Mary's.

4. e.g., *Indifferent* as he was to the weather, he still felt the cold of the mainland winter. *Terrible* though his punishment was, he endured it without a murmur. *Delightful* as the countryside appeared, I did not like the bus journey. *Complicated* though the knitting pattern seemed, she purled and plained with twinkling speed. *Strange* though it may appear, she dropped not a single stitch.

5. e.g., Whatsoever is found we shall share fifty-fifty. – S. Whatsoever you find to do, do it with all your might. – C. At whatsoever moment you call on me I'll come. – A.

6.

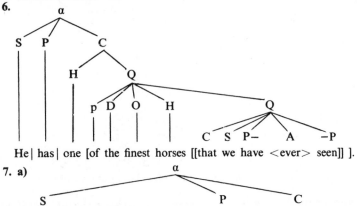

He | has | one [of the finest horses [[that we have <ever> seen]]].

7. a)

The excuse [[he gave]] [for his lateness] | was | [[that he was not early]].

b)

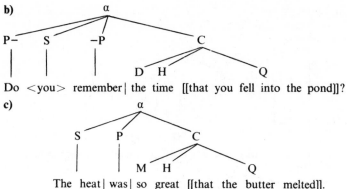

Do <you> remember| the time [[that you fell into the pond]]?

c)

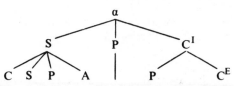

The heat| was| so great [[that the butter melted]].

d) *and so on.*

CHAPTER 18

1. e.g., The hostess *making* no objection, we had a further helping of crêpes suzettes. Not *feeling* very well, we retired to bed.

2. a) 18.22 (b)

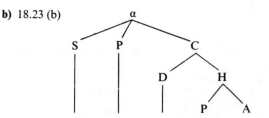

[[What I dislike most]]| is| [[darning| smelly old socks]].

b) 18.23 (b)

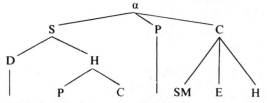

We| appreciate| your| [[writing| to us]].

Cynthia's [[passing| her exams]]| is| most welcome news.

c) 18.23 (c)

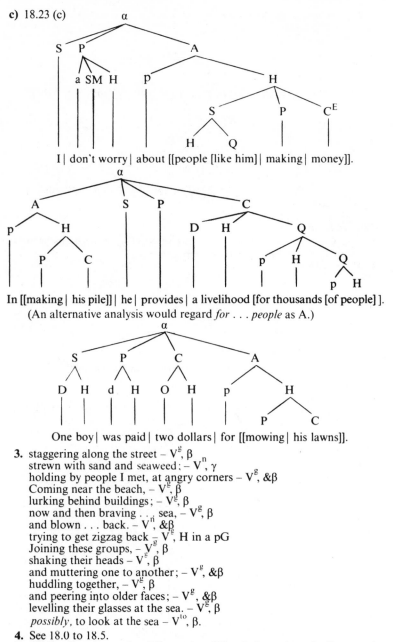

I | don't worry | about [[people [like him]] | making | money]].

In [[making | his pile]] | he | provides | a livelihood [for thousands [of people]]].
(An alternative analysis would regard *for . . . people* as A.)

One boy | was paid | two dollars | for [[mowing | his lawns]].

3. staggering along the street – V^g, β
strewn with sand and seaweed; – V^n, γ
holding by people I met, at angry corners – V^g, &β
Coming near the beach, – V^g, β
lurking behind buildings; – V^g, β
now and then braving . . . sea, – V^g, β
and blown . . . back. – V^n, &β
trying to get zigzag back – V^g, H in a pG
Joining these groups, – V^g, β
shaking their heads – V^g, β
and muttering one to another; – V^g, &β
huddling together, – V^g, β
and peering into older faces; – V^g, &β
levelling their glasses at the sea. – V^g, β
possibly, to look at the sea – V^{to}, β.

4. See 18.0 to 18.5.
5. *While off work,* you should be resting. *When in Rome* do as the Romans do.

6. *Without food in the cupboard or money in his pocket,* he was in a bad way. *With all the traffic in the street* it is impossible to sleep. *With Peter in charge,* we had a good leader.

7.

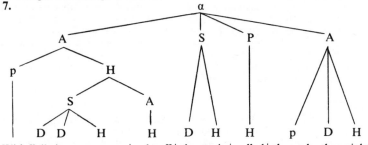

With [[all its passengers | asleep]] | the train | rolled | through the night.

CHAPTER 19

1. a) whether N.Z. can . . . years. **(b)** that the issues should . . . way. **(c)** to categorise such information . . . headings. **(d)** letting your hair down now and then. **(e)** to come. **(f)** to have four different levels of readership.

2. a) what falls to pieces. **(b)** Why we did so. **(c)** What he needs. **(d)** What matters. **(e)** What destroys the meaning.

3. a)

S P   C   = S

It | is | [[telling the truth]] | [[that matters]].

b)

S P   C   = S

It | is | the last sentence | [[which destroys the meaning]].

4. a) It is anybody's guess what they have done with the booty. **(b)** It is quite obvious that you have made a mistake. **(c)** It is the second theorem that should be discussed. **(d)** It would be absurd to act in this way. **(e)** It takes more than a few coloured trimmings to make a statistical report interesting.

5. a) They | thought | it | strange | [[that the meeting had not been arranged earlier]]. $\overset{S}{}$ $\overset{P}{}$ $\overset{C^E}{}$ $\overset{C^I}{}$ $\overset{=C^E}{}$ **(b)** We | consider | it | unwise | [[to proceed with the plan any further]]. $\overset{S}{}$ $\overset{P}{}$ $\overset{C^E}{}$ $\overset{C^I}{}$ $\overset{=C^E}{}$ **(c)** However, | the committee | deemed | it | expedient | [[to continue the project]]. $\overset{A}{}$ $\overset{S}{}$ $\overset{P}{}$ $\overset{C^E}{}$ $\overset{C^I}{}$ $\overset{=C^E}{}$

6. e.g., There's something odd going on in that scrum. There is a good deal of influenza about now. If you don't get this exercise right, there'll be weeping and wailing. There are some queer people over there.

7. a) *It* refers to *That,* and is therefore a referring subject. **(b)** *It* has an appositional subject in the *that* clause, as is shown by: That most of the troubles were centred in territories formerly British | is | ironic. **(c)** Similarly with *it* and the *that* clause. The fact that in the rewrite *that* becomes *when* does not destroy the appositional relation.

8. *It* was most annoying. What? That the children were not asleep. *It* therefore refers to preceding sentence. *It* was obvious – *it* is in apposition to the *that* clause following. *There* was James . . ., and *there* they were all talking. – This is a rather unusual use of *there*. By position *there* appears to be a substitute subject, but by its emphasis and demonstrative meaning, it appears to be an adjunct. Either of these analyses would serve. *It* was almost eleven – non-referring subject. *There* was not much use – substitute subject; doing anything about *it* now – referring use, H of a pG. *It* was foolish – substitute subject, in apposition to *to bother*. *There* – AG at A. *It* – substitute subject. *There* are – substitute subject. *It* at C refers to *a cat*.

CHAPTER 20

1. a) What disgusting luck for the burglar! **(b)** What a fool he looked! **(c)** How quickly all Julia's friends congratulated her.
2. e.g., What shall we do with the drunken sailor? What mistake did he make? Who was he drinking with? How did he know? What boat shall we put him on? Have you stopped teasing your brother? Never did sun more beautifully steep . . . Yet did I never breathe its pure serene . . . Full many a glorious morning have I seen . . .
3. a) There entertain him all the Saints above.
Now trips a lady, and now struts a lord.
Too rare, too rare, grow now my visits here.

Down goes the scrum, and in goes the ball.
Up the straight go the leaders.

b) Who is he that cometh like an honoured guest?
Where now are those tall poplars?

CHAPTER 21

1. *Whose?* is C^{I} in 'That is whose?' Another possibility is S; i.e., 'Whose is that?' Whether it is C or S depends on whether it is regarded as a transform of 'That is whose?' or 'Whose is that?' *This your bag?* is an elliptical transform of either *Is this your bag?* or *This is your bag?*
2. Catenative: Latin *catena*, a chain: *catenare*, to connect like links; hence occurring in a connected series. e.g., Would you like to be made to continue to work more carefully?
3. There are probably very few. Note, *We heard tell that . . . , Let's go see . . .*
4. e.g., forget, choose, want. expect.
5. All except *hate*.
6. *dislike* does not, *loathe* is doubtful.
7. a) Did you remember shooting the ducks? **(b)** Did you remember to shoot the ducks? In (a) the ducks have been shot. In (b) the ducks may still be alive.
8. I am glad to oblige you. You were lucky to find me home. All the pupils appeared keen to do their best. He looked eager to join in the fun.
9. a) This question may be difficult to answer. ⟶
It may be difficult to answer this question. ⟶
To answer this question may be difficult.

b) All the alternatives suggested are impossible to remember. ⟶
It is impossible to remember all the alternatives suggested. ⟶
To remember all the alternatives suggested is impossible.

    c) Kittens are delightful to watch when . . .   ——➤
    It is delightful to watch kittens when . . .   ——➤
    To watch kittens when . . . is delightful.

10. *see:* e.g., hear, watch, observe . . . ; *expect:* command, order, advise, compel; *find:* catch, stop, resent, start.

11. Multi-predicated: (a), (d). Alpha beta: (b), (c), (e).

CHAPTER 22

1. In (iii), (ix), (xiii) *it* is a substitute subject. In (vi), *it* refers directly to *service and servility*. In (x) *it* is substitute complement for the *if* clause.

2. e.g., like *however;* consequently, meanwhile, unfortunately, perhaps; also some pG's: in the same way, on the other hand. E.g., like *and:* neither, nor, yet.

3. a) e.g., certainly, indeed, assuredly. **(b)** e.g., however, of course.

4. i) Linkers, e.g., We spent a pleasant day. The weather, *though,* could have been better.
It was raining heavily. *However,* the temperature remained high.
I admitted my error. *Equally,* the other driver had made a mistake.
'I should like to see that picture.' '*Then* will you come with me tonight?'
ii) Non-linkers, e.g., This exercise is easy, *though* tedious.
It must be done, *however* ridiculous it seems.
The driver admitted he was *equally* to blame.
The *then* president framed this regulation.

5. a) *relayed* is related to *sent over*, *strange light* to *laser beam; relayed* and *sent over* are synonymous; *laser beam* is included in *strange light*. **(b)** *This* refers to whole of preceding sentence; an identity relationship. **(c)** *a pile of stones* is related to *objects;* an inclusion relationship. *To give expression* refers to *ways of communicating:* synonymous.

6. The three sentences are linked by the repetition of *language,* which is more general in the second sentence than in the first. The meaning of *language* differs again in the third sentence. The second and third sentences show relationship between *universal* and *there has never existed a group of men*. Conclusion: an example of faulty coherence, because of varying meanings given to *language;* what is said of *spoken language* has little to do with the second sentence.

INDEX